Chicano Popular Culture

Adela de la Torre,

EDITOR

Other books in the series:

Mexican Americans and Health: ¡Sana! ¡Sana!
   Adela de la Torre & Antonio L. Estrada

Mexican Americans and the U.S. Economy: Quest for buenos días
   Arturo González

Mexican Americans and the Law: ¡El pueblo unido jamás será vencido!
   Reynaldo Anaya Valencia, Sonia R. García, Henry Flores, and
   José Roberto Juárez Jr.

Chicana/o Identity in a Changing U.S. Society: ¿Quién soy? ¿Quiénes somos?
   Aída Hurtado and Patricia Gurin

Mexican Americans and the Environment: Tierra y vida
   Devon G. Peña

Chicano Popular Culture

Que Hable el Pueblo

Charles M. Tatum

The University of Arizona Press   Tucson

The University of Arizona Press
© 2001 The Arizona Board of Regents

⊛ This book is printed on acid-free, archival-quality paper.
Manufactured in the United States of America

06   05   6   5   4   3   2

Library of Congress Cataloging-in-Publication Data
Tatum, Charles M.
   Chicano popular culture : que hable el pueblo / Charles M. Tatum.
      p. cm. — (The Mexican American experience)
   Includes bibliographical references and index.
   ISBN 0-8165-1983-8 (pbk. : acid-free paper)
   1. Mexican Americans—Social life and customs. 2. Mexican
Americans—Intellectual life. 3. Popular culture—United States—History.
4. Mexican American arts—History. 5. Mexican Americans in literature.
6. Mexican Americans in motion pictures. I. Title. II. Series.
   E184.M5 T38 2001
   973'.046872—dc21
2001001220

■ CONTENTS

FIGURES

■ LIST OF ACRONYMS

CARA	Chicano Art: Resistance and Affirmation
CSO	Community Service Organization
FCC	Federal Communications Commission
HBO	Home Box Office
INS	Immigration and Naturalization Service
LRUP	La Raza Unida Party
LULAC	League of United Latin American Citizens
MALDEF	Mexican American Legal Defense and Education Fund
MAM	Mexican American Movement
MAYO	Mexican American Youth Association
NAACP	National Association for the Advancement of Colored People
NCLR	National Council of La Raza
NEH	National Endowment for the Humanities
NFWA	National Farm Workers Association
PBS	Public Broadcasting Service
SAG	Screen Actors Guild
SAP	Second Audio Program
SICC	Spanish International Communications Corporation
SIN	Spanish International Network
TRPI	Tomás Rivera Policy Institute
UMAS	United Mexican American Students

Introduction

THE STUDY OF POPULAR CULTURE

We are immersed in popular culture during most of our waking hours. It is on radio, television, and our computers when we access the Internet, in newspapers, on streets and highways in the form of advertisements and billboards, in movie theaters, at music concerts and sports events, in supermarkets and shopping malls, and at religious festivals and celebrations. It is found throughout our homes in the kitchen, the playroom, and a teenager's bedroom as posters of rock groups, actors, and sports heroes. Madonna, Michael Jordan, Gloria Estefan, Ricky Martin, Joe Montana, Sammy Sosa, and Jennifer López are all subjects of popular culture. In short, we experience popular culture with all of our senses almost every day of our lives.

Why is it important to study popular culture? One answer is that the popular culture that surrounds us can tell us a great deal about ourselves — our traditions, roots, history, economics, political life, prejudices, values, and attitudes. This is especially true when we examine aspects of popular culture analytically; that is, when we pause long enough to study it in a historical context. Such study can tell us much not only about the larger society we live in, but also about age groups, men and women, regions of the country, and ethnic groups. In this book, you will learn that Chicano popular culture is sometimes very different from and sometimes quite similar to the popular culture of other U.S. ethnic minorities and that of the dominant Anglo society. By studying popular culture, then, you will have a wide-open window of opportunity to learn about the uniqueness of the fastest-growing U.S. minority population.

Labels and Terms

In the chapters that follow, you will encounter a variety of terms of identification: "Mexican," "Mexican national," "American of Mexican descent," "Mexican American," "Mexican origin," "Spanish speaking," "Tejano,"

"Nuevo Mexicano," "Chicano" ("Tejana," "Nuevo Mexicana," and "Chicana," the grammatical feminine equivalents in Spanish, are also used in this book), "Latino," and "Hispanic." These terms can be confusing and misleading without a brief explanation of how they are used in this book. "Mexican" and "Mexican national" are synonymous terms that refer to a person who has retained his or her citizenship of the country of Mexico and resides in Mexico, is temporarily in the United States, or even resides in the United States without becoming a citizen. "American of Mexican descent," "Mexican American," and "Mexican origin" are also synonyms and therefore used interchangeably in this book. They refer to an American citizen who generally resides in the United States and whose parents (or only one parent) are of Mexican descent. Such a person may be a naturalized U.S. citizen, a first-generation citizen, or one whose family roots extend as far back as the sixteenth century.

"Chicano" is a very special term that deserves more explanation. Before about the mid-1960s, the term was used by some Mexican Americans to describe in a disrespectful way recently arrived immigrants from Mexico who were thought to be socially inferior, less educated, Mexican Indian, or *mestizo* (of mixed Mexican Indian and European blood). The term is derived from *mexicano* (Mexican), which is in turn derived from the Meshica Indians. According to Mexican legend, the Meshica founded Mexico City, the political and cultural center of the country. The use of the term by Mexican Americans had racial overtones because of the inferiority they attributed to immigrants of whole or partial Indian origin. Cultural nationalists and other activists in the mid-1960s adopted the term as an expression of ethnic pride and used it to identify themselves in a positive way as descendants of Mexican Indians. In the same way, black cultural nationalists adopted the term Afro-American (today usually African American) to associate themselves with their cultural and ethnic origins in Africa. The term Chicano is still commonly used today for self-identification and frequently as a synonym for Mexican American, the term preferred by many Americans of Mexican descent.

Others self-identify as "Latino" or "Hispanic," very broad and inclusive terms that refer to Americans of Mexican, Central American, South American, and even Spanish descent. These last two terms will be used from time to time in the following pages to characterize, for example, a popular culture form, trend, celebration, etc., that includes Americans of Mexican descent but is not restricted to this group.

■ Historical Background

Mexican Americans are but one of several minorities (e.g., African Americans, Native Americans, Asian Americans, Puerto Rican Americans) in the United States to be denied their civil and constitutional rights. As early as the beginning of the nineteenth century with the initial contacts with Mexicans on the frontier, Anglo Americans began to construct Mexicans, especially Mexicans of a mixed-race background, as members of a different and inferior race. This initial contempt became overt racism in the decades of annexation and conquest of Mexico's northern territories. Popular culture in the form of orally transmitted poetry, folktales, proverbs, and other sayings was already well established in Mexico's northern territories during the early part of the nineteenth century.

Mexico Loses Its Northern Territories

When Mexico declared its independence from Spain in 1821, the present states of Texas, New Mexico, Arizona, and California, as well as parts of Utah, Nevada, Colorado, Oklahoma, and Kansas, became part of this new nation's vast hinterland. In the next thirty-three years they became, in turn, part of the United States

Texas was the first territory to go, a process that began with the arrival in 1821 of four hundred non-Hispanic Catholic families as part of an agreement signed between Stephen F. Austin and the new Mexican government (Mexico had just won its independence from Spain). The Anglo population grew to about twenty thousand by 1830, and began to agitate for an independent republic. Many had strong feelings that the Mexican government's Spanish-language legal procedures and general neglect of their concerns placed Anglos at a distinct disadvantage in their relationship to the Spanish-speaking Mexican population. In 1836, Anglo as well as some Mexican Texans declared their independence from Mexico and established the Republic of Texas (also known as the Lone Star Republic). Anglo Texans defeated General Antonio López de Santa Anna and his Mexican troops at the Battle of San Jacinto.

Mexican officials never recognized the Republic of Texas and were fearful that the U.S. government had conspired with the rebellious Texans as part of a long-term political and military strategy to take over much of the rest of Mexico's northern territories. The Mexicans' fears were confirmed when in 1845 the U.S. Congress ratified a treaty to annex Texas.

The expansionist war against Mexico began in all of its intensity shortly thereafter when U.S. President James K. Polk sent General Zachary Taylor to block the mouth of the Rio Grande River (known then and still today in Mexico as the Río Bravo). Mexican troops retaliated by crossing the river, attacking U.S. troops, and inflicting heavy casualties. Polk then requested and was granted support from Congress to officially declare war on Mexico. U.S. troops invaded Mexico in four different directions, and over the next three years bitter battles were fought in Mexican territory, culminating in the invasion and occupation of Mexico City. The Mexican government reluctantly signed the Treaty of Guadalupe Hidalgo in February 1848, officially ending the war and ceding to the United States for a modest payment of fifteen million dollars the territories of New Mexico, Arizona, California, and parts of Nevada, Utah, and Colorado. In 1853, the Mexican government sold additional lands in southwestern New Mexico and southern Arizona to the United States under the provisions of the Gadsden Purchase treaty.

The Denial of Civil and Constitutional Rights

The 1836 Texas Constitution, the Treaty of Guadalupe Hidalgo, and the Gadsden Purchase treaty all were supposed to protect the civil and constitutional rights of Mexicans in the newly acquired lands, but the historical record offers abundant examples of how these rights were routinely violated and how Anglo racism toward mestizo and Indian-origin Mexicans and Mexican Americans created a legacy of bitterness and conflict that has lasted to this day. Of the tens of thousands of Mexicans living in the newly acquired territories, only about three thousand took advantage of the Mexican government's offer to repatriate them to Mexico. The rest stayed and became U.S. citizens.

Due in large part to the refusal of Anglo Americans to accept the majority of these new citizens as equals, U.S. officials at all levels of government often ignored treaty agreements that gave Mexican Americans the same rights as all U.S. citizens under the Constitution. Even in New Mexico, where a sizeable Mexican American population in comparison to the Anglo population allowed Mexican Americans to retain much political power and forge coalitions with Anglo leaders and power brokers, the Spanish-speaking population fared poorly. Many Hispanic communities in New Mexico and elsewhere in the Southwest held communal land grants that the Spanish crown had given them many decades before in an attempt to encourage the settlement of New Spain's northern territories. In the nineteenth century Anglo political, legal, and banking rings conspired to deprive them of these lands. The many Spanish-language newspapers that were founded in the second half of the nineteenth century amply documented cases of injustice and protested insidious discrimination and racism perpetrated against Mexican Americans.

As land values rose with the dramatic increase in the Anglo population, competition for landownership became more intense. Ownership of land for grazing livestock, farming, and mining inevitably became caught up in a web of intrigue and corruption as Anglo (and even some wealthy Mexican American) political, financial, and legal power brokers conspired to force community and individual Mexican American landowners to give up their lands due to bankruptcy or the inability to satisfy deed requirements in a new and often alien legal system. The requirements for proving landownership in Mexico and the United States differed considerably, putting Mexican Americans at a great disadvantage in their new country. When Congress passed the 1862 Homestead Act, many of the original landowners, especially those in California, suddenly found that Anglos had settled on their land and that they had little recourse through the courts to remove them. To add to the Mexican Americans' legal difficulties, the court proceedings and trials were often conducted entirely in English, a language that most of the Southwest's recent U.S. citizens did not understand or speak well enough to effectively defend themselves.

The widespread loss of land was a grave injustice, but there were other more egregious racial crimes against the Mexican American population during the nineteenth century. For example, Texas Anglos commonly lynched blacks, Mexicans, and Mexican Americans, a practice that increased significantly after the Civil War and continued until the end of the century. The Chicano historian Arnoldo De León, who has studied this and other forms of Anglo racism in Texas, states, "Lynchings of blacks and Mexicans were accompanied by ritualistic tortures and sadism not displayed in other lynchings—such treatment being justified by reference to the supposed sexual threat posed by the blacks and the cruelty and depravity of Mexicans" (De León 1983, 91). In California and Arizona, Anglo vigilante groups also took the law into their own hands and hanged Mexicans and Mexican Americans. When they were tried in the criminal justice system, members of the Spanish-speaking population received poor legal representation and disproportionately long sentences.

Resistance to Injustice

The loss of land and other injustices perpetrated against Mexican Americans from the nineteenth century forward were not passively accepted by the Mexican-origin population. For example, in New Mexico Mexican Americans organized into bands of hooded night riders known as Las Gorras Blancas (The White Hoods) who harassed Anglo land developers by destroying their fences and even derailing their supply trains. These bands in New Mexico and elsewhere in the Southwest have been thoroughly studied by contemporary Chicano historians, who have named them *social bandits* because they often led the resistance against Anglo oppression. Some of the best-known social bandit leaders were Juan Nepomuceno Cortina and Joaquín Murieta. Cortina, a landowner in the Brownsville, Texas, area, frequently led raids against Anglo landowners and the officials who protected them. He also vigorously defended Mexican Americans against other injustices and openly urged the Spanish-speaking population to defend itself by taking up arms. Murieta was a Mexican miner who came to California shortly after the 1848 gold rush. Like Cortina, he became the leader of a small guerrilla band that would target Anglos who had been identified for their mistreatment of Mexican and Mexican American miners and others. Popular culture in the form of newspapers and music amply documented the exploits of Cortina and other social bandits during all of the nineteenth and the beginning of the twentieth centuries.

Along with resisting economic and political domination, Mexican Americans in the Southwest actively struggled to maintain their culture, and as F. Arturo Rosales has pointed out, "The most crucial measure for resisting cultural domination for Southwest Mexicans was the maintenance of Spanish" (Rosales 1996, 17). The most effective vehicle for doing so was the Spanish-language press that thrived across the Southwest from the mid-nineteenth century through the first quarter of the twentieth century. This topic will be discussed in detail in chapter 4: "Newspapers, Radio, and Television," but it is important to note here that the maintenance of Spanish through the Spanish-language press formed part of a general campaign by Mexican Americans to resist both injustices and the loss of their unique identity as a people of Mexican origin.

Mexican Immigration

Up until about the 1890s, there was little immigration from Mexico across the U.S.–Mexican border to the United States. This began to change as both the Mexican and the U.S. railroad systems expanded, thereby affording a large number of Mexican workers—many of them from deep in Mexico—relatively inexpensive and readily accessible transportation to the border and within certain regions of the United States. By 1900, 127,000 Mexican-born immigrants had added significantly to the approximately 200,000 Mexican Americans native to the Southwest (Rosales 1996, 20). Mexican immigrants or seasonal workers from Mexico along with the native population became the main sources of labor for the growing commercial agricultural business—farms and ranches owned by corporations rather than by individual landowners or families. This was especially true in Texas and in the fertile central valleys of California, which the availability of water for irrigation had transformed. Industrial mining in California as well as Arizona, Colorado, and New Mexico also attracted skilled Mexican miners and unskilled laborers.

The violent revolution that erupted in Mexico in 1910 dramatically increased the flow of Mexican immigration to the United States. The tyrannical thirty-year regime of Mexican President Porfirio Díaz came to an end with the election of Francisco Madero, a liberal and reform-minded intellectual. Unfortunately, he was assassinated in 1911 by Díaz supporters. During the next seven years, the entire country suffered through a violent and bloody struggle as the presidency changed several times and revolutionary and government forces fought numerous battles throughout the country. Hundreds of thousands of men were enlisted to fight on one side or the other, leaving women and children to fend for themselves. In addition, the civilian population in several regions of the country was frequently caught in the political and military cross fire between opposing forces, adding to their suffering and distress. Many civilians and military deserters took flight, seeking refuge along the U.S.–Mexican border and eventually in the United States itself. Some returned to Mexico after the revolution ended, but the majority stayed, adding significantly to the immigrant population that had formed in the United States at the end of the nineteenth century. In 1910, 210,000 Mexican nationals lived in the United States but by 1930 there were approximately one million (Rosales 1996, 43). The flight of Mexicans from Mexico to the United States was fictionalized decades later by many Chicano writers including José Antonio Villarreal, whose novel *Pocho* is discussed in the chapter on popular literature (see chapter 5).

Many who stayed were drawn by the promise of employment in the booming war economy; the United States had entered the war against Germany in 1917, and key manufacturing industries needed to replace the hundreds of thousands of able-bodied American citizens who had joined the armed forces. The war economy also afforded U.S.–born Mexican Americans the opportunity to improve their employment status and overall economic situation. Mexicans and Mexican Americans alike—who until World War I had been employed primarily in agriculture, mining, and the railroads in the Southwest—now were pulled to midwestern industrial cities such as Chicago and Detroit to work in skilled positions in such sectors as the rapidly growing automobile industry and meatpacking. It was at this time that Mexican/Mexican American communities began to form in large cities outside of the Southwest, communities that are still growing and vibrant today. Popular culture in the form of music and newspapers thrived among Mexican Americans in urban sites throughout the Southwest and the Midwest during the first quarter of the twentieth century.

Nativist Attacks

Despite the great opportunities that an expanding U.S. economy offered both Mexican nationals and Mexican Americans, both groups suffered greatly at the hands of Anglo society even during the best of times. During downturns in the economy after the end of World War I, the U.S. government, which had been eager to attract workers from Mexico during boom times, made it difficult for Mexican citizens to cross the border or to become U.S. citizens. The rise of *nativism,* especially along the U.S.–Mexican border, singled out Mexican nationals and Mexican Americans as targets for vicious and often fatal attacks and blamed them for depriving Anglo Americans of jobs. Such nativist attitudes are unfortunately still prevalent today and are manifested officially in legislation such as California's Proposition 63, making English the state's official language, California's "light up the border" campaign supposedly intended to deter illegal immigration, and the vigilante groups that have surged along the Arizona-Sonora border to discourage Mexican undocumented workers from crossing into the United States. Nativism reached its most extreme expression during the Great Depression of the 1930s, when about 600,000 Mexican nationals (even children born in the United States and therefore citizens) were deported to Mexico. This represented about a third of the total Mexican national population residing in the United States (Rosales 1996, 49).

"The Other Mexico"

The Mexican immigrant population that remained in the United States in the 1930s developed a somewhat separate identity from that of Mexican Americans. Whereas many Mexican Americans seemed eager to try to assimilate into the dominant Anglo culture by, for example, insisting that their children speak only English, the immigrant population for the most part closely identified with Mexico, its history, traditions, and language. This cultivation in the United States of all things Mexican was known as *México lindo* (beautiful Mexico) and the immigrant community saw itself as *El México de afuera* (the other Mexico).

It was the *mutualista,* or mutual aid society, that provided most immigrants with a connection to their mother country and served to bring them together to meet their survival needs in a new and alien country. Cultural activities, education, health care, insurance coverage, legal protection and advocacy before police and immigration authorities, and anti-defamation activities were the main functions of these associations. Mutualistas, which formed in all the major cities in the Southwest and Midwest, also succeeded in bringing together Mexican nationals from different social classes to form a common bond, a feat that no organization had been able to achieve in Mexico.

Mexican Americanism

Beginning in the 1940s and gaining strength in the 1950s, Mexican immigrants gradually surrendered their México de afuera ideology for one that identified them as permanent residents of a new country, residents who could now freely and eagerly join with the U.S.–born Mexican American population to create a powerful social and political force with which the dominant society would have to reckon. This new ideology, commonly referred to as "Mexican Americanism," was actively promoted by new organizations such as the League of United Latin American Citizens (LULAC) and, after War World II, the American GI Forum. LULAC was founded during the Great Depression and has functioned as an effective civil rights organization mainly on behalf of Mexican Americans.

World War II (1939–1945) was the key event that gave Mexican Americanism its strong impetus and urgency. Hundreds of thousands of Mexican Americans from rural and urban areas throughout the Southwest and Midwest joined the various branches of the military and went abroad to serve their country bravely in both the European and Pacific theaters of the war. Meanwhile, at home in the United States, Mexican American women—most of them for the first time—assumed major family financial responsibilities and took jobs in war and other industries. Hispanics in general, and Mexican Americans in particular, were highly decorated and suffered casualties in numbers disproportionate to their population.

By war's end, the wave of Mexican American soldiers who returned to the United States, together with those at home who had proudly served the war effort through their civilian jobs, had developed a very different set of expectations of U.S. society than those that had predominated before the war. Mexican Americans in great numbers now demanded their full due as citizens, citizens who had fought, died, and worked shoulder-to-shoulder with Anglo citizens whose rights had always been guaranteed. Discrimination and racism remained the greatest obstacles to full citizenship, and LULAC, the American GI Forum, and other organizations such as the Mexican American Movement (MAM) provided advocacy on behalf of Mexican Americans who now demanded a much greater share of the American Dream. MAM, formed in the 1930s in California under the auspices of the YMCA, had as its goals "to improve conditions among our Mexican American and Mexican people living in the United States" and to pursue "citizenship, higher education . . . and a more active participation in civic and cultural activities by those of our national descent" (quoted in Gutiérrez 1995, 136). The organization's newspaper, *The Mexican Voice,* effectively propagated the view that Americans of Mexican descent needed to improve themselves in order to be accepted and to succeed in the United States (Rosales 1996, 101). Although this may strike us today as a conservative political stance that did not challenge the status quo of the exclusion of minorities from full participation in U.S. society, MAM's views were typical of the postwar period, at least for many middle- and upper-class Mexican Americans. The tension between Mexican Americans eager to assimilate into Anglo society and those who chose to remain more faithful to their Mexican roots is reflected in the different strands of music popular with each group after World War II. Spanish-language radio stations were important in popularizing these divergent musical tastes.

After World War II the struggle against rampant discrimination against all minorities in employment, housing, and education became a major rallying cry for Mexican Americans. Organizations, associations, and legal defense committees began to systematically challenge racist practices. For example, a LULAC–sponsored initiative succeeded in desegregating many schools in southern California in 1946. LULAC was also instrumental in desegregating public schools in Texas, where it already had a good record of success from before the war. Under pressure from Mexican American groups, some Arizona schools ended segregationist practices (Rosales 1996, 104–5).

Mexican Americans also enjoyed some successes in electoral politics, as leaders and political strategists began registering a larger number of Mexican-origin citizens and encouraging them to use their collective power at the ballot box in municipal, state, and federal elections. Edward Roybal won a seat on the Los Angeles City Council and would go on to be elected to the U.S. House of Representatives. Voting as a block, Mexican American voters in El Paso elected Raymond Telles as mayor in 1957, and Eligio "Kika" de la Garza and Henry B. González were elected to the House of Representatives in the 1960s. The electoral obstacles were not as formidable in New Mexico as elsewhere due to the large concentration of Mexican Americans; candidates had enjoyed success there since statehood in 1910. In 1919, Mexican-born Octaviano Larrazolo was elected governor of New Mexico; Dennis Chávez served in the U.S. Senate from the 1930s until his death in 1962, and Joseph Montoya was elected to the Senate in 1964 and stayed until the 1970s.

The Chicano Movement

The 1960s brought a dramatic shift in Mexican American politics with the rise of the so-called *movimiento chicano* (Chicano Movement), a term often used to describe a highly complex social and political process that manifested itself in several different ways during the 1960s and 1970s:

- The unionization of farmworkers in the agricultural fields of California, Texas, and elsewhere in the Southwest led by César Chávez, Dolores Huerta, and others
- The Crusade for Justice founded by Denver activist Rodolfo "Corky" Gonzales
- The Alianza Federal de Mercedes (Federal Alliance of Land Grants) inspired by Reies López Tijerina and based mainly in New Mexico
- La Raza Unida Party founded by José Angel Gutiérrez and others in Texas

- The high school walkouts and demands by high school and college students for curricular reform and the establishment of Chicano Studies programs
- The Chicano Moratorium against the war in Vietnam

There were many other leaders, occurrences, variations on the preceding, and expressions of protest, but what they had in common has been described by one perceptive Chicano social critic in the following way:

> Anguished by a lack of social mobility, frustrated by insensitive institutions which fostered discrimination and racism, and exploited in economic terms, the Chicano community engaged in a total evaluation of its relationship to the dominant society. The development of an assertive stance and mobilization towards a new style of political activity were the beginnings of a new social, economic, and artistic resurgence. (Ybarra-Frausto 1977, 82)

Much of Chicano popular music, radio, newspapers, and literature reflected the deep discontent of the Chicano Movement and the resulting artistic resurgence.

The Chicano Movement took place against a backdrop in the United States throughout the 1960s and the early 1970s of a general discontent among a sizeable part of the population with established political and social institutions (e.g., government and the two-party system, the nuclear family, schools, and churches). The Civil Rights Movement, the rise of Black Power, the American Indian Movement, feminism, and other militant forms of political protest played key roles as well. During much of the latter part of the 1960s, social unrest, demonstrations, and riots in large urban areas heightened tensions between minorities and Anglo society. Finally, the profound discontent surrounding the war in Vietnam on the part of millions of Americans of every race and sector of society led to a general sense of disillusionment and loss of faith in the U.S. government that had repeatedly lied to its citizens about many different aspects of the war.

Different Manifestations of the Chicano Movement

César Chávez is generally recognized as the first leader of the Chicano Movement. He was born in Yuma, Arizona, in 1921 to poor farmworker parents. As a child, he labored beside them in the fields of California and very early developed a strong sense of social justice. As a young man, he was trained by the Community Service Organization (cso) in the tactics of organizing. He cut his teeth as an organizer among California's meatpackers but soon turned to organizing farmworkers. His efforts and those of other organizers such as Dolores Huerta, also cso–trained, began in 1962. Over the next three decades, the union he helped to found, the National Farm Workers Association (NFWA) enjoyed many successes in their dealings with large growers and other agriculturally related businesses. Through union-negotiated contracts, labor conditions and wages for thousands of farmworkers across the Southwest improved dramatically.

Rodolfo "Corky" Gonzales, another early Chicano leader, was born in 1928 in Denver, Colorado, to migrant-worker parents. He took up boxing at age fifteen in order to escape the despair and unpromising future of growing up poor and Chicano in an urban barrio. Gonzales became a very successful professional boxer after World War II but retired in 1953 to launch a political career first in organized politics and later as a Chicano activist. He held several important Democratic Party positions, including becoming the party's first Mexican American district captain in Denver. Gonzales eventually became disillusioned with the political process and the inability and unwillingness of established Democratic Party officials to deal meaningfully with minority rights. He left the party as his stance against discrimination became more radical. In 1966, he founded the Crusade for Justice, a service-oriented cultural center that challenged the Denver city government and the Democratic Party to become more committed to eradicating poverty and dealing effectively with racial injustice. The Crusade for Justice sponsored the First Annual Chicano Youth Conference in 1969, which was attended by more than fifteen hundred Chicano community and university activists from throughout the Southwest. Through his organization and its sponsored events, Gonzales encouraged young Chicanos to join the struggle to claim their rights as American citizens.

Reies López Tijerina, a Tejano born in 1926, was trained as a minister and in the mid-1960s organized a New Mexico–based movement, the Alianza Federal de Mercedes, whose purpose was to regain the lands that Spanish-speaking New Mexicans had lost in the nineteenth and early part of the twentieth centuries due to the legal, political, and economic deceit discussed earlier in this chapter. A charismatic orator and persuasive leader, Tijerina established a following mainly among northern New Mexico's rural Mexican Americans. Although he was not ultimately successful in restoring land to the original owners, he did galvanize a militant group of loyal followers who for a time seemed on the verge of creating an effective political force, particularly in the rural communities of Tierra Amarilla and other northern New Mexican counties. Tijerina was indicted and convicted of several alleged crimes against the state of New Mexico and the U.S. Forest Service. He served his time and faded from the public eye. The Alianza became overwhelmed with legal problems and eventually disbanded in the 1970s.

La Raza Unida Party (LRUP), founded by José Angel Gutiérrez and other Tejano activists, was probably the most successful example of Chicano Movement participation in electoral politics during the 1960s and early 1970s. The underlying ideology of LRUP relied heavily on cultural elements with which Texas Chicanos could identify: the role of the family, Tejano music, Mexican history, and the Spanish language. It was a pragmatic nationalism that distanced itself from counterculture identification and Marxist rhetoric (Rosales 1996, 233). In 1970, Gutiérrez and other LRUP leaders targeted the Crystal City school board and city council for the party's first incursion into electoral politics—they succeeded in electing their candidates to both. LRUP also enjoyed more modest gains in neighboring counties and municipalities. In later years, LRUP broadened its participation in Texas by fielding a gubernatorial and other candidates in the 1972 statewide election. Although this effort ultimately did not succeed, it did give the party the opportunity to take its message of change to Mexican Americans across Texas. LRUP did garner some modest electoral victories in California and in other states but never became a national political force that seriously challenged the two-party system.

Along with their teachers and professors, high school and college students were at the forefront of the movimiento, stamping it with a strong imprint of cultural nationalism, political radicalism, and militancy. For example, in March 1968, a loosely organized group of Chicano high school students staged a coordinated walkout in several Los Angeles high schools, demanding among other things, curricular reform. José Angel Gutiérrez and other activists who were instrumental in founding LRUP had cut their political teeth in the mid-1960s in the Texas-based Mexican American Youth Association (MAYO). Student groups, such as southern California's United Mexican American Students (UMAS), were formed on high school and college campuses in the late 1960s and early 1970s throughout the Southwest. In March 1969, Gonzales's Crusade for Justice convened the Chicano Youth Conference, which brought together students and other

Chicano youth to celebrate and promote their separateness and cultural nationalism. One of the concrete achievements of the conference was the decision to hold a national protest day against the war in Vietnam.

A second conference held at the University of California, Santa Barbara, scarcely a month after the Denver gathering provided a concrete agenda for curricular changes in higher education, including a call for the creation of Chicano Studies programs on high school and college campuses across California. The participants in this conference issued a cultural manifesto, "El Plan de Santa Bárbara" (The Plan of Santa Barbara). "El Plan de Santa Bárbara" and a handful of other documents and declarations of the late 1960s had a profound influence on the Chicano Movement's political, educational, and cultural nature. This influence will be seen clearly in the following chapters.

By 1970, mass demonstrations against U.S. military involvement in Vietnam were occurring all across the country. Chicanos joined this wave of protests in August 1970 by holding the National Chicano Moratorium march in Los Angeles and simultaneously in other southwestern cities. On August 29, more than thirty thousand protesters marched through the streets of Los Angeles and later congregated in Laguna Park in East Los Angeles. The largely peaceful meeting ended tragically when police charged and dispersed the crowd. Three people were killed, many more were injured, and hundreds were arrested. Rubén Salazar, a prominent Chicano reporter for the *Los Angeles Times*, was killed in a separate but related police action. The Moratorium and the confrontation with the police served to galvanize the Chicano community throughout the Southwest against the war in Vietnam.

Chicanos Since the Chicano Movement

Although a sizeable number of Americans of Mexican descent did not participate in any of the various aspects of the Chicano Movement—many actively opposed it—it is fair to say that for a few years their lives were at least indirectly affected in the sense that official Washington as well as Anglo public perceptions were positively altered toward this increasingly visible ethnic minority. What is certain is that the past thirty years offer a very mixed list of successes and failures regarding the status of Chicanos in U.S. society.

On the positive side, more Chicanos have attended and graduated from college and received postgraduate degrees than before 1970. They are consequently more highly represented in the public, professional, educational, and business sectors than previously. For example, the Clinton administration appointed several Chicanos to cabinet posts: Henry Cisneros, Federico Peña, and Bill Richardson. Manuel Pacheco served as president of the University of Arizona and as chancellor of the University of Missouri system, the first Chicano to be selected for such a prestigious post. As you will see in the following chapters, Chicanos are also more visible in areas such as radio, television, newspapers, the literary world, and the music and film industries.

On the negative side, the high school dropout rate for Chicanos has not improved appreciably over the past three decades and the percentage of Chicanos living at or below the poverty level has actually increased in the "new economy" of the 1990s, in which the gap between rich and poor has widened and deepened. Nativism has persisted against immigrants from all underdeveloped countries including Mexico and Central America. California's Proposition 187 denying health and educational services to undocumented immigrants passed in 1994 bolstered by attacks on Mexican nationals and poor Chicanos. In 1996 California also passed Proposition 209, which went far in dismantling the state's commitment to Affirmative Action that had aided thousands of Chicanos, women, and others to advance in education and employment.

■ Organization of This Book

The book you are about to read and study is organized into six chapters, and each chapter is in turn divided into short sections designed for reasonable reading assignments. Chapter 1 presents some widely accepted definitions of popular culture as well as some of the most interesting and provocative theories of popular culture, including some recently developed by Chicano scholars. An understanding of definitions and theories will assist you in gaining a deeper appreciation for and being better prepared to discuss the material covered in subsequent chapters. Chapter 2 traces the history of Mexican American popular music from its origins in the sixteenth century through the end of the twentieth century. Chapter 3 provides a background to contemporary Chicano cinema, beginning with a summary of the stereotyping of Mexicans, Latinos, and Chicanos in U.S. cinema over the past seventy-five years. Most of the chapter is about the development of Chicano cinema in the past thirty years. Chapter 4 covers three important media: radio, television, and newspapers. Each medium could easily fill an entire chapter, but the interrelationship among the three lends itself to discussion in one chapter. Chapter 5 deals with a small but representative sampling of Chicano literature: those works and authors who have been popular among Chicano and non-Chicano readers alike, with an emphasis on novels, short stories, theater, and poetry published during the past thirty years. Chapter 6 takes a look at popular religious and secular celebrations, festivals, and art. Mural and graffiti art is discussed in considerable detail due to the prominent role it has played in Chicano cultural expression since about 1970. A short conclusion is followed by a reference list that is designed to provide you with many resources for further study. In addition you will find a short list of suggested readings at the end of each chapter.

A brief word here about why some forms of Chicano popular culture are not covered in this book. The limitation of space was a major consideration; not everything could be included without significantly adding to the book's length. The decision was made to include popular culture forms about which a great deal is known and consequently about which a full and informed discussion could be provided. Correspondingly, certain forms were excluded because they have not been carefully studied. Other forms were excluded because they appeal to a relatively narrow audience. For example, Chicano comic books are not included because they have neither been studied very thoroughly nor are they read extensively outside of certain urban areas such as Los Angeles. Humor was excluded because it has not been systematically studied and would have required substantial research in order to be discussed intelligently and sensitively as a chapter in this book. Another excluded topic is food, undoubtedly an important form of popular culture. However, there is little typically Chicano about the food one finds in homes and restaurants in the Southwest or wherever there are concentrations of Chicanos. The varieties of cuisine we find are really Mexican regional foods. Food is simply too vast and elusive a topic to be handled in a single chapter. You will probably think of other forms of popular culture that might have been included and perhaps a future edition of this book will include some of them.

■ Suggested Readings

De León, Arnoldo. 1983. *They Called Them Greasers: Anglo Attitudes Towards Mexicans in Texas, 1821–1900.* Austin: University of Texas Press.

Kanellos, Nicolás. 1994. *The Hispanic Almanac.* Detroit: Visible Ink.

Rosales, F. Arturo. 1996. *Chicano! The History of the Mexican American Civil Rights Movement.* Houston: Arte Público Press.

Chicano Popular Culture

Definitions and Theoretical Approaches to Popular Culture

Before beginning the study of any field (e.g., literature, sociology, psychology, math, or biology), it is always a good idea to know something about how those who are considered authorities define the field and what theories they have developed about it. Popular culture is no exception. Before you study the various forms of Chicano popular culture, it would be to your advantage to have a grasp of some definitions of popular culture and how various scholars and other intellectuals have thought about it over the past few decades. In this chapter, a few basic definitions and theories of popular culture are introduced to you to serve as a guide to the wide variety of material included in later chapters.

Definitions of Popular Culture

In addition to *popular culture,* there are several other terms with which you should be familiar: *high culture, low culture, folk culture,* and *mass culture.* Scholars who study culture have engaged in endless debates—debates that still rage—about these terms. It is not appropriate in this short introduction to deal in detail with the confusing array of differences, ambiguities, and nuances that have characterized these debates. The discussion that follows, then, is general and necessarily superficial. My purpose is to provide a useful and applicable overview of definitions that will help in your understanding of various forms of Chicano popular culture in later chapters.

Some scholars draw a clear distinction between what they consider high culture and low culture. As the adjective implies, they include cultural activities that appeal to an educated and sophisticated audience under the rubric of *high culture.* They often cite opera, ballet, certain kinds of literature, symphonic music, theater, and art collected and exhibited in private galleries and museums as examples of high culture, because these are thought to appeal to audiences that have refined tastes and highly developed aesthetic sensibilities. Some scholars also attribute these tastes and sensibilities to the artists, musicians, novelists, poets, ballet dancers and classical musicians who create and participate in high culture forms. In contrast scholars characterize as *low culture* activities that in their opinion are created to appeal to audiences whose tastes and sensibilities they consider not to be sophisticated or refined; examples are large sporting events, soap operas, and rock-and-roll concerts. These scholars consider individuals who create low culture as being interested primarily in the qualities that will attract large numbers of consumers who are not well educated or aesthetically sophisticated. A society's upper classes (those who control political and economic power) generally share this hierarchical view of culture.

Scholars commonly define *folk culture* as the practices of small groups within a larger society. For example, Mexico has numerous Indian subcultures (e.g., Tarascan, Tarahumaran, Huichol, Mayo, Yaqui), some of which have highly developed forms of music, dance, and art. Scholars would generally classify these forms as folk culture. They are not widespread throughout Mexican society but are limited to the locales where these Indian groups historically have had their greatest influence. In Spanish the term *cultura popular* is synonymous with the English term *folk culture* and should not be confused with popular culture.

Popular culture is an elusive term perhaps harder to define than high, low, or folk culture. Some scholars, often referred to as mass culture critics, believe that popular culture can be defined as folk culture in societies that have not yet undergone a process of industrialization. These scholars would therefore consider the cultural practices of Mexican Indian subgroups to be folk culture. Scholars such as the Germans Theodor Adorno and Max Horkheimer define popular culture as synonymous with *mass culture;* that is, culture produced by culture industries such as television and advertising for "mass" consumers in order to keep these consumers buying products and accepting ideas that keep a capitalist economy such as that of the United States strong and stable. We commonly refer to Adorno, Horkheimer, and their colleagues as the Frankfurt school because they came together in 1923 at the University of Frankfurt in Germany to form the Institute for Social Research. Many of these scholars came to the United States in 1933 to escape German Nazism and then returned to Frankfurt after the defeat of Hitler.

Closely related to the Frankfurt school definition of popular culture as mass culture is that of other thinkers such as the Italian Antonio Gramsci and the German Louis Althusser. These scholars considered popular culture as a form of what they called the *dominant ideology* through which the dominant classes—a country's aristocracy or the very rich who own vast amounts of a country's wealth—control the other social classes. The dominant classes exercise control over the means of production such as manufacturing, large corporations, and culture industries such as television, newspapers, cinema, and radio that shape the attitudes and behaviors of mass consumers.

Other scholars, commonly referred to as *cultural populists,* tend to define popular culture as the ways in which consumers receive the messages sent to them by culture industries. These scholars maintain that rather than "consuming" or interpreting these messages as cultural industries intend them to, consumers subvert the messages by interpreting them in ways that are personally meaningful and even beneficial. Thus they see popular culture as expressing the interests, experiences, and values of ordinary people.

In addition to these definitions of popular culture, there are numerous others that reflect specific points of view. A good example is the feminist definition, which views popular culture as patriarchal ideology that is largely controlled by men and that works antagonistically against women.

■ Theoretical Approaches to Popular Culture

Just as it is not my intent to provide in this limited introduction an exhaustive or in-depth discussion of the various definitions of popular culture, my overview of selected theories of popular culture will also be brief. Your familiarity with these theories will help you more clearly understand and appreciate the various forms of Chicano popular culture discussed in the following chapters.

The various theoretical approaches to popular culture all deal with the following questions:

- What or who determines the form and dissemination of popular culture?

- Where does popular culture come from?

- Are the people responsible for its creation as a way of expressing their lived experiences, interests, preoccupations, attitudes, and priorities?

- Alternatively, is popular culture imposed on the people by powerful forces over which they have no control?

- Do the wealthy and politically powerful elites create values and priorities and force those less powerful in a society to accept them as a way of exercising social control?

- Does popular culture as it is transmitted and disseminated to the masses sacrifice quality, artistic and intellectual values, and integrity to profit motives and ease of marketing?

- Are commercial considerations more important than quality when a cultural industry produces a popular culture form for purchase or consumption by consumers?

- Is the real purpose of popular culture to function as a means of social control to get consumers and citizens to accept and adhere to ideas that will guarantee the continued political and economic power of the elite?

- Is popular culture a form of rebellion, resistance, and subversion of powerful forces that try to control our lives?

I will not provide definitive answers to these questions here, but I hope that you will gain a greater appreciation for the complexity of approaching popular culture and that you will keep in mind the various theories of popular culture as you study and discuss the content of subsequent chapters.

In very general terms, there are two dominant views of the production and consumption of popular culture: (a) it is imposed by powerful forces— forces of domination—from above upon the social classes with subordinate social, political, and economic status; or (b) it is produced by and for subordinated peoples themselves. The first view is by the far the most widely accepted today. Supported by mass culture theorists—scholars who study mass media such as radio, television, the movie industry, and the music industry—this theory evolved out of concepts developed by individuals associated with the University of Frankfurt Institute for Social Research.

The writings of Theodor Adorno are particularly important, especially "Culture Industry Reconsidered" (Adorno 1975), a reconsideration of his earlier thinking. In this essay, Adorno associates mass culture with "culture industries" in order to distinguish it from popular culture, which he considers to be a spontaneous expression arising directly from the masses. His analysis of culture industries reveals his utter disdain for their manifestations, especially when contrasted to forms of high culture. Those who control culture industries merge the spheres of high and low art (spheres that Adorno thinks have justifiably been separate for thousands of years) into consumable products for the masses. Such products are readily available to be passed on to consumers from above because culture industries boast technical capabilities as well as administrative and economic concentrations of power. Contrary to what those who control the culture industries would have us believe, the consumer is the object rather than the subject of a process that cynically lulls us into accepting "the master's voice." The owners of a culture industry have no interest in the specific content or formation of individual artistic expression but rather in transforming works into various cultural commodities such as radio programs or movies. Cultural works have value only in relation to their potential as commodities to be foisted on the masses, particularly the masses in the most economically developed countries, where consumers have more buying power.

In general, cultural theorists who tend to equate popular culture with mass culture claim that the processes of industrialization and urbanization have brought about radical transformations in the social fabric uniting common citizens. The rise of large-scale and assembly-line types of production or manufacturing (e.g., the auto industry) together with the growth of large, densely populated cities have increasingly forced people to leave their homes and neighborhoods to commute to work daily by car or public transportation. This way of life has eroded the strong social ties that individuals traditionally had within their local communities and has also threatened their values and family life. Mass culture theorists and others have described this transformation as the *atomization* of society, because industrialization and urbanization have forced people to relate to each other like so many atoms in a chemical compound. They lack meaningful relationships with each other and respond to each other as if they were so many atoms bouncing off others in meaningless ways without moral or social direction. The village, the family, and the church have lost the ability to influence the formation and retention of values. Social elites have taken advantage of this vacuum by using mass media to persuade and manipulate people more completely and systematically than was possible before industrialization and urbanization became so prevalent. Those who own or control mass media are now able to exercise tremendous power in forming the attitudes, values, and even behaviors of the people in a mass society.

A useful overview of the thinking of those who adhere to a mass culture consideration of popular culture includes the following characteristics:

1. Power and techniques to manipulate a culture industry are concentrated in a few hands, and many are employed to carry out its most nefarious ends.
2. Artistic creativity has been snuffed out in favor of cultural products mass-produced for a large and unthinking audience of consumers.
3. Individuals' worth in society is judged solely on the basis of their potential as consumers, and they are merely passive receivers of cultural products, unable to make judgments or meaningful discriminations.
4. Electronic and print media play increasingly important roles in creating a pseudo-world in which our experiences are reorganized into stereotypes and distortions of ourselves and our reality.
5. The world created by mass media is unambiguously defined so that subtle distinctions become increasingly blurred.
6. Folk culture and popular culture, which arise from below, are merged with high art into a mass culture that has no respect for any traditions, artistic and intellectual values, or aesthetics that do not serve its purposes.
7. Conformity is emphasized over true expressions of individuality. The cult of personality of actors, beauty queens, politicians, sports heroes, etc., dominates.
8. Consumers live passively in a dreamlike world stripped of their own aspirations and sense of themselves (Hall and Whannel 1964, chap. 13).

This is, indeed, a most depressing picture of a society in which various cultural products play an important role as commodities designed to maintain a false sense of reality and to satisfy passive consumer tastes. Despite the differences in the several theories of mass and popular culture that have became prominent during the past thirty years, they do seem to share a common sense of a "total culture" in which mass and popular culture and consumer culture are shaped. Moreover, many scholars of mass and popular culture tend to see themselves in the role of cultural saviors committed to rescuing mass consumers from themselves by developing a set of cultural standards that would challenge and replace those embedded in the cultural products such as television programs, movies, and magazine advertisements produced by mass culture industries. These scholars are sometimes even suspicious of democratic government because of the egalitarian effects it can have on traditional hierarchies; that is, a democratic government can displace the influence that proponents of high culture can have on the masses. For example, there are those who have expressed their displeasure with some of the programs that the National Endowment for the Humanities and the National Endowment for the Arts have funded.

The preceding theoretical approaches tend to view popular culture in general as a cultural phenomenon that is imposed from above. These approaches generally betray a fundamental misunderstanding of the role of the audience in popular culture. The audience is viewed as passive, vulnerable, exploitable, a mass of consumers that receives, accepts, and often behaves in response to the messages that culture industries send them. Consumers are like robots mindlessly responding to messages as though they were commands.

A radically different view of popular culture often referred to as *cultural populism* holds an entirely different view of consumers and popular culture. Cultural populists argue that popular culture "cannot be understood as a culture which is imposed upon the thoughts and actions of people" (Strinati 1995, 255). It cannot be understood unless it is viewed as a genuine expression of the views and values of the common people rather than as a set of views and values that is imposed from above. This theoretical approach to popular culture clashes with many of the other approaches that take the view that popular culture is imposed on consumers by social elites and the culture industries they control. To the contrary, cultural populists view popular culture as the authentic culture of the people because it originates with the people.

The Englishman John Fiske is one proponent of the cultural populist approach. He believes that popular culture "is made by subordinate peoples in their own interests out of resources that also, contradictorily, serve the economic interests of the dominant." Part of popular culture is always outside the control of dominant political and social forces, for it is a culture of conflict that always "involves the struggle to make social meanings that are in the interests of the subordinate and that are not those preferred by the dominant ideology" (Fiske 1989, 2). Creators and consumers of popular culture have the choice of either resisting or evading structures of dominance such as those of government or of culture industries. He offers as examples of this choice girl fans of Madonna who resist patriarchal meanings of female sexuality by constructing their own oppositional ones (Fiske 1989, 22). Fiske asserts that meanings can never be identified in a popular culture text—he defines "text" broadly to include everything from images on billboards to movies, television programs, and advertisements in magazines—but must be constructed within wider social life and in relation to other texts. Moreover, popular texts are inadequate in themselves and are completed only when taken up by people within their everyday culture. Readers, viewers, and listeners give meaning to these texts only when the textual messages are relevant to their everyday lives. Fiske views relevance as central to popular culture, for it minimizes the differences between text and life, aesthetics, and everyday experience. Relevance is produced for consumers from the intersection of the textual and the social (Fiske 1989). The subordinate classes, which for Fiske constitute the majority of producers and consumers of popular culture, hold the power to construct oppositional meanings; that is, meanings that are quite contrary to those that the culture industries intend to embed in their texts (Fiske 1989, 6, 10).

Stuart Hall, an English compatriot of Fiske's, refers to these intended meanings as *preferred readings* and, like Fiske, he believes that audiences may—and often do—arrive at alternative or even oppositional readings of the same text (Hall 1980). Hall, Fiske, and other cultural populist scholars have demonstrated this by carrying out empirical studies that examine how actual audiences read actual texts. They have discovered that popular culture forms are open, allowing different subcultures or different audiences to interpret texts or messages in ways that often meet the needs and specific circumstances of their subcultures (Mukerji and Schudson 1991, 41). This potential to resist intended messages or meanings in texts differentiates Fiske and Hall's consumers from those envisioned by scholars such as Adorno, Horkheimer, Gramsci, and Althusser.

Fiske's optimistic view of the production and consumption of popular culture as having the power to construct oppositional meanings is at least partially shared by Argentinean/Mexican anthropologist Néstor García Canclini and by Chicano scholars Américo Paredes, Ramón Saldívar, and José Limón. In his 1982 study, *Las culturas populares en el capitalismo,* García Canclini examines the transformations that indigenous Mexican arts, crafts, and popular festivals have undergone in a developing industrialized economy. Like Fiske, he believes that not only does culture represent a society, it also serves the function of "re-elaborating" social structures and inventing new ones (García Canclini 1982, 43). He demonstrates how in the past few decades Tarascan and other Indian groups' production of arts and crafts and the celebration of their festivals have lost their symbolic meaning through, among other things, their reification (i.e., being turned into objects to be observed) in museums and their reproduction for economic purposes by dominant capitalist interests. His program for initiating an adversarial basis for popular cultural forms includes the organization of the Mexican Indian producers of these forms into cooperatives and unions, allowing them to reassert the control over the means of production and distribution they once had.

Américo Paredes (1915–1999) was a distinguished Chicano scholar who for many decades was a professor at the University of Texas at Austin. There he taught folklore and other courses in the Department of English to many generations of undergraduate and graduate students, several of whom became university professors and well-known scholars in their own right. In his groundbreaking work, *With His Pistol in His Hand: A Border Ballad and Its Hero* (1958) Paredes studied the ballad or *corrido* of Gregorio Cortez, an early-twentieth-century popular hero among the Mexican American and Mexican population of the Lower Rio Grande Valley on the U.S.–Mexican border. (I shall deal in greater detail with this popular hero and the corrido tradition that grew up around him in chapter 2 on Chicano popular music.) Whereas today corridos are transmitted by means of the printed page, radio, television, film, and recorded music, at the beginning of this century and earlier, they were performed socially in all-male settings such as *cantinas* (barrooms) and barbecues. Paredes believed that heroic corridos such as the ballad of Gregorio Cortez were written anonymously by *corridistas* (performers of corridos) who focused on events that clearly reflected the values of their community. The heroic corrido, then, was a popular culture form that had its origins in a subordinate group, the Mexican American population in Texas in the early twentieth century. And given the places where it was performed, it seems obvious that it was celebrated as a form of protest by an exploited population. Their deep resentment over the treatment Gregorio Cortez and his family received from Anglo lawmen reflected resentments over the unjust and exploitative treatment of the entire Mexican American population of the Lower Rio Grande Valley. Popular culture served to express seething collective discontent. Like other cultural populists, Paredes definitely believed that popular culture—at least the corrido—began as a form created by Chicanos to resist the hegemonic forces of the dominant society.

More recently, Chicano scholars José Limón and Ramón Saldívar have reinforced Paredes's very original view that the heroic Mexican corrido is a popular culture form that came into being quite spontaneously from "below" to express collective values, resistance, and social protest. Limón (1992, 30) characterizes this type of ballad as "an expressive instrument of social struggle." In his analysis of the heroic corrido of Mexico and its transformation into Chicano poetic texts of the 1960s, Limón draws on the work of the English Marxist Raymond Williams, specifically his great contribution to cultural theory that allows us "to see how the subordinate groups are dialectically related to domination in cultural terms and how this relationship can be transformed over time" (Limón 1992, 41). Limón argues that later Chicano poetic texts took on much of the status and quality of the residual Mexican culture and contain much of the oppositional character of the earlier heroic corrido, which waned in popularity from the 1930s to the 1960s. As Limón's mentor at the University of Texas at Austin, Paredes was instrumental in transmitting knowledge of the Mexican epic ballad to a new generation of scholars and poets, who would draw on the contestatory and oppositional thrust of this poetic/song form as a precursor to Civil Rights–era poetics.

Like Limón, the Chicano literary critic Ramón Saldívar credits Paredes's classic study of the border ballad as "crucial in historical, aesthetic, and theoretical terms" (Saldívar 1990, 27). Whereas Limón focuses on the importance of Paredes's work in understanding post-1960s Chicano poetry, Saldívar cites Paredes as fundamental to our understanding of the contemporary development of Chicano prose fiction, particularly the novel. The border ballad is for Saldívar a popular creative expression and formulation of the sociocultural conditions under which Chicanos lived during the latter half of the nineteenth and the first part of the twentieth centuries. And just as importantly, the border ballad expresses the Chicano population's resistance in the twentieth century to those imposed conditions. The border ballad is thus a precursor to modern Chicano prose fiction, which is also a strong and persistent expression of resistance to unjust conditions. In other words, for Saldívar, as for Paredes and Limón, certain Chicano popular culture forms are produced by and for the subordinate classes as ways not only of rejecting dominant Anglo values but of resisting exploitative economic conditions.

I will revisit in the following chapters the definitions and theoretical approaches discussed in this chapter as I examine specific forms of Chicano popular culture. The questions at the end of each chapter will encourage you to think about how the definitions and theoretical approaches apply to these forms. It will be helpful to reread this chapter as you think about how to reply to the questions.

■ Discussion Questions

1. Do you agree that there is a legitimate distinction between high and low culture? Why or why not?

2. Implicit in the separation between high and low culture is a suggestion that high culture is "purer" or superior because it is not mass-produced. Do you believe mass production devalues culture? Why or why not?

3. Mass culture theorists would argue that popular culture is imposed on consumers from above by culture industries. If you were arguing for this position, what evidence would you cite to support it?

4. The opposite view, cultural populism, would argue that popular culture arises from the people and may express values oppositional to the social elite. If you were arguing for this position, what evidence would you cite to support It?

5. Several Chicano scholars have argued that Mexican/Chicano popular culture serves to express opposition to the dominant Anglo culture. Do you believe that popular culture might serve different purposes among subordinate minority groups than it does in the dominant Anglo society? Why or why not?

■ Suggested Readings

Fiske, John. 1989. *Reading the Popular*. Boston: Unwin and Hyman.

Hall, Stuart, and Paddy Whannel. 1964. *The Popular Arts*. London: Hutchison.

Limón, José. 1992. *Mexican Ballads, Chicano Poems: History and Influence in Mexican-American Social Poetry*. Berkeley and Los Angeles: University of California Press.

Paredes, Américo. 1958. *With His Pistol in His Hand: A Border Ballad and Its Hero*. Austin: University of Texas Press.

Saldívar, Ramón. 1990. *Chicano Narrative: The Dialectics of Difference*. Madison: University of Wisconsin Press.

Strinati, Dominic. 1995. *An Introduction to the Theories of Popular Culture*. London and New York: Routledge.

2

Music

Like other forms of popular culture, music expresses profoundly the values, spirituality, sentiments, joys, tragedies, and struggles of a people. Words put to song, instrumental music, melodies, and music that accompanies dance and other performances collectively have helped to form the rich cultural tapestry of Chicano popular culture from the sixteenth century to the present. This chapter will cover this broad sweep of popular music, beginning with Spanish and Mexican folk music transplanted to the Southwest and ending with the latest forms of Chicano music popular today among a wide generational range of rural and urban dwellers. Some of this music has survived over the centuries, whereas other music results from new forms and adaptations being created spontaneously by men and women eager to carry on a vibrant musical tradition.

Popular Hispanic Folk Music of the Southwest

In reconstructing the rich history of popular Hispanic folk music in the Southwest, we are fortunate to be able to draw upon the results of the extensive fieldwork conducted throughout the twentieth century by musicologists and folklorists. Arthur Campa, Rubén Cobos, Aurelio Espinosa, Vicente Mendoza, Américo Paredes, and John Donald Robb are among the most important scholars responsible for providing us with much of what we know about Mexican and Chicano music. These and other researchers devoted much of their careers to fanning out across the Southwest with nothing more than recorders (wire recorders early on and sophisticated tape recorders later on) and pencils and writing tablets. They interviewed and recorded hundreds of men and women who willingly sang their songs, played their musical instruments, and most importantly, imparted invaluable information about the music they had heard as children, had preserved over a lifetime, and were teaching their sons and daughters, who in turn would pass on these musical traditions to future generations.

These devoted scholars, like archaeologists, would spend weeks at a time in the small and sometimes very isolated towns of northern New Mexico, southern Colorado, the Texas Rio Grande Valley, and elsewhere across the Southwest seeking out and getting to know the musicians and singers who were carrying on the musical traditions they had inherited from prior generations. We are grateful to these hardy and determined scholars but, of course, we owe our greatest debt to those men and women who made themselves available to be interviewed and who were willing to sing and play their music.

The popular Hispanic folk music of the Southwest has deep roots in Spain and Mexico, but it is a living cultural form that is forever changing and adapting to new social conditions and musical currents (Robb 1980, 5). Some of the forms that the original settlers brought with them from Spain to Mexico in the sixteenth century, and later brought north to the Southwest, have been preserved. But most of these forms have changed or have been altered over the past several hundred years as inventive and innovative musicians have modernized the music and adapted it to their circumstances. We also know that some forms of music from the Spanish and Mexican traditions simply have been lost due to neglect or lack of interest.

The most common forms of popular Hispanic folk music found in the Southwest are the *canción,* the *décima,* the *romance,* and the *corrido.* All of these forms tend to be secular (i.e., non-religious), but there are also forms of religious music such as *alabados* and *alabanzas* that even today are performed on the occasion of holy days and functions.

The Canción

The canción is introspective in nature and is usually found in the form of *coplas,* or four-line verses (Robb 1980, 201). It is the ideal song form for lovers who wish to express their deep-felt sentiments for each other. After about 1920, the *canción ranchera,* a variation on the traditional canción that addressed social issues, acquired great popularity along both sides of the Texas-Mexican border as well as in the Los Angeles area. It became the song form of choice among the disenfranchised masses.

Along with the corrido (discussed later), the canción ranchera provided the Spanish-speaking population a voice in its transition from a rural, subsistence economy to an urban, capitalist culture (Peña 1999b, 53). Lydia Mendoza, the legendary Tejana known to her fans as "La Alondra de la Frontera" (The Lark of the Border) was instrumental in popularizing the canción ranchera; these songs formed an important part of her impressive repertoire.

The Décima

The décima is a form of folk song especially popular in New Mexico, where it flourished during the nineteenth and the early part of the twentieth centuries. It was one of the most popular song forms in fifteenth-century Spain and has had a very strong presence in Mexico and Latin America, where it is still commonly heard. A décima refers to a ten-line stanza of poetry, and the song form generally consists of forty-four lines (an introductory four-verse stanza followed by four ten-line stanzas). The décima deals with a wide range of subject matter, including themes that are philosophical, religious, lyrical, and political. Humorous décimas typically would satirize an individual's weakness or foolish act. A decimero would frequently challenge the target of the satire or his/her defender to respond in kind with a décima, thereby setting up a song duel that tested the originality and wit of contending composers.

In the Lower Rio Grande Valley, celebrated *decimeros* (composers and singers of décimas) often performed at public and social functions on both sides of the border. The Verduzco and the Cisneros families were particularly famous for their performances at dances, weddings, wakes, novenas (prayers used in saying a rosary), and children's funerals. As late as 1940, an elderly Verduzco was still composing and selling his décimas (Paredes 1993, 235–36). The Spanish-speaking population of the Lower Rio Grande Valley gradually lost interest in the décima, however, and by the turn of the century had replaced it with the corrido as a popular song form. In New Mexico, though, the décima continued to thrive well into the twentieth century. Even today it is occasionally heard in the small mountain towns of northern New Mexico and southern Colorado.

A related aspect of the popular Hispanic folk music tradition was the *trovo,* or song contest, in which contestants, or *trovadores* (troubadours), matched their wits as they created humorous *trovas,* short verses that served to parody their rivals or some other agreed-upon subject. The troubadours had to be good singers and quick versifiers, and had to possess an equally sharp wit in order to be competitive. They sang verses of their own composition but also well-known Spanish romances and décimas. Sometimes they would improvise on a familiar ballad, adapting it to a specific set of circumstances. Some nineteenth- and early-twentieth-century troubadours became famous in west Texas and New Mexico, adopting colorful names such as "El Zurdo" (Lefty), "Cienfuegos" (One Hundred Fires), "El Viejo Vilmas" (Old Vilmas), Chiloria, and "El Pelón" (Baldy). El Pelón's real name was thought to be Jesús Gonzales, born close to Santa Fe in 1844. One of his manuscripts, written on rawhide, was discovered in a cave in 1934. Little is known about Chiloria, and what information we have about El Viejo Vilmas comes from his trovos and the long series of verses he composed.

One scholar has documented that troubadours often traveled with wagon supply trains making the trek along the Santa Fe Trail from Chihuahua City to Santa Fe (Robb 1980, 462). Sometimes two or more wagon trains would meet and pitch camp together. After the chores had been completed and the evening meal finished, troubadours from each of the trains would sit around a campfire and compete. After running through the songs and verses they knew, they would begin to make up verses extemporaneously, sometimes challenging each other by asking questions or making fun of the members of the wagon trains, who would have formed a tight circle around them to enjoy the evening's entertainment.

Alabados and Alabanzas

Songs and melodies that are explicitly religious include alabados and alabanzas. The alabados address the various events of the Passion of Christ commemorated every year during Holy Week. Alabados are commonly associated with the Penitentes (Penitents), a Roman Catholic religious sect that exists even today in the remote villages of northern New Mexico and southern Colorado. As the name implies, members of this sect practice acts of penance. Extreme acts of penance, such as flagellation and even crucifixion, sometimes took place during Holy Week, although such practices have been banned by the Catholic Church hierarchy. The alabanzas, on the other hand, are songs that praise either the Virgin Mary or the saints. Each village has its own unique melody and slightly different words for both alabados and alabanzas; what unifies these song forms is the religious subject matter addressed in the song texts.

The Romance

The romance, or ballad, is a brief narrative song form with lines that are generally of eight syllables. It is usually of an episodic character; that is, it deals with an occurrence or series of occurrences that happened or are supposed to have happened. In addition to being episodic, it is usually to the point, concise, and lively as it narrates an event, sings the praises of a hero, or expresses religious sentiments. The romance had already established a long and distinguished history in Spain centuries before the arrival of the Spanish in the New World.

The Corrido

A ballad form closely related to the romance is the corrido. According to eminent Chicano scholar Américo Paredes, the romance was still strong in Spain when the Spanish conquerors arrived in Mexico in the sixteenth century. They brought with them a form of the original romance, and by the middle of the sixteenth century some Mexican Indian tribes were composing their own romances (Paredes 1993, 129).

Romance corridos were composed to commemorate the Spanish colonization of Florida in 1745 and the independence of Mexico from Spain more than seventy years later. Paredes and others have documented that the romance corrido—by the nineteenth century it had come to be known simply as the corrido—then underwent a period of decline in Mexico after the 1848 Mexican War. The corrido would enjoy a period of renewed popularity from about 1875 to the beginning of the Mexican Revolution of 1910. After about 1930, the corrido in Mexico became highly commercialized with the advent of commercial radio, the increasing popularity of movies, and the establishment of a thriving recording industry. Most of the corridos heard today on radio, television, and in other mass media have developed into song forms that sometimes have little resemblance to the traditional corridos composed and sung during the early part of the century. Many of the traditional corridos have, of course, survived and their music and words, readily available on tape and compact disk recordings, coexist alongside contemporary corridos.

Along both sides of the U.S.–Mexican border, the corrido had a different history than it did in the interior of Mexico. It became a popular form of expression among the Spanish-speaking population along the Lower Rio Grande border about the same time that its popularity was on the decline in Mexico. This increase in popularity was related to the increased immigration into Texas after 1848 of Anglos from other parts of the United States. At this time corridos began to be used to record in song the increasing incidents of social conflict arising from Anglo social and racial oppression of the Mexican American population. The corrido be-

■ Fig. 1. A distraught and exhausted Gregorio Cortez (played by Edward James Olmos) rests after evading a large posse that has been pursuing him for many days. (From the 1983 Embassy Pictures movie poster; reprinted courtesy of David Maciel.)

came a form of cultural resistance composed and sung in Spanish at a wide variety of public and private events. It clearly reflected the heightened tension, and occasional armed resistance, associated with the intercultural conflict between Anglos and Texans of Mexican descent.

We can credit Américo Paredes for conducting thorough research on the border ballad and explaining to generations of his students and the public the importance of the corrido to the Spanish-speaking population on both sides of the U.S.–Mexican border. He determined that the most important and most popular of these ballads were based on the historical events surrounding the life of Gregorio Cortez, a Texas-Mexican rancher who lived with his family in central Texas at the beginning of the twentieth century (see figure 1). As narrated in "El corrido de Gregorio Cortez" (The Ballad of Gregorio Cortez), a simple misunderstanding between Anglo lawmen and Gregorio and his brother leads to gunshots and the death of both his brother and a deputy sheriff. Gregorio flees for his life, pursued by a large Anglo posse. Due to his skill as a horseman and his familiarity with the terrain, he eludes his pursuers for several weeks until he is finally captured and jailed. *Corridistas* (balladeers) composed several versions of this series of events, but all highlight Gregorio Cortez's bravery, loyalty, gentleness as a husband and father, defiance of Anglo authorities, and victimization as a member of an oppressed group.

It is evident that the use of the corrido to express intercultural conflict along the U.S.–Mexican border continued well into the twentieth century. Such corridos continued to be composed and sung until after World War II, but wartime corridos differ from the earlier songs in important ways. In the pre–World War II period, the protagonist of a corrido was "invariably presented as a potent, larger-than-life hero who in a symbolic sense avenged the collective insults against his people," a pattern exemplified in "El corrido de Gregorio Cortez" (Peña 1992–1996, 202). This hero is replaced in later corridos by a relatively weak character who is portrayed as a more-or-less helpless victim.

The shift in the role of the protagonist can be explained by the profound changes that took place in the socioeconomic circumstances of the Chicano population relative to those of the dominant society between 1900 and about 1950. Beginning at the end of the Depression in the early 1930s, Mexican Americans along the U.S.–Mexican border moved by the thousands from rural settings and small villages to large urban centers such as Houston, San Antonio, El Paso, Phoenix, and Los Angeles. Due in part to Mexican Americans' increasing dependence on manufacturing jobs in cities and in part to the return to the United States after World War II of thousands of Mexican American veterans who had fought valiantly in overseas war operations from 1942 to 1945, the expectations of the Mexican American population changed. Urban Mexican Americans—especially veterans—expected more opportunities from the country they had defended and died for. Although they were more willing than before to assimilate into this society, they demanded that it be much more accommodating. At the same time, political organizations that advocated for Mexican Americans became stronger and more effective. One scholar has suggested that these socioeconomic and political developments contributed in a very important way to a change in the role of the corrido from a form that uplifted a battered cultural image to one that rallied support for activist political causes (Peña 1992–1996, 202).

The Mexican American population along the U.S.–Mexican border was the "passive beneficiary" of the exploits of Gregorio Cortez and other larger-than-life corrido heroes. In contrast, the new, victimized corrido protagonist served to rally the population to defend itself against racism, economic exploitation, and social injustice. The following corrido, "Los rinches" (a derogatory term for the Texas Rangers), is an example of this new role. (Reprinted with permission of Texas A&M University Press from Manuel Peña, *Música Tejana*, 1999b, 81–82):

Voy a cantarles, señores	Gentlemen, I'm going to sing for you
De dos pobres infortunios,	about two unfortunate souls,
y de algo que sucedió	and something that happened
el día primero de junio.	on the first day of June.
En el condado de Estrella.	In the county of Starr
en merito Río Grande	right in Rio Grande City
junio del '67	in June of '67
sucedió un hecho de sangre.	a bloody event took place.
Es una triste verdad	It is the sad truth
de vanos pobres campesinos	about some poor farm workers
que brutalmente golpearon	who were brutally beaten
esos rinches asesinos.	by those murderous Rangers.
Decía Magdaleno Dimas	Said Magdaleno Dimas,
—Yo no puse resistencia	"I didn't offer any resistance;
rendido y bien asustado	subdued and very frightened;
me golpearon sin conciencia.	Still they beat me without mercy."
Decía Benjamín Rodríguez	Then said Benjamín Rodríguez
sin hacer ningún estremo:	without making a move,
—Ya no me peguen cobardes,	"Don't hit me anymore, you cowards,
en nombre del ser supremo.	in the name of the Almighty."
Esos rinches maldecidos	Those cursed Rangers
los mandó el gobernador	were sent by the governor
a proteger los melones	to protect the melons
de un rico conservador.	of a rich conservative.
Mr. Connally, señores,	Mr. Connally, gentlemen,
es el mal gobernador,	is the evil governor,
que aborrece al mexicano	who hates the Mexican

y se burla del dolor.	and is contemptuous of our pain.
Me despido, mis hermanos,	I take my leave, my brothers,
con dolor del corazón.	with an aching heart.
Como buenos mexicanos,	Like good Mexicans,
pertenezcan a la unión.	join the union.

The corrido as a song form continues to thrive today along the U.S.–Mexican border, across the Southwest, and even in the Midwest and Northwest, where there are significant concentrations of Chicanos. There are countless recordings of corridos that deal with racism, politics, intercultural and police violence, drugs and illegal drug running, the plight of undocumented Mexican and Central American workers, poverty and economic exploitation, and a wide range of other social topics. In addition to these corridos, it is not uncommon to hear on Spanish-language radio and television stations corridos about assassinations, movie stars, social outcasts, fights, sports figures, horse races—just about every imaginable topic. There are even corrido contests such as the one held in Tucson until recently during the Tucson Heritage Experience Festival, an annual community ethnic cultural festival.

◼ Música Tejana

Up to this point, I have briefly discussed some important song forms that were either brought to the Hispanic Southwest by Spanish and later Mexican settlers or that evolved from these song forms. In this section, I give an overview of a regional artistic phenomenon—*música Tejana*—because of its importance in Texas and to a much lesser degree across the Southwest from the middle of the nineteenth century to the end of the twentieth century.

Texas can be described as a kind of Chicano musical epicenter from which the influence of musical styles, instrumentation, and performers radiates outward. In Albuquerque, Tucson, Phoenix, Los Angeles, and many other communities in between, there are men and women of all ages listening to the top hits on their radios; watching television dance and performance programs; buying records; and attending live music performances at dance venues, high school auditoriums, and concert halls.

Those interested in Chicano popular music owe a great debt of gratitude to scholar Manuel Peña, who in three books and countless articles (see Peña 1985, 1992–1996, 1999a, 1999b) has carefully documented Tejano music from the mid-nineteenth century forward. It is only appropriate that the following overview of Tejano music begin with a quote from Peña: "Among the Mexican Americans who inhabit the American Southwest—the states of California, Arizona, New Mexico, Colorado, and Texas—one group has distinguished itself for its strongly innovative musical spirit: the Texas-Mexicans, or tejanos as they sometimes call themselves" (Peña 1999b, 14).

Peña perceptively documents how music as a form of expressive culture grew out of a complex combination of historical circumstances surrounding the conflict between Anglo Texans and Texas-Mexicans before and after the Mexican War of 1846–1848. As a result of the Treaty of Guadalupe Hidalgo, which ended the war, the Mexicans who had resided in what was formerly northern Mexico suddenly became citizens of the United States. Although on paper the treaty guaranteed their rights, in reality they found themselves subordinated within a new social order dominated by Anglo Texans. The Tejanos were thus at what Peña aptly calls "ground zero" in the explosive clash between Anglo and Mexican social systems in the Southwest.

Because armed resistance to these oppressive conditions was rarely viable—although there were certainly instances of it—Texas-Mexicans and the waves of Mexican immigrants who later followed "ultimately forged a unique expressive culture, ranging from bilingualism to the musical forms" that Peña describes in his book *Música Tejana* (1999b, 16).

As we shall see, the changes in the social status of Mexican Americans in Texas over the next century brought with them different forms of music that reflected deep class fissures between working-class Tejanos and middle- and upper-class Tejanos intent on assimilating themselves into the dominant culture.

Conjunto

I have already discussed the nineteenth- and early-twentieth-century border corrido as a uniquely Chicano song form that both reflected the deep antagonism that Tejanos had toward Anglos and served as a form of resistance. Like the corrido, the Texas-Mexican conjunto is another powerful oppositional form of culture (Peña 1999b, 21). Later in its history, the conjunto also came to reflect the emerging class differences within the Tejano population. Thus, this uniquely Tejano music served as a form of resistance against Anglo values and oppressive conditions as well as a way for working-class Tejanos to distinguish themselves from those Tejanos they considered more *agringados* (anglicized) in their dress, speech, values, customs, and ultimately, musical preferences.

Conjunto is an accordion ensemble that originally also included a guitar or bajo sexto (a basslike, twelve-stringed instrument with, like the accordion, a strong Mexican identity), and a *tambora de rancho,* an improvised drum made from materials such as goatskin heads, wire rims, mallets, and henequen (twine made from agave fiber). The accordion, the basic instrument of conjunto ensembles, made its appearance in Texas-Mexican music around the middle of the nineteenth century. Some musicologists believe that it was introduced by the Polish, German, and Czech immigrants who settled around San Antonio in the 1840s, but Peña believes that the instrument was imported from northern Mexico, where German immigrants had popularized it after the 1860s (Peña 1985, 35–36). Whatever its origin, the accordion was an ideal instrument because it was portable, relatively easy to learn, and needed no accompaniment. It was common for accordionists to play at functions such as weddings and other festive occasions, and by the beginning of the twentieth century, the accordion was the preferred instrument of rural and working-class Tejanos. A bajo sexto and tambora de rancho were added to the ensemble's instrumentation early in the century. Around this time the conjunto began to establish a musical tradition and to distinguish itself as the music of the common people, along with corridos and canciones about political topics.

Peña identifies the 1920s as the "watershed years" for Texas-Mexican music due mainly to the influence of large American recording companies on recording and distribution. Companies such as Decca and subsidiaries of RCA and Columbia set up recording studios in San Antonio and Dallas, as well as Los Angeles. These recording companies would place advertisements in local newspapers and employ the services of Mexican American talent brokers to attract, audition, and record popular Mexican and Tejano musicians and singers. The advent of Spanish-language broadcasting coupled with the popularization of electronically produced music by means of relatively inexpensive home phonographs catapulted conjunto music across the Southwest.

Narciso Martínez is generally considered the father of conjunto music, although others such as Bruno Villarreal and José Rodríguez were also known for their excellent accordion playing. Martínez was the most prolific and most popular accordionist after 1935 (Peña 1985, 55). He was born on October 29, 1911, in Reynosa, Tamaulipas, Mexico, across the border from McAllen, Texas. His parents brought him over to Texas in that year, and he has lived in the United States since then. Although he has refused to become a naturalized American citizen, he has always considered himself to be, in his own words, a *méxico-americano*. Like many conjunto musicians, he was raised in a working-class family, received almost no schooling, and was self-taught on the accordion. By 1935, he had mastered the two-button accordion and had launched his career. As his reputation continued to grow, Martínez was soon dubbed "El Huracán del Valle" (The Hurricane of the Valley) by his fans. Despite the success of his recordings, he profited little from his recording contracts, which were commonly written to benefit the recording companies rather than the Tejano performers.

Martínez is representative of many successful conjunto musicians who never really achieved the kind of star status we associate with contemporary singers and musicians. As a consequence, their ties to their working class roots remained strong. Martínez remained popular during the 1940s and 1950s, and was one of the first conjunto musicians to tour outside Texas to New Mexico, Arizona, and California (Peña 1985, 59).

In his analysis of the development of conjunto music, Peña stresses that despite the significant popularity of Narciso Martínez and other musicians, this type of music remained a collective folk phenomenon. He states that "a consensus was continuously being worked out between performers and the public that sustained them. All performers, and audiences alike, were working-class folk who shared a strong sense of ethnic and, to a certain extent, class consciousness" (Peña 1985, 64).

After World War II, the major recording companies such as RCA began to turn away from conjunto music in favor of what they viewed as a much more lucrative Hispanic music market in Mexico. RCA and other companies closed down their studios in Texas and opened new ones in Mexico City. Radio stations throughout the Southwest did, however, continue to play conjunto music in response to listener demand.

The exit of large commercial recording companies had a silver lining for conjunto music, as enterprising Mexican American talent searchers and businessmen set up their own recording studios that, while not nearly as large or successful as RCA or Columbia, did manage to capture a local Texas market. Despite the failure of many of these small companies, some such as Falcón and Ideal succeeded and were instrumental in propagating Tejano music (Peña 1985, 72).

Two men, Valerio Longoria and Tony de la Rosa, were central to the development of conjunto music after World War II. Longoria was born in 1924 in a small town between Corpus Christi and San Antonio. He spent much of his youth accompanying his father on the migrant stream, and what he lacked in formal education he made up for in musical talent. He first learned to play the guitar and was performing with musical groups by the age of eight. He then mastered the accordion. Longoria served in the U.S. Army in Germany during World War II, then returned to Texas and signed a recording contract. According to Peña, he was perhaps the first accordionist to combine singing talent with his playing. This was important because in song forms such as the canción corrida and the canción ranchera, the lyrics he sung would often replace the accordion itself.

As famous and as influential as Longoria was in the recent stages of development of conjunto music, Tony de la Rosa's mark on this music is even more enduring (Peña 1985, 85). He was born close to Corpus Christi and by the time he was sixteen had begun playing as an independent accordionist. He was to become the best-known conjunto accordionist throughout the 1950s as he traveled through much of the United States and Mexico. To his groups he added the electric bass and the electrified bajo sexto as standard ensemble instruments. This innovation was especially important in effectively projecting the instruments in large dance halls, which increasingly were equipped with public address systems and microphones that enhanced the singing and amplified the accordion (Peña 1985, 85–89).

Whereas conjunto music underwent dramatic changes between 1930 and 1960, most musicians since about 1960 have not significantly altered the music but have been content to rework the innovations made by Longoria, de la Rosa, and others in the 1950s. Peña attributes this turn toward musical conservatism to social forces. Once conjunto music had attained its maturity by 1960, it had become irrevocably identified as Tejano working-class music, a music that satisfied the musical needs of this class. And because the material and economic conditions of workers have not changed appreciably since the 1960s, their aesthetic needs have not changed either (Peña 1985, 101).

Orquesta Tejana

Conjunto was the preferred form of music of working-class Chicanos in Texas and throughout the Southwest from about the 1930s through the 1960s and is still popular today, especially among Tejanos who adhere closely to their class identity and traditional Mexican values. *Orquesta* (orchestral) music, on the other hand, became increasingly popular, first among Tejanos and later among Chicanos everywhere who became eager to shed their working-class origins and identity and begin to assimilate into the dominant culture.

The development of orquesta music roughly parallels that of conjunto but differs from it in an important way: rather than being built "from the ground up," orquesta had ready-made Mexican and American models to imitate. As Peña (1999b, 118) has observed, orchestral ensembles, ranging from symphonic units to brass bands, were already well established in both countries by the end of the nineteenth century. As orquesta music evolved, it began to acquire a bicultural identity that reflected the bicultural drive characteristic of middle-class Chicanos who strived to be comfortable in many important ways—language, customs, dress, food—in both Anglo and Chicano societies.

Orquesta groups from the late nineteenth century through the 1920s tended to be string (mainly violin) ensembles. As large American swing bands began to dominate the U.S. music scene in the 1930s, it was only a matter of time before orquestas in Texas and elsewhere began modeling themselves on this new and exciting music and dance style called *swing*. Around 1930, the instrumentation of orquestas changed to that of big American swing bands and switched from strings to almost exclusively wind instruments. Beto Villa, considered the father of native orquesta Tejana, began recording in 1947 in a style that Peña (1999b, 119) identifies as "Tex-Mex Ranchero," a sound that influenced orquesta music across the Southwest for decades to come. Finally, in the late 1960s, the group Little Joe and the Latinaires (renamed Little Joe y la Familia in the 1970s) gave rise to what has become known as La Onda Chicana (The Chicano Wave). By the mid-1980s, orchestral music, including La Onda Chicana, lost its popularity among Chicanos and went into a period of sharp decline.

The key for successful orquestas has been to mediate between traditional Chicano/Mexican culture and Anglo culture. Although many middle-class Mexican Americans aspired to become more assimilated into the dominant society, they were not entirely comfortable abandoning the values and cultural practices of their families. Successful orquestas thus had to walk a fine line and produce a music that reflected and responded to the bicultural desires of its audience.

La Onda Chicana

Orchestras in the Southwest and even the Midwest in the 1950s and the 1960s typically juxtaposed the two styles of orquesta and American pop music. Alternation between American versus Mexican, middle-class versus working-class characterized orquesta music for more than two decades until the sociocultural forces of the mid-1960s that led to the Chicano Movement offered a different solution: a synthesis of musical styles and traditions.

Musicians such as Little Joe Hernández and Sunny Ozuna began experimenting with a new style of orquesta that incorporated American pop musical traditions directly into their compositions. Little Joe joined a Texas group, David Coronado and the Latinaires, as a guitarist, and in 1957 the group recorded a rock tune, "Safari," parts 1 and 2, which may have been the first rock and roll tune recorded by a Tejano group (Peña 1999b, 153). In 1963, Sunny Ozuna and his group Sunny and the Sunliners recorded a rock tune, "Talk to Me," that catapulted them and Tejano onto the top-forty charts.

By 1967, Little Joe had become leader of his group and had dropped the name Latinaires in favor of La Familia, a strong indication of how the Chicano Movement's strong resistance to assimilation had influenced young musicians as well as artists and writers. The cultural nationalism of the Chicano Movement, which emphasized a return to Indo-Mexican and traditional values—including the reemergence of the family as a strong cultural institution—led Little Joe to formally change the name of his group. Other changes occurred as well, changes that would characterize the emerging musical style called La Onda Chicana: long hair, hippie clothing, and overt militancy. In 1972, Little Joe y la Familia recorded a rock album, *Para la Gente,* that included the cut "Las nubes" (The Clouds), an immensely popular tune. The tune represents a genuine synthesis: the *ranchero*-flavored instrumental introduction to the piece with two trumpets, trombone, two saxophones, plus rhythm section of electric guitar, electric bass, Hammond organ, and trap-drums gives way to a string ensemble. The effect created constantly threatens to dissolve the basic ranchero style. Jazz-oriented licks constantly interrupt and interact with ranchero style throughout the rest of the piece in what Peña calls "bimusicality" closely related to the linguistic code-switching (dual use of English and Spanish) that the Chicano Movement made acceptable and exalted as a valid form of Chicano speech (Peña 1999b, 167–69). It is understandable, then, why "Las nubes" was elevated to anthem status.

Unlike Little Joe Hernández, Sunny Ozuna remained staunchly middle class during his career and never identified with the cultural nationalism of the Chicano Movement. Sunny and his group, Sunny and the Sunliners, continued throughout the 1960s and 1970s to project an image of sophistication, and his audiences typically would attend his concerts dressed in coats and ties and formal gowns—no long-haired hippies and the odor of marijuana smoke wafting through the air. In addition to polkas, they played boleros, cumbias, and cha-cha-chas in swing style, as well as a wide variety of Afro-Caribbean, Brazilian, and Latin American musical genres. Sunny and the Sunliners adopted what Peña has identified as a "bimusical" solution, drawing on traditional polca ranchera—a musical style originating in and associated with Mexican rural life—as well as other musical traditions but never achieving a synthesis in the way that Little Joe y la Familia had (Peña 1999b, 174).

Tejano Music of the Post-Chicano Era

The American political landscape changed dramatically after the mid-1970s, and Chicanos and Chicano music were not immune to these changes. "Tejano" became in the 1990s the umbrella term under which various Texas-Mexican and other Chicano groups were labeled. Tejano combines Mexican polkas, *baladas* (love songs in slow tempo), and cumbias with elements of rock, pop, country, and even reggae and rap. The traditional role of música Tejana as an organic cultural expression now gave way to the desire of musicians and their major label sponsors to become successful and profitable mass-market commodities. Even as highly successful musical entertainers struggled to recognize their traditional roots in Texas-Mexican culture, they were forced to adjust their musical styles to appeal to a much more ethnically and class-diverse audience. Nonetheless, there are important variations among groups who fall under the Tejano music umbrella.

Some groups, such as La Mafia and Emilio Navaira, have relied more heavily on the polca ranchera than other groups; Mazz and other groups have favored the balada. Selena, the "Queen of Tejano," relied heavily on commercially successful Latino genres such as the cumbia. In addition to the differences among these groups and musical figures, some accordion-based groups remained faithful to the early traditional forms such as conjunto and orquesta, while so-called progressive conjunto groups deviated somewhat from the basic ensemble by incorporating synthesized keyboards and a broad repertoire of songs (Peña 1999b, 185–86).

The intense commercialization of Tejano music in the last fifteen years is based largely on the success of what are often referred to as the "Big Four" of the Tejano recording industry: Selena, Emilio Navaira, La Mafia, and Mazz. For example, Selena's last recording, the pop-rock album *Dreaming of You,* was the top album in the Billboard 200 charts, selling 331,000 copies by the end of its first week on the market (Burr 1995, 39). Prior to 1990, top Tejano performers were lucky to sell 20,000 units. The mass-music industry into which the Big Four were plugged had developed close control of the market, airplay on radio and television, and circuits of distribution.

Selena

Selena Quintanilla Pérez was born in Freeport, Texas, in 1971. Selena was already performing publicly in 1983 at the age of twelve, and two years later she and the musical group Los Dinos recorded their first hit, "Dame un beso" (Give Me a Kiss). In 1987, she was named Female Entertainer of the Year by the Tejano Music Awards, the first of several years she would win the title. In 1989, she also won the Female Vocalist of the Year title. Several major commercial recording companies began to vie for her contract, and it was Capitol/EMI that succeeded in signing her (Patoski 1996, 95). She continued to blaze a path in Tejano music history. By 1994, her album *Amor Prohibido* (Forbidden Love) had knocked Gloria Estefán's *Mi Tierra* (My Land) off the number-one spot on the charts and by March 1995 had sold more than 400,000 units. In February 1995 she and Los Dinos attracted more than 60,000 people to a concert at the Houston Livestock and Rodeo Show at the Astrodome. It would be her last concert. On March 12, 1995, she was fatally shot by Yolanda Saldívar, who had started the Selena Fan Club.

Joe Nick Patoski, who wrote the 1996 biography *Selena,* comments that as Selena grew older and more physically mature, her image began to be transformed from the barrio girl-next-door to a full-blown sexual commodity (Patoski 1996, 95–98). She would capitalize on her sexuality for the rest of her short career until her untimely death in 1995. The selling of her image combined with a fine singing voice propelled her to an unprecedented level of popularity for a Tejano or Tejana musical figure. Her untimely death propelled her to "queen" status, and even today her fans continue to pay her homage in much the same way—but not to the same degree—that fans continue to remember and revere Elvis Presley. A steady stream of fans continues to visit her family's recording studio, Q Productions, in Corpus Christi every business day. There are several Selena websites and several official and unofficial biographies that, with the exception of the one by Patoski, paint a highly romanticized and idealized image of her. Her family is building a museum in her honor at their studio and has donated a black leather outfit of hers to the Smithsonian National Museum of American History. In 1998, fifty Sears stores conducted a market test of the Selena Spring Collection of junior sportswear—denim bottoms, skirts, and shorts; apparently Sears plans to carry the line nationwide and perhaps even in Puerto Rico and Mexico. It is even rumored that a Selena Barbie Doll is in the works. The filming of a movie based on Selena's short life began in San Antonio in October 1996 and opened across the Southwest in April 1997. It starred Jennifer López as Selena and Edward James Olmos as her father, Abraham.

Chicano Music on the West Coast

If Texas was the most important center for the development of Chicano popular music from the late nineteenth century through the 1990s, it was not by any means the only site of musical activity. Especially since about 1960, California—particularly Los Angeles—has produced several musical genres and numerous groups, musicians, songwriters, and individual singing artists. This is not to say they all were from California, only that many of them eventually ended up in the Los Angeles area because it was the center of the recording industry and had a huge and enthusiastic Chicano population that supported its musical artists. Eduardo "Lalo" Guerrero and Ritchie Valens (Valenzuela), were two Mexican Americans who broke into the California recording industry early, the former in the 1940s and the latter in the 1950s. Although they were different in their musical tastes, both of them should be considered pioneers in terms of their success in an Anglo-dominated industry.

Eduardo "Lalo" Guerrero

Eduardo "Lalo" Guerrero is a good example of a musician who left his native state of Arizona for Los Angeles as a young man to fulfill his desire to become a successful recording artist. Guerrero was born in Barrio Libre (the Free Barrio) in Tucson in 1916. His father, head boilermaker in the roundhouse of the Tucson Southern Pacific Railroad, worked tirelessly to support his family of five children, which was to grow to seventeen children by the time Guerrero was a young man. His mother, Doña Conchita, taught Guerrero to play the guitar when he was fourteen years old, but he began his career as a performer when he was in grammar school. His mother died when he was a young man and his father contracted Lou Gehrig's disease (amyotrophic lateral sclerosis).

Guerrero and his brother Frank relocated from Tucson to Los Angeles when he was eighteen. He recorded exclusively in Spanish for a few years, and his records sold modestly in the southern California market. His first recording as a solo singer was in 1948, and his songs soon began to get airplay on Spanish-language radio stations in the Los Angeles area. His popularity grew and he was soon performing in many venues as the featured artist.

Despite the predominance of Spanish-language recordings he made during the late 1940s and 1950s, Guerrero desired to be primarily a performer of stock American tunes of that era. His idols as a high school student had been Rudy Vallee, Al Jolson, Eddie Cantor, and later, Bing Crosby (Reyes and Waldman 1998, 7). Imperial Records asked Guerrero to begin recording in English and to change his professional name to Don Edwards. The experiment flopped, however, and he went back to recording and playing for Mexican American audiences through the 1950s. At the same time, he recorded a parody of the "Ballad of Davy Crockett," which had been popularized by Bill Hayes and Fess Parker. Guerrero's version, which was called the "Ballad of Pancho López," was a success and eventually sold more than 500,000 copies. He performed it on the "Tonight Show" hosted in the mid-1950s by Steve Allen as well as on the "Art Linkletter Show."

Twenty years later, cultural nationalists and others would harshly criticize Guerrero for this song because it appeared to make fun of Chicanos (Reyes and Waldman 1998, 8). Some argued that he was merely satirizing an American icon— Crockett—while others resented the humor being directed at Chicanos. Guerrero also wrote and recorded other parodies in the late 1950s, including "Tacos for Two" (a parody of "Tea for Two"), "There's No Tortillas" ("Yes, We Have No Bananas"), "Pancho Claus," and "I Left My Car in San Francisco" (a parody of the Tony Bennett standard "I Left My Heart in San Francisco"). In 1960, he was able to open his own nightclub, Lalo's Place, in Los Angeles financed from the proceeds of his recording and performing successes.

Despite the criticism of his "Pancho López" parody, Chicano students of the Chicano Movement era generally considered Guerrero to be a pioneer in the music field, and Chicano organizations invited him to speak on college campuses during the 1960s and 1970s; now more than eighty years old, he is still performing on college campuses. At the same time, Guerrero has continued to perform for largely Anglo audiences at venues such as luxurious restaurants in Los Angeles, Palm Springs, and elsewhere.

Guerrero has never considered himself a militant, but he has taken strong stands on occasion in order to combat negative stereotyping and overt racism. For example, he composed and sang "No Chicanos on TV" as a protest against the television industry's practice of relegating Chicano characters to minor (and usually negatively stereotyped) roles.

Guerrero received numerous awards throughout his career, not only for his contribution to American musical culture but also for his public stands on social issues. The Latino organization Nosotros (founded by actor Ricardo Montalbán) awarded him two Golden Eagle Awards in 1980 and 1989. The Smithsonian Institution declared him a "National Folk Treasure" in 1980. President and Mrs. Bush awarded him a National Heritage Fellowship in 1991. He was inducted into the Tejano Music Hall of Fame in 1992. Mexican President Ernesto Zedillo presented him the 1998 Cultural Institute Lifetime Achievement Award, and in the same year the National Council of La Raza (NCLR) recognized him with an ALMA award. Perhaps Guerrero's crowning honor was receiving the National Medal of the Arts awarded at a White House ceremony on February 7, 1997. In making the award, President William Clinton said, "Presented by the president of the United States of America for a distinguished music career that spans over sixty years, two cultures, and a wealth of different musical styles. With humor, passion, and profound insight, he has entertained and enlightened generations of audiences giving powerful voice to the joys and sorrows of the Mexican American experience."

Ritchie Valens (Richard Valenzuela)

Richard Valenzuela was not the first Chicano musician to excel at R&B or rock and roll in the Los Angeles area, but he certainly was one of the most talented rock and roll musicians of all time and probably one of the most confident as well (Reyes and Waldman 1998, 37). Valenzuela was born and raised in Pacoima, a suburb of Los Angeles in the San Fernando Valley. He learned to play the guitar and already as a high school student was performing at high school dances and other local venues. Music promoter Bob Keane, following a tip about a talented performer, attended one of Valenzuela's performances in Pacoima, very much liked what he heard, and invited the young man to record some songs for him. He liked "Come On, Let's Go," a song that Valenzuela had written. Keane took Valenzuela to Gold Star Studios in Hollywood where he recorded the song. Thanks to Keane, who was well connected in the recording business, the song was soon being heard on commercial radio stations in Los Angeles. Valenzuela's career was launched, and to make him more attractive to a general audience, Keane asked him to anglicize his name to Ritchie Valens.

The anglicizing of surnames had been occurring in the movie and recording industries for decades, starting with Jewish studio moguls who changed their names in the 1920s as a protection against anti-Semitism (Reyes and Waldman 1998, 39). Keane's desire to change Valenzuela's name was probably motivated more by commercial gain than protection against racism, however.

By late 1958, Valens was being invited to perform at concerts and dances all over southern California. He then recorded "La Bamba" and "Donna," which together with "Come On, Let's Go" were to form the trilogy of songs for which Valens is best remembered. The 45-rpm single with "La Bamba" on one side and "Donna" on the other became one of the best-selling 45s of all time. In late 1958, Valens toured the Midwest and East, appearing on "American Bandstand" and in Alan Freed's Christmas show at the Paramount Theater in New York City. Valens's short but very intensive and successful career came to a tragic end on February 3, 1959, when the small plane carrying him, Buddy Holly, and J. P. "Big Bopper" Richardson crashed into a snow-covered Iowa cornfield.

Fig. 2. Lou Diamond Phillips portrays Ritchie Valens in the movie *La Bamba,* singing the song by the same name that contributed to Valens's fame. (1987 Columbia Pictures movie poster reprinted courtesy of David Maciel.)

It is difficult to trace any measurable influence that Valens had on the development of Chicano rock and roll in the 1960s and 1970s. Those musicians who were close to him were very hesitant to play his big hits after his death lest they be accused of exploiting his name. This is not to say that public officials, politicians, and music promoters have not invoked his name over the years to enhance their own reputations or simply to pay homage to him as a great Chicano musician.

Since the 1980s, a virtual industry has been created around the figure of Ritchie Valens. The release in 1987 of the movie *La Bamba* (discussed in greater detail in chapter 3 on cinema) starring Lou Diamond Phillips as Valens began what was to become a revival of his image (see figure 2). In

1991 the U.S. Postal Service dedicated a stamp to him, and in 1994 the Ritchie Valens Community Center Building was formally dedicated at a park in his hometown of Pacoima.

West Coast Chicano Music in the 1960s

The two Chicano acts that were most prominent and that had the greatest impact on Chicano rock and roll music in Los Angeles in the 1960s were Cannibal and the Headhunters and Thee Midniters. Both of these groups had nationwide hit records (Reyes and Waldman 1998, 69).

Cannibal and the Headhunters was made up of four musicians, three of them from the tough Ramona Gardens housing project in East Los Angeles: Richard "Scar" López, Bobby "Rabbit" Jaramillo, Joe Jaramillo, and Frankie García from Aliso Village near East Los Angeles. The Headhunters' most celebrated recording was their version of "Land of 1,000 Dances," which quickly became a standard in East Los Angeles. It also did well elsewhere, finally climbing as high as thirty on the Billboard charts. The group toured throughout the Southwest, the Midwest, the East, and the South, playing at venues (e.g., the Kentucky Bluegrass State Fair) where no Chicano entertainer—including Guerrero and Valens—had appeared before. Perhaps the pinnacle of their success and recognition was being invited to join the final leg of the Beatles' tour of America in 1965. They performed with the young British group at Shea Stadium in New York as well as at the Hollywood Bowl in Los Angeles. The group finally broke up in 1966 over a money dispute with their promoter Eddie Davis (Reyes and Waldman 1998, 73).

According to Chicano music historian Steven Loza (1993, 99), from 1964 to 1970 the musical group Thee Midniters "were considered by many to be the most significant rock and roll band to emanate from the Mexican community in Los Angeles." Although this eight-piece group released only four albums, they performed hundreds of concerts, which allowed them to develop a polished stage presence with well-rehearsed, choreographed moves and tailored suits like those of the young Beatles, the group that was sweeping the United States. They were immensely popular throughout southern California yet did not profit greatly from their record sales. One of their most popular singles was "Whittier Boulevard," named after one of East Los Angeles's most popular cruising streets.

The band brought together a group of very talented musicians including lead singer Willie García, lead guitarist George Domínguez, drummer George Salazar, and saxophonists Romeo Prado and Larry Rendón, who wrote the music that gave the band a highly unusual jazz tinge (Reyes and Waldman 1998, 85–86).

The band regularly performed at the Hollywood Palladium as part of Sunday-evening salsa concerts. They learned and played a wide range of markedly different musical styles, reflecting how eclectic Chicano rock and roll was during the 1960s. Toward the end of their existence as a band Thee Midniters released the "Ballad of César Chávez" (1968) in recognition of the leader's role in improving the lot of farmworkers across the Southwest. Later that year they released "Chicano Power" as a gesture toward the Chicano Movement.

West Coast Chicano Music in the 1970s

The profound changes in cultural perspective that the Chicano Movement of the late 1960s and early 1970s had on high school and college campuses and in the barrios of cities throughout the Southwest were reflected in Chicano music of the period. Bands and individual performers no longer tried to disguise their identity as Americans of Mexican descent. The days of anglicizing one's name were over; the names of new bands no longer were designed to appeal to a broad Anglo audience. Even some established bands changed their names to reflect a newfound pride in Chicanismo.

For the most part, Chicano musical performers aligned themselves with the ethnic or cultural nationalism of the Chicano Movement. Such an alignment was not without its problems. Bands and individual performers did not want to be (or appear to be) disloyal to the spirit and political agenda of cultural nationalism that Chicanos of all generations—but particularly the young music audiences—were embracing. On the other hand, they also felt compelled to remain consistent with the style and range of American and Anglo-American sources that formed the basis of their music. Their musical models, after all, had always been Anglo or black performers (Reyes and Waldman 1998, 105).

At the same time, many Anglo and black bands and performers were themselves beginning to reflect the values and political agenda of the New Left of which the Chicano Movement was one manifestation. As Reyes and Waldman (1998, 105) have observed, "The rock charts started to read like student demands." A sampling of titles of rock and soul hits of the late

1960s and early 1970s illustrates this point: "People Got to Be Free," "It's Your Thing," "War," "Say It Loud—I'm Black and Proud," the Rolling Stones' "Street Fighting Man," and the Beatles' "Revolution."

For many Chicano musicians of the late 1960s and early 1970s, Spanish or Indian names, Mexican songs, and Latin rhythms constituted a statement of their ethnic identity or of how they wanted to be perceived by the Chicano community (Reyes and Waldman 1998, 112). Two bands that formed during this time embody this change: Tierra and El Chicano. These bands not only reflected their cultural orientation in their names, but they also were an essential part of the political events taking place on campuses and in the barrio. Tierra, for example, performed at Cal State Los Angeles during the September 16 (Mexican Independence Day) fiestas in 1970 and 1971. In general, both bands played at political rallies and celebrations of important Mexican historical events; but, of course, they continued to play at dances. The fine line that these two (and many other) bands walked was to reflect their pride in their Mexican heritage through their choice of venues and musical selections while at the same time trying to stay current and successful in the larger American popular music market. Tierra played dances, rallies, and celebrations in East Los Angeles but also toured the East Coast with black soul and R&B bands.

El Chicano was formed in 1969 and, like Tierra, continued playing and recording through the mid-1990s. Bobby Espinosa, one of its founders, is a skilled jazz organist and gave the band from its inception a jazz-tinged sound. One of its early hits, "Viva tirado," got the band invited to perform at jazz festivals in the Midwest. Their Los Angeles–based Chicano audience understood that the band played a variety of music—jazz, blues, and rock and roll—that did not necessarily reflect its highly symbolic name. Audiences elsewhere in the Southwest where the band toured were often disappointed that it did not play Tejano or popular Mexican music, however.

After the early 1970s, the political agenda of most Chicanos shifted away from cultural nationalism toward making progress within the established political order. Sponsoring candidates and running voter registration drives replaced street demonstrations and sit-ins on campuses. This is not to say that Chicano organizers and their recent converts to a newfound pride in Indo-Mexican culture did not continue to pursue their agenda, but the emphasis definitely shifted toward making and consolidating gains within the municipal, state, and national political systems.

Likewise, successful Chicano bands formed in the mid-1970s did not turn their backs on the successes, values, and symbols of the Chicano Movement and its cultural nationalism. A well-known band, Ruben and the Jets, achieved what Reyes and Waldman (1998, 126) call a "new musical synthesis, combining the classic Chicano sound—mainly black-based R&B—with visual representations of Chicano pride." The issues of politics and ethnic identity and pride formed an essential part of the repertoire of these and other Chicano bands from the 1970s forward; no longer could they satisfy their audiences by singing only about typical subjects such as love, sex, and parties.

Frank Zappa produced Ruben and the Jets and he together with Ruben Guevara, the band's leader, gave the band's music a kind of sharp edge that clearly differentiated it from the softer sounds of 1960s bands such as Thee Midniters. By 1973, the band was touring with Three Dog Night and playing huge venues such as the Royals Stadium in Kansas City before 43,000 fans (Reyes and Waldman 1998, 127). The band had developed a unique way of making Chicano standards from the 1950s and 1960s sound new by giving them an R&B sound. Their album covers were also designed to honor the 1950s and the 1970s simultaneously. Ruben Guevara was largely responsible for the band's success in synthesizing the currents of two musical eras. He was also the prime agent in what came to be known as the "Eastside Renaissance," which centered around music (along with murals, literature, theater, and politics) as a symbol of Chicano power, behavior, and culture (Loza 1993, 111). In other words, music served its community as much more than mere entertainment. After the breakup of Ruben and the Jets, Guevara went on to form his own group, Con Safos (slang for "the same to you"), a defiant name and symbol (C/S) that he extended to represent Chicano self-determination, self-reliance, and self-realization; that is, self-empowerment. He composed "C/S," which is a composite of the historical urban struggle of Chicanos against an oppressive Anglo society (Loza 1993, 112).

West Coast Chicano Music in the 1980s

According to Loza, the success of Luis Valdez's play *Zoot Suit* (discussed in greater detail in chapter 5), which premiered in the late 1970s at the Mark Taper Forum at the Music Center in downtown Los Angeles and at the Aquarius Theater in Hollywood, contributed to the musical awareness of Los Angeles Chicanos. This was especially true when the play was made into a movie by the same name. The score for both the play and the motion picture—much of it composed by Lalo Guerrero and Daniel Valdez, Luis Valdez's brother—recalled the musical atmosphere of the anti–Vietnam War period and the pachuco subculture (a youth gang culture) in Los Angeles. The 1981 movie starred Chicano actor Edward James Olmos as the Pachuco figure.

Some 1980s examples of Chicano musical expression from the Los Angeles area are the following groups: The Brat, Los Illegals, The Undertakers, and the Plugz (now known as Los Cruzados). These and many other groups have tended to rely on punk rock and new wave styles, although none of the bands has entirely abandoned the Chicano/Mexican musical tradition. The punk rock espousal of anarchy, contradiction, and rebellion as a cry for social, political, and cultural revolutions was not entirely alien to some of the messages contained in the music influenced directly by the Chicano Movement. What was different was the outrageous dress and demeanor of many Chicano punk rockers. New wave, which is an outgrowth of punk and its espousal of social change, offered Chicano music groups a way to remain socially committed and yet pursue a wider, non-Chicano audience (Loza 1993, 111). Los Cruzados, Felix and the Katz, Odd Squad, The Undertakers, Loli Lux and the Bears, The Brat, and Los Illegals are all Los Angeles–based bands that have adopted the message and esoteric style of new wave.

LOS LOBOS Of all contemporary West Coast Chicano musical groups, perhaps the most enduring, the most adaptable, the closest knit, and the most resilient has been Los Lobos. The original members of the band were Conrad Lozano, David Hidalgo, Louie Pérez, and César Rosas. They began where so many other Chicano bands began: in a family living room jamming and talking about music. They were discovered in 1973 by promoter Fernando Mosqueda, who "had faith in Los Lobos long before they had faith in themselves" (Reyes and Waldman 1998, 145). At that point, they were just some friends who would get together to talk, listen to old Mexican recordings, and practice a few Mexican songs. Mosqueda got them their first real concert at a Veterans of Foreign Wars hall in Compton, California. They came up with the name Los Lobos, the name they still have today.

Up to that point, the various members of the band had played in funk bands, hard and soft rock bands, and Beatles-like bands, but this would be the first time they had performed Mexican music for money and in public. Their dress and style was more funk than mariachi, their repertoire was very limited, and they did not speak Spanish. Despite not meeting the dress and style expectations of their audience, they did well. What they lacked in Mexican authenticity they made up for in confidence. For the next eight years, they increased their Mexican music repertoire to 150 songs and played hundreds of gigs in both large and small venues. They were also beginning to listen to punk groups, including the Sex Pistols, and to attend shows at punk clubs in Hollywood. They met Phil Alvin, singer and guitarist for the Blasters, a popular rock and roll group from Los Angeles. He encouraged them to record and send him a rock demo tape. As a result, they were soon engaged to open at the Whisky, one of Hollywood's hottest clubs. Once again—as eight years before—they rose to the challenge, playing a mix of Tejano and original songs.

Los Lobos has endured as a close-knit group of friends who have not let internal jealousies, the demands of marriage and relationships, the failure to land recording contracts, and money tear them apart. According to Reyes and Waldman (1998, 147), "They moved slowly, but they never quit. That persistence and dogged determination set Los Lobos apart from earlier Chicano bands, who tended to get frustrated or impatient if good things did not happen soon, or again and again."

The members of Los Lobos were similar to at least some other Chicano musicians from Los Angeles in two respects: they listened to a broad spectrum of music—including James Brown, Aretha Franklin, the Rolling Stones, the Beatles, and Led Zeppelin—and they were diverse in their musical backgrounds. This rich mixture of musical tastes allowed them to diversify and adapt to current musical changes during their many years together. It also allowed the group to remain unpredictable and to delight in upsetting the expectations of their audiences. Their audiences soon caught on and sometimes would request songs that were not part of the repertoire for a given performance (e.g., rock and roll at a traditional Mexican ballad performance).

In the late 1970s, Los Lobos finally recast themselves as a rock band, which allowed them to draw more fans and sell more albums. They recorded the soundtrack for the 1987 movie *La Bamba,* which required them to play some 1950s standards such as "Come On, Let's Go" and "That's My Little Suzie." Not wishing to be typecast as simply a Chicano rock band or a band that played only Mexican traditional music, they recorded in the late 1980s *La Pistola y el Corazón* (The Pistol and the Heart) and then quickly another rock album. During the 1990s, they recorded two musically innovative albums, *Kiko* (1992) and *Colossal Head* (1996).

Los Lobos has largely succeeded in not being pigeonholed as a band that plays a certain kind of music. During the 1980s their better-known songs can be classified as folk rock or country rock. During the 1990s some of the songs on their *Colossal Head* album sound somewhat like punk (e.g., "Más y más") but also remind older listeners of late-1960s blues. They also continue to compose, record, and perform songs that return them to their 1980s folk rock and country rock days (Reyes and Waldman 1998, 154).

SANTANA   Like Los Lobos, Santana has endured since the early 1970s and continues to tour the United States and internationally while at the same time producing award-winning albums. Carlos Santana, the group's founder, was born in 1947 in Mexico, where his father, an accomplished mariachi violinist, introduced him to traditional Mexican music and the basics of music theory. The family moved to Tijuana in 1955, where Carlos quickly learned to play guitar and soon was studying and imitating the sounds of the great black blues singers: B.B. King, T-Bone Walker, and John Lee Hooker. He began playing in local Tijuana and San Diego bands that were playing predominantly popular 1950s rock and roll songs. In 1960, his family moved to San Francisco, but Carlos stayed in Tijuana to hone his musical skills in local clubs. He also learned English, which allowed him to enroll in school in San Francisco a year later. He vigorously developed his musical style, a style that was to become the basis for the Santana Blues Band he would form in 1966.

San Francisco in the mid-1960s was not only a mecca for America's drug and alternative living scene but also a center of musical diversity and excitement. Santana and his band became immediately popular in San Francisco. They played the Filmore West, one of the most important West Coast venues for rock and roll bands. In 1969, the band performed at the New York Woodstock Festival, introducing an East Coast audience to Santana's brand of Latin-flavored rock.

Over the next twenty years, Santana and his band would produce eight gold and seven platinum albums. Carlos Santana alone and together with his band would win numerous awards including the Billboard Century Award (1996), Chicano Lifetime Achievement Award (1997), induction into the Rock and Roll Hall of Fame (1998), and the Medallion of Excellence Award for community service presented by the Hispanic Congressional Caucus. Carlos won a Best Rock Instrumental Performance Grammy in 1988. The band's most recent album *Supernatural* won the Grammy Award for Album of the Year in 2000. Santana and his band won a total of eight Grammy Awards in 2000, tying the record set by Michael Jackson in 1983.

Carlos Santana individually and the band collectively have sold more than 40 million albums and have performed for well more than 20 million people, outstanding achievements even in this age of musical superstars. The band has performed in more than fifty foreign countries including at the 1987 Rock 'n' Roll Summit, the first joint U.S.–Soviet rock concert. They have played for numerous charities and worthy causes including Blues for Salvador, San Francisco earthquake relief, Tijuana orphans, the rights of indigenous peoples, and education for Latino youth (in association with the Hispanic Media and Education Group).

West Coast Chicano Music in the 1990s

Groups like Los Lobos and Santana cannot be conveniently categorized or limited to one decade or another of Chicano music; as I have pointed out, they have endured for close to thirty years. Still, in this section I address some trends in West Coast Chicano music during the last decade of the twentieth century.

Los Angeles continued to be the center of Chicano musical activity on the West Coast during the 1990s. One observer of this music scene has characterized it in the following way: "While musically there is little that binds many of the rock, hip hop, punk, blues, ska, and fold bands that make up the core of L.A.'s underground Chicano music scene—aside from the occasional bilingual lyric and traditional Latin American or indigenous musical inflection—philosophically and conceptually they are united" (Doss 1998, 192). Of the approximately two dozen bands that make up this music scene the most prominent are Ozomatli, Quetzal, Aztlán Underground, Lysa Flores, Cactus Flower, Ollin, Quinto Sol, Blues Experiment, JABOM, and Announcing Predictions. They tend to produce music that reflects their members' hybrid identity in the Los Angeles area. That they are Americans of Mexican descent raised in an urban environment that has bombarded them for years with messages, values, and attitudes common to urban dwellers across the United States is captured in the following quote, "We may be wearing *guayaberas* [a formal shirt worn in Mexico], but we're also wearing Doc Martens and nose rings" (Doss 1998, 192). This expresses succinctly the hybrid identity of many of the Chicano musicians whose song themes range from the dangers of urban life to environmental concerns, racial unity, unfulfilling sex, genocide, and love. The website of Son Del Barrio, a Chicano recording label, reflects this hybridity in its description of the Chicano Groove musical genre it specializes in: "Chicano Groove reflects the sublime and sometimes schizophrenic reality of a bicultural, bilingual generation. Rhythmically, it will capture the hearts and imaginations of an increasingly diverse audience of music fans" (www.sondelbarrio.com).

These bands produce music that is an urban blend of traditional and modern, retro and futuristic and includes a wide range of styles, traditions, and genres: rock and roll, soul, Mexican *jarochos,* conga beats, punk, and others. Many of the bands consider themselves to be underground and on the fringes of the Los Angeles recording industry. They tend to form their own recording consortiums that draw on local promoters and local musical talent, but this trend may change in the next decade as major labels begin to seek them out. The bands try to play in small venues—galleries and restaurants—that appeal to young Chicanos who will appreciate the "Chicano cultural subtext in their music, a sensibility shaped by negatives: neither this nor that, always on the border" (Doss 1998, 193). Many of the group members identify as Chicanos but in doing so they do not necessarily associate themselves with the cultural nationalism and pride in Indo-Mexican traditions of the 1960s Chicano Movement—their parents' generation—but rather with a late-1990s urban Chicano with spiked hair and pierced nose and tongue. Many of the bands, however, have taken Indian names (e.g., Quetzal, Ozomatli, Aztlán) and have incorporated indigenous Mexican and Andean instruments into their repertoire in order to identify with their indigenous roots as well as to produce a music that avoids the sanitized sound of the contemporary music that most commercial radio stations play.

◼ Trans-Regional Chicano Music

In this section, I discuss music and performers that are not strongly identified with a region but that are commonly played or at least listened to wherever Chicanos are concentrated in the Southwest, Midwest, Northwest, and even the East Coast.

Mariachi is the form of Chicano music that is currently the most quintessential; that is, it is found almost everywhere in the United States and seems to appeal to Chicanos regardless of class and social status, whether assimilated or first or second-generation immigrants from Mexico, and whether English/Spanish bilingual or monolingual in English or Spanish.

Música de mariachi is Mexican in origin and is associated closely with west Mexico, the state of Jalisco, and the city of Guadalajara. Before 1940, the instrumentation of a mariachi group usually consisted of certain stringed instruments—violins, a large harp, a *guitarra de golpe* (a struck guitar), a curve-spined *vihuela* (a five-stringed guitar), and a *guitarrón* (a big guitar with a bass sound)—and sometimes a drum. The trumpet was added to the instrumentation for all serious groups after the 1940s (Sheehy 1999, 45–47). The musicians, who generally were not professionally trained, typically played for dances, birthdays, baptisms, and weddings, sometimes for free, sometimes for a modest wage.

During and after the Mexican Revolution (1910–1920), mariachi musicians and groups began emigrating from west Mexico to both Mexico City and the United States. Recordings of this regional music began appearing in Mexico City, and beginning in the 1920s and 1930s mariachi music became quite common in popular Mexican films and in stage shows in Mexico City. Movies such as *Allá en el rancho grande* (Out There on the Big Ranch [1936]) featuring *charros* (Mexican cowboys) and some of Mexico's most famous actor-singers (e.g., Jorge Negrete and Pedro Infante) were very important in popularizing mariachi music. Mexico City's powerful radio station xEw began broadcasting mariachi music nationwide in 1930. After 1940, mariachi groups became more professional and more commercialized; they began to tour and perform across Mexico and to sign profitable recording contracts. The Mariachi Vargas de Tecalitlán was perhaps the prototype of the new mariachi group.

Mariachi groups today—wherever they are found—typically dress in what is known as a *traje de charro,* an elegant suit consisting of tight-fitting pants lined with silver buttons running down the length of the pant leg, a fancy white shirt, a short coat, cowboy boots, and optionally, a large charro hat.

Mariachi music began its rise to popularity in the Southwest with the large-scale immigration of Mexicans, including many from west Mexico, to the United States during and after the Mexican Revolution. The showing of Mexican charro films in southwestern cities from the 1930s through the 1950s combined with xew's broadcasts across the U.S.–Mexican border simply reinforced and increased the popularity of this music. As in Mexico, amateur musicians have always played mariachi music at social functions, but since about the 1960s professional groups have formed, mariachi festivals have sprung up, and college and high school mariachi programs have been created. All of this activity has established a solid foundation for the continuation of the mariachi music tradition in the United States.

Tucson has been one of the centers of mariachi music for more than thirty years. In 1964, a Catholic priest organized the first young mariachi group in the area. In 1971, Randy Carrillo, a young musician, organized Mariachi Cobre, a professional group that today is probably the best-known U.S.–based mariachi band. The original group consisted of Carrillo, his brother Steve, their friend Mack Ruiz, and Frank Grijalva, the group's musical arranger. In 1981, the group and local community leaders and promoters established the International Mariachi Conference, which has taken place in Tucson annually ever since, attracting the finest mariachi performers in Mexico and the United States, including Mariachi Cobre. Since 1982, the Epcot Center at Disney World in Orlando, Florida, has featured Mariachi Cobre. Mariachi Cobre often appears on the same stage as other famous groups such as Mariachi Los Camperos de Nati Cano and Mexico's Mariachi Vargas. They have also accompanied such famous recording artists as Linda Ronstadt (a native Tucsonan), Lucha Villa, Lola Beltrán, and Vikki Carr. In 2000, Mariachi Cobre played at concerts and festivals throughout the United States, including Phoenix, Minneapolis, the Hollywood Bowl, and San Jose, California.

Tucson is not alone in offering opportunities for mariachi musicians. High schools throughout California and Texas have mariachi programs, as do colleges and universities such as Stanford University and Texas Tech University. Mariachi festivals are held all over the United States throughout the year. In 2000, festivals were held in Corpus Christi, Texas; Phoenix, Arizona; Whittier, California; Houston, Texas; Fresno, California; Brackenridge, Texas; Wanatchee, Washington; Anaheim (Disneyland), California; Lubbock, Texas; San Jose, California; Albuquerque, New Mexico; Santa Barbara, California; Chicago, Illinois; Las Vegas, Nevada; Washington, D.C.; and Las Cruces, New Mexico. There are many professional groups throughout the Southwest.

Vikki Carr

Vikki Carr is not a name that many popular music listeners would normally associate with Chicano popular music. Born Florencia Bisenta de Casillas Martínez Cardona in 1940 in El Paso, Texas, she—like Ritchie Valens—is an example of the West Coast recording industry practice in the 1950s of "sanitizing" Chicano performers by anglicizing their Spanish names to make them more acceptable to a general Anglo audience. Carr has enjoyed great success as a recording artist. She left El Paso for Los Angeles as a teenager and very soon began her singing career touring with a band. She signed her first recording contract with Liberty Records in 1961, and by 1967 she was an international recording star especially popular in Australia and Great Britain (where she was invited to perform for Queen Elizabeth II in London). The following year, she performed at sold-out concerts in Germany, Spain, France, Australia, and Japan.

Her popularity in the United States continued to increase, and she has performed at the White House before four presidents. She has recorded numerous best-selling English-language records including fifteen gold albums. In 1985, she won a Grammy for her Spanish-language album *Simplemente Mujer* (Simply a Woman), and other Spanish-language albums have garnered her gold, platinum, and even diamond awards. The *Los Angeles Times* named her Woman of the Year in 1970. Among her other awards are the 1972 American Guild of Variety Artists Entertainer of the Year Award, the 1984 Hispanic Woman of the Year Award, and the 1991 Boy Scouts of America Award. She has founded the Vikki Carr Foundation and contributed to many charitable causes over her long career. She remains active today as a recording artist, performing before both English- and Spanish-language audiences and recording albums in both languages (Kanellos 1994, 595).

Linda Ronstadt

Linda Ronstadt was born in 1946 in Tucson, where she now lives with her two adopted children. She attended the University of Arizona for a short time before setting out for Los Angeles, where she formed a group called the Stone Poneys in the mid-1960s. Beginning in the 1970s, Ronstadt produced many memorable ballads, country and western songs, and romantic renditions accompanied by the Nelson Riddle Orchestra. She even turned briefly to popular opera. She established herself as one of the most popular female rock and roll singers with hits such as "Desperado," "Blue Bayou," and "Poor, Poor Pitiful Me."

Ronstadt's experimentation with a broad range of musical styles has earned her critical acclaim, including a Grammy for best country performance for her 1986 album *Trio,* which she produced with Dolly Parton and Emmylou Harris. In 1987, she released the album *Canciones de mi padre* (My Father's Songs), a tribute to her Mexican/Mexican American background on her father's side. The songs on this album are mainly popular mariachi songs such "Por un amor" (For a Love), "Tú solo tú" (Only You), "Dos arbolitos" (Two Little Trees), "El sol que tú eres" (The Sun That You Are), and "Hay unos ojos" (There Are Some Eyes). A few years later, in 1991, she recorded *Más canciones,* which included additional popular Mexican songs such as "Mi ranchito" (My Little Ranch), "Siempre hace frío" (It's Always Cold), and "El camino" (The Road). This same year, she starred in *La pastorela,* a contemporary version of the traditional Christmas-season play.

Like other forms of popular culture, Chicano popular music today constantly undergoes changes and adapts to new circumstances, incorporating trends that rapidly cross the stage of American popular music. Sometimes Chicano musicians reach back to earlier decades to seek musical and cultural inspiration in the artistic expression that sustained prior generations. Sometimes they seek to be on the cutting edge of the latest wave of new music. Their music is always creative and expressive of a wide range of personal as well as collective sentiments.

■ **Discussion Questions**

1. Would the popular Hispanic folk music brought to Southwest by the Spaniards be an example that a cultural populist or a mass culture theorist might use to illustrate these respective theories of popular culture?

2. What role did decimeros and trovadores play in Hispanic society, especially in rural areas?

3. What forms of music were successfully transplanted from Spain to the Southwest?

4. Discuss the role of the corrido along the U.S.–Mexican border in general and the importance of "El corrido de Gregorio Cortez" in particular.

5. Why can Texas be described as an epicenter of Mexican American music?

6. How would a cultural theorist who adheres to Adorno's concept of culture view mass-produced conjunto music?

7. Why did orquesta Tejana music appeal to a different audience than did conjunto music?

8. Describe the characteristics of La Onda Chicana music and contrast it with the music of the post–Chicano Movement era in Texas.

9. Did Selena's huge commercial success compromise her social message?

10. Discuss Lalo Guerrero's contribution to Chicano music.

11. What impact did the Chicano Movement have on West Coast music in the 1960s and early 1970s?

12. What accounts for the popularity over several decades of Los Lobos and Santana? Do they have anything in common?

◼ Suggested Readings

Loza, Steven. 1993. *Barrio Rhythm: Mexican American Music in Los Angeles.* Urbana: University of Illinois Press.

Peña, Manuel. 1985. *The Texas-Mexican Conjunto: History of a Working-Class Music.* Austin: University of Texas Press.

— —. 1999. *Música Tejana.* College Station: Texas A&M University Press.

Reyes, David, and Tom Waldman. 1998. *Land of a Thousand Dances: Chicano Rock 'n' Roll from Southern California.* Albuquerque: University of New Mexico Press.

Robb, John Donald. 1980. *Hispanic Folk Music of New Mexico and the Southwest.* Norman: University of Oklahoma Press.

Schechter, John M. 1999. *Music in Latin American Culture: Regional Traditions.* New York: Schirmer Books.

3

Cinema

Unlike popular music and some other forms of Chicano popular culture, cinema had a late start. It was not until the mid-1960s that Chicano directors, producers, and actors began to make short films and documentaries. In this chapter, I briefly discuss these beginning artistic efforts as well as more ambitious short films, documentaries, and videos produced in the past twenty years. I then provide a more detailed discussion and analysis of selected feature-length films that have appealed to Chicano and non-Chicano audiences alike.

To better understand and appreciate the emergence of Chicano cinema and its focus on creating an authentic and historically accurate view of Americans of Mexican descent I begin this chapter with a short history of racial and ethnic stereotyping in American movies, with an emphasis on Hollywood stereotypes of Mexicans and Mexican Americans from about 1910 through the 1970s. This material is important because Anglo perceptions of their southern neighbors and this ethnic group were based in large part on the images Hollywood had conveyed to audiences for decades on the silver screen.

Race and Ethnicity in American Movies

The movies have been an important part of American popular culture since the end of the nineteenth century, when cinema emerged as a distinct technology of projecting motion pictures onto a screen (Musser 1991, 109). The first films relied heavily on optical effects to create illusions for delighted audiences, but with advances in cinema technology these films gave way to longer, more complex films that told a story, including comedies based on racial and ethnic stereotypes.

These very early twentieth-century comedies grew out of a long practice in American culture of degrading non–Anglo-Saxon population groups in popular genres as diverse as the comic strips and vaudeville acts. Audiences who flocked to the first film comedies were already familiar with and primed to accept and laugh at the negative stereotypical images of ethnic groups projected onto the screens of theaters throughout the country (Musser 1991, 43).

As cinema scholar Gary Keller (1985, 5–6) has pointed out, "The earliest cinema fulfilled a number of functions with respect to race, ethnicity, and gender. Some of these functions were contradictory, but this should not be surprising because film did not depict race and ethnicity from one ideological point of view or set of assumptions." The most important consideration for theater owners and film creators and distributors was that their products be commercially viable; that is, profitable.

Films making fun of race, ethnicity, and women were highly popular and therefore profitable, but the emerging film industry had to be careful not to alienate its American born middle-class audience by going too far with its use of negative stereotypes. Some films were made to appeal to an audience that could afford to buy tickets (an audience that generally did not include blacks, Hispanics, American Indians, Jews, Asians, or recent immigrants from Italy, Ireland, Poland, Germany, Norway, or other European countries). Others were made to appeal to at least northern European immigrants. These films seemed designed to instruct white immigrant audiences about American culture and how best and most quickly to assimilate into it by abandoning their own local, insular cultures (Musser 1991). There is little doubt, however, that the film industry in the early 1900s was not interested in appealing to or attracting non-Anglo groups that included blacks, American Indians, Hispanics (except those of European Spanish origin), and Asians.

In 1915, D. W. Griffith produced a three-hour epic film, *The Birth of a Nation,* that became a model for American cinematic epics dealing with race and ethnicity. Griffith's film, which reflected his own racist attitudes, created horribly distorted and negative stereotypes of Southern blacks while depicting Southern whites (especially Klu Klux Klansmen) as heroic and virtuous. He used illusion and other technological advances in filmmaking to outrage and at the same time to titillate his audience in a way that live theater, fiction, poetry, or journalism had not been able to do (Kanellos 1994, 499).

The Birth of a Nation apparently satisfied the cultural, racial, and aesthetic needs of white, middle-class moviegoers who, through their attendance, made it one of the most successful film spectacles of the period. Other filmmakers followed Griffith's example by creating their own epics—many of them Westerns—that often pitted Mexicans, African

Americans, and American Indians against white "civilizers" such as settlers, explorers, cowboys, and the U.S. Army. The inevitable defeat of racial and ethnic minority groups by representatives of Anglo-Saxon civilization drove home to audiences the social and cultural message that their mores and values were ultimately superior to those of "primitive" cultures.

Hollywood's Portrayal of Mexicans and Mexican Americans from the 1910s through the 1970s

From the earliest days, the vast majority of roles for Mexican American actors in Hollywood formula films were the Castilian *caballero* (romantic male), dark lady, greaser-gangster, social problem, Good Samaritan, and brown avenger. Typically, the Mexican Americans who played these roles were killed, mocked, punished, seduced, or saved from poverty, moral ruin, or death by Anglo actors playing socially redeeming roles. As I discuss later, some progressive films were exceptions to these kinds of films, but these generally were not produced by larger and more dominant Hollywood movie companies.

Castilian Caballero Films

The Castilian caballero films began in 1914 with the feature-length film *The Caballero's Way*. This film genre featured figures such as Zorro, Don Arturo Bodega, and later, the Cisco Kid. The heroes of these movies, who are identified as Castilian (thus Caucasians of Spanish European origin), follow the predictable formula of putting down, denigrating, and patronizing mestizos. The Cisco Kid cycle of caballero films began in the silent movie era with *The Caballero's Way* and *The Border Terror* (1919), but most of the films in this genre were made during the sound era. César Romero, a Cuban American actor born in New York City, made three films between 1939 and 1941, the Spanish-born actor Duncan Renaldo did eight between 1945 and 1950, and Chicano actor Gilbert Roland (born Luis Antonio Dámaso de Alonso) did six between 1946 and 1947.

The Cisco Kid lead role was typically a romantic male who aggressively sought and usually conquered at least one beautiful woman per film, but although he might have flirted with Anglo women, conquering them simply did not fit within the Hollywood code or the caballero film formula.

Dark Lady Films

The so-called dark lady films made their appearance in the 1930s and quickly became popular with the viewing public. Lupe Vélez, called by her Hollywood publicists the "Mexican Spitfire" (she was born in 1908 in San Luis Potosí, Mexico), became the most popular of the dark ladies. She made eight movies in the Mexican Spitfire series before she died at the early age of thirty-six. Rita Hayworth (born Margarita Carmen Cansino in New York City in 1918) got her start as a dark lady, her most notable performance being in a barroom scene in *Hit the Saddle* (1937). She successfully made the transition from ethnic minority to mainstream actress, a process that required her to lose her Latina identity, including changing her surname to Hayworth. Raquel Welch (born Raquel Tejada in Chicago in 1940) would later undergo the same transition from Latina actress to mainstream love goddess.

Greaser-Gangster Films

The Hollywood gangster movie genre of the 1930s produced an ethnic equivalent, the so-called greaser-gangster movie. *Greaser* is, of course, a highly negative epithet commonly used to denigrate Chicanos and Mexicans even today. The use of the term in movies has been traced to a film made as early as 1907. Filmmakers first used the term as part of a film's title in 1908 with *The Greaser's Gauntlet,* then produced an entire series of greaser films between 1908 and 1918, including *Ah Sing and the Greaser, Tony the Greaser, The Greaser and the Weakling,* and *The Girl and the Greaser.* Filmmakers finally stopped using the epithet in movie titles but only after many protests by film insiders, Mexican American groups, and even the Mexican government.

The greaser as a character, however, did not disappear from the screen but instead evolved into the greaser-gangster. Unlike his Anglo counterparts—James Cagney, George Raft, and Humphrey Bogart—the greaser-gangster protagonist was portrayed as shifty, untrustworthy, treacherous, ugly, crude, oily (the origin of the term "greaser"), and totally disloyal even to other gangsters. Leo Carrillo (a Mexican American born in Los Angeles in the early 1900s) became the most popular greaser-gangster, portraying a lying, murdering border thief in almost thirty films. Finally, the Mexican government protested the way its justice system had been portrayed in the film *Girl of the Rio* (1932) (Kanellos 1994, 504–6).

Social Problem Films

The film industry was affected to some extent by the waves of social unrest that swept over the United States from the early 1930s (the end of one of the worst depressions the country had ever experienced) through the Second World War and up to the rise of McCarthyism, a devastating and sometimes hysterical period of anticommunism that destroyed the careers of thousands of intellectuals, politicians, and entertainment figures including many involved in the film industry.

Hollywood responded to the unrest and heightened social consciousness among the general population by creating a new genre, the social problem film. In characteristic fashion, filmmakers responded cautiously, producing films that still fit comfortably within the formula that had regulated the film industry almost since the beginning of its short history. Industry conventions dictated that films not advocate for substantive social transformation, but rather promote the notion that some of society's social and political institutions needed limited change.

Hollywood compiled a very mixed record of success in terms of its treatment of Mexican Americans and Mexicans in its social problem films. For example, *Bordertown* (1935) continued the tradition of using an Anglo in a lead role written for a non-Anglo, and rather than focusing on the oppression of Mexican Americans, the film places much greater emphasis on solving the murder mystery that is integral to its plot. At the end of the film, Johnny, the Mexican American protagonist who has experienced both success and disillusionment in the Anglo world, returns to his barrio to live out his life among his own people. The film implicitly applauds his decision, thus conveying its message that "stoic acquiescence to the status quo" is preferable to "the aspiration for social change" (Kanellos 1994, 508). On the positive side, social problem films did at least produce some strong and psychologically complex Chicano roles, including several Mexican American protagonists in *Giant* (1956), the family of Leo Mimosa in Billy Wilder's *The Big Carnival* (1951), and the actors Katy Jurado and Pina Pellicer in *One-Eyed Jacks* (1961).

Good Samaritan Films

Continuing a pattern that had begun during the silent film era, Hollywood created several films in the 1930s in which well-intentioned Anglos would save ethnic-minority victims from some threatening situation, exploitative boss, or the like. Many Hopalong Cassidy, Gene Autry, Lone Ranger, Roy Rogers, and Tex Ritter films featured these Western cowboy heroes defending the rights of hapless Mexican Americans, Mexicans, and Native Americans (Kanellos 1994, 507–9). These Anglo Good Samaritans could be depended on to chase away, discourage, or otherwise neutralize evil-doers who did not respect the downtrodden. The problem with these films was that the downtrodden were not allowed to act on their own behalf, to serve as their own agents of change against oppressive conditions. In effect, Mexican American and Mexican characters were portrayed as childlike beings incapable of controlling their own personal or social destinies.

Progressive Films

There are at least two films, *The Lawless* (1950) and *Salt of the Earth* (1954), that deal realistically and in a hard-hitting way with Mexican American social problems. It is significant that both were independently produced and therefore did not have to conform to the usual Hollywood norms. The first was a low-budget independent film released by Paramount, and the second was produced and made totally outside of the major studio system by individuals—actors, writer Michael Wilson, producer Paul Jarrico, and director Herbert J. Biberman—who had been blacklisted by Senator McCarthy and his allies in the film industry.

Both films expose and deal forthrightly with some of the underlying social causes of racism against Mexican Americans and of their underclass economic status, in contrast to other well-intentioned but misguided films that attributed racism, discrimination, and exploitation to an individual sociopath, cruel businessman, heartless mine foreman, or similar character.

The Lawless, directed by Joseph Losey and scripted by blacklisted Daniel Mainwaring (who was forced to use a pseudonym to hide his true identity), revolves around the lives of Mexican American and Mexican fruit pickers whose subsistence wages make it impossible for them to afford adequate housing and a dignified standard of living. *The Lawless* is a very progressive film that deals explicitly with the violation of the fruit pickers' labor rights by Anglo industrial (mining) interests. *The Lawless,* which is set in a Mexican American community in an agricultural area, has as its central episode a dance that Anglo toughs disrupt. A brawl ensues, resulting in the arrest of several Mexican Americans and one Anglo. Blame for the brawl is assigned to the Mexican American "fruit tramps" after prominent Anglos intervene in the police investigation. In addition to its portrayal of the abuses of the justice system, an important aspect of this film is the psychological depth it gives to both the Mexican American and the Anglo characters, including the policemen and the fruit pickers. It avoids simplistically depicting Chicanos as good and Anglos as evil.

Progressive film historians and social critics alike have hailed *Salt of the Earth,* based on a successful New Mexico miners' strike, as one of the most important films of its era. Its unrelenting message is one of resistance against a capitalist enterprise that has stolen land from its original Mexican American owners and then exploited them as low-wage earners in the zinc mine excavated on that land. Through a system similar to debt-peonage, whereby workers and their families are charged heavily and unfairly for living in company-owned housing and buying goods at the company store, the mining company is able to trap the miners in a seemingly endless cycle of debt that forces them to remain dependent on their Anglo overseers. The company houses are hovels without adequate sanitation and plumbing, and the mine's safety provisions are minimal, especially for the largely Mexican American and Mexican workers who are forced to work under the most dangerous conditions or lose their jobs.

The miners mount a protest against these working conditions, but the Anglo company manager brings them back into line by warning that he will quickly find scab (nonunion) workers to replace them. The miners go out on strike, walk picket lines, and try to bring the manager to the negotiating table. The local Anglo police are brought in by the mining company to "monitor" the strike. They disrupt the picket line and arrest the strike leaders on trumped-up charges of resisting arrest. Later, the police evict the strikers from their homes.

The Mexican American and Mexican women in the mining community play a major role in rallying their men to resist the company, to strike, and to maintain discipline on the picket line. They become fearless and active protagonists on their own behalf, a role unprecedented up to that point in any film about Mexican Americans. The part of their leader, Esperanza Quintero, is played by Mexican actress Rosaura Revueltas.

As an independently produced film, *Salt of the Earth* clearly went far beyond the constraints of Hollywood social problem films and provided a model for progressive filmmaking for decades to come. It quickly became and has remained an underground classic viewed at film festivals and in college courses throughout the Southwest.

The Lawless and especially *Salt of the Earth* provided audiences an alternative view of Mexican Americans that went beyond that of Hollywood's social problem films. As limited as social problem films were in depicting Mexican Americans as helpless children often rescued by brave and altruistic Anglo heroes, they were far better than many films of other genres that continued to be produced up until the Civil Rights Movement of the early 1960s.

Brown Avenger Films

A new stereotype emerged in Westerns and other films in the 1960s: the brown avenger. This filmic figure was a spinoff of the "superstud" movie protagonist that Hollywood created in the 1950s and the 1960s in response to the ever-increasing numbers of Chicanos, other Latinos, and African Americans in their movie audiences. The Civil Rights Movement of the early 1960s was also a factor that contributed to the creation of some very strong Latino and African American male roles. On the one hand, Hollywood claimed that it was simply responding to the desires of its increasingly diverse audience as well as to pressure from groups such as the NAACP (National Association for the Advancement of Colored People) to replace formally passive and subservient African American and Latino roles with new active roles such as police officers, civil servants, students, and workers. On the other hand, Hollywood exploited the climate of black and brown militancy of the era to create characters who, although they might be emotionally satisfying to their audience, also displayed some very negative traits such as insensitivity toward women, brutality, and violent dispositions.

In a sense, Hollywood used the cover of the Civil Rights Movement to create black and brown avengers, another stereotype with some definite antisocial tendencies. A new hip, black audience responded enthusiastically, applauding actors such as Jim Brown, Melvin Van Peebles, and Richard Roundtree in 1960s films such as *Shaft* and *Super Fly*. The same market pressures of changing demographics, the Civil Rights Movement, and increasing militancy of the Chicano population encouraged Hollywood to create the brown macho figure, the counterpart of the black stud. So-called Super-Mex roles were common in Westerns. A prime example was Jorge Rivero in *Rio Lobo* (1970), who brings Anglo evildoers to justice through his skill with guns and martial arts. Following a long Hollywood tradition, Anglo actors continued playing Chicano/Mexican roles (Keller 1985, 37–39).

■ Chicano Cinema

The 1960s Civil Rights Movement was largely responsible for the unprecedented actions of the U.S. film industry to increase the hiring of ethnic
minorities in cinematic professions. Regarding Chicanos, a 1969 U.S. Equal
Employment Opportunity Commission report found that only 3 percent of
the workforce at major Hollywood studios was Spanish-surnamed. During
the late 1960s and early 1970s, lobbying organizations such as LULAC,
the Mexican American Legal Defense and Education Fund (MALDEF), the
National Council of La Raza (NCLR), and others dramatically increased
the pressure on the film industry to accelerate and increase the hiring of
Chicanos.

Chicano media activist groups in the Los Angeles area (e.g., CARISSMA
and JUSTICIA) along with a group of concerned Latino actors known as
Nosotros and organized by the Mexican-born actor Ricardo Montalbán
applied even greater pressure on the film industry to change the portrayal
of Chicanos on screen. The film industry responded with token gestures to
hire more Chicanos, primarily through the creation of internship programs. At the same time, university film programs such as those at University of California, Los Angeles (UCLA) and the University of Southern
California created special admissions programs for Chicanos and other
ethnic minority students interested in filmmaking. Jesús Treviño, a prominent Chicano filmmaker, believes that these three occurrences became "the
chief resource for the emergence of Chicano cinema" (Keller 1985, 46–47).

Young Chicano filmmakers such as Treviño served their apprentice-
ships in film school and in lower-level positions in the film industry
through the production of documentaries and community-interest shows
on a variety of subjects, most of them not specifically Chicano in content. Many of these filmmakers had been student and community activists
during the militant phase of the Chicano Movement, and consequently
brought to their filmmaking a commitment to social change and a heightened sensibility that strongly motivated them to produce uniquely Chicano
cinema (Keller 1985, 47).

There are many actors, directors, producers, cinematographers, editors,
and others who over the past three decades have been associated with
Chicano cinema, and I will discuss their roles and contributions in more
detail as I focus on individual films. A partial list would include Jesús
Treviño, Moctezuma Esparza, Luis Valdez and his brother Daniel Valdez,

José Luis Ruiz, Ricardo Soto, Paul Espinosa, Daniel Salazar, Sylvia Morales, Ricardo Trujillo, Carlos Avila, Edward James Olmos, and Mercedes Sabio. Among the non-Chicanos who have contributed to the emergence and continuation of Chicano cinema are Les Blank, Gary Greenberg, Robert Young, and Isaac Artenstein.

As you will see from the overview of short features, documentaries, and full-length feature films listed in the appendix at the end of this chapter, it is very difficult to generalize about the underlying themes, content, and story lines of Chicano cinema since the late 1960s. Nonetheless, scholars such as Keller have identified a general trend. He views at least the first wave of Chicano cinema as "a response to the extraordinary efforts on the part of both Mexican cinema and United States cinema (not acting independently, but primarily as instruments of government and/or society) to alternately repress, caricature, or otherwise distort or reject the authentic personae and history of an entire people" (Keller 1985, 48).

■ Chicano Feature-Length Films Since the 1970s

Chicano feature-length films produced no earlier than the 1970s fall into two broad categories: (a) independent productions that have been produced and directed outside of the established Hollywood studios; and (b) films that Chicano film historians and critics have identified as "Hollywood Hispanic" films. The latter are hybrid films that combine Chicano expertise– and sometimes control—with Hollywood production values and distribution. These filmic productions are more closely affiliated with Chicano independent films than with the average Hollywood production that makes use of Chicano material (Keller 1994, 207). As we will see, since the early 1970s, independent productions have been far more numerous than Hollywood Hispanic films.

Financing and Production

The financing of the production of a film, especially a feature-length film, is an expensive undertaking and a daunting process. The Hollywood film industry historically has secured funding from groups of investors who invest in films as they would in any other business. The greater the risk that a film will not succeed financially at the box office (and more recently in subsidiary markets such as video sales and foreign distribution), the more difficult it is for film producers to raise the necessary financial backing for its production. There are also a very limited number of private and public foundations that support financially modest filmmaking projects. Thus, independent Chicano filmmakers not affiliated with the Hollywood studio system have gone to different funding sources over the past thirty years to finance their film projects: Hollywood non-film studio investors for *Zoot Suit;* Mexican official financial sources for *Raíces de sangre* (Blood Roots); the National Endowment for the Humanities (NEH) and the Corporation for Public Broadcasting for *Seguín* and *The Ballad of Gregorio Cortez;* and fund-raising from private, non-Hollywood sources for *Once in a Lifetime*.

As Gary Keller (1994) has pointed out, the "independence" of Chicano filmmakers is very relative. They may not depend on the traditional Hollywood studio system for financing, production, and distribution, but they are subject to the politics and priorities of the investors, agencies, and foundations that financially underwrite their films, and although the control these entities exercise is often more complex or subtle than that exercised by Hollywood, it exists and by its very nature has threatened the total independence of the Chicano filmmaker.

Authenticity

Film critic Chon Noriega has drawn on the Chicano art movement from the mid-1960s to the early 1980s to devise a conceptual framework for defining *authenticity* in Chicano cinema. The four characteristics of Chicano art that he believes can also be applied to cinema are resistance, maintenance, affirmation, and *mestizaje* (recognition of and pride in Chicano culture's Indo-Mexican history and legacy as well as its Spanish European past). He views these four elements as tactics that can be used to respond culturally to political, economic, legal, and social oppression by the dominant society. Noriega concludes that to determine a film and a filmmaker's authenticity, these four characteristics must be measured across the following spectrum of a film's history: production, exhibition, signification, and reception (Noriega 1992, 167–74).

PRODUCTION. Production involves the filmmaker's ability to raise sufficient funding to produce a film, and Noriega is rightfully concerned that Chicano filmmakers not be overly beholden to investors, foundations, or agencies that could compromise a film's content or distribution.

EXHIBITION.   Exhibition concerns the filmmaker's ability to control the distribution of a film, including its showing at festivals and its ability to reach a mainstream audience, a highly desirable objective for Chicano cinema.

SIGNIFICATION.   Signification means that Chicano filmmakers should attempt and be allowed to provide an accurate view of Chicano history or contemporary events within a film's narrative structure (a feature-length film generally relies on its narrative nature to tell a persuasive and moving story about a historical event or true story). Chicano filmmakers should attempt to construct an image that is counter to the popular and often distorted image of Chicanos perpetuated by mainstream cinema. In this vein, I have already discussed Hollywood's propensity to portray negative stereotypes of Mexicans and Mexican Americans over its past century of making films.

RECEPTION.   By reception, Noriega means that filmmakers and distributors (as well as professors of cinema) need to be more aware of the diversity of Chicano/Latino audiences and how they might react differently to the same film (e.g., certain groups might resent a film's characterization of them as "Hispanic" or "Chicano.")

Keller (1994) offers a different but not unrelated set of characteristics that could be used to define Chicano cinema and the extent of a filmmaker's social commitment and the authenticity of the film:

THE DECONSTRUCTION AND SUBVERSION OF HOLLYWOOD GENRES AND FORMULAS.   Keller makes the point that already Chicano filmmakers have produced films that subvert the stock genres and formulas that Hollywood has used for decades in making Western, "bad Mexican" or greaser, and border immigration films and musicals.

THE INNOVATIVE USE OF SPANISH AND ENGLISH (AND SOMETIMES INDIGENOUS LANGUAGES).   From the 1970s on, Chicano filmmakers have incorporated into their films code-switching or the grammatically viable combination of English and Spanish. This has become a fundamental aspect of many films and one that linguistically marks the film as Chicano because it mirrors the spoken language of millions of Americans of Mexican descent. The bilingual, bicultural audience is thus very receptive to this use of language.

THE INNOVATIVE USE OF CHICANO MUSIC. Traditional and hybrid forms of music such as the corrido and the conjunto serve not only to background but also to foreground a film's content and to situate its audience within a Chicano cultural space.

THE INNOVATIVE USE OF MISE EN SCENE AND MONTAGE. Mise-en-scène, or "putting the scene," involves filling a screen space not only with Chicano images but also with the aural and visual texture of Chicano culture, including music, language, home altars, food, and neighborhoods. Numerous Chicano documentaries and some feature-length films begin with a montage of Chicano culture and history.

Keller cites other aspects of Chicano cinema that distinguish it from stock Hollywood films—even recent ones—that may contain Chicano content (Keller 1994, 208–9):

■ The recuperation of Chicano history

■ Close attention to the political dimensions of the topics treated

■ A commitment to dealing with sometimes controversial topics that may threaten or diminish success at the box office

■ The willingness to employ large numbers of Chicanos in all aspects of film production, including actors, editors, and production crews

■ The filming of Chicanos in real-life situations and settings such as the barrio filled with everyday sounds, language, and music

Independent Chicano filmmakers have produced more than thirty feature-length films in the past three decades. Of these, I will discuss the following films in this section: *Raíces de sangre, Alambrista!, Seguín, The Ballad of Gregorio Cortez, El Norte, Break of Dawn, El Mariachi, . . . And the Earth Did Not Swallow Him,* and *Selena.* I will also consider four Hollywood Hispanic films: *Zoot Suit, American Me, La Bamba,* and *Born in East L.A.*

Raíces de sangre (1977)

Raíces de sangre is one of earliest Chicano feature-length films as well as one of the earliest and most successful collaborations between Chicano and Mexican film artists. It was written and directed by Jesús Treviño and financed and produced by the Banco Nacional Cinematográfico (The Mexican Cinema Bank). *Raíces de sangre* is the story of Carlos Rivera, a

DOS GRANDES FUERZAS
AL FIN UNIDAS..!

RICHARD YÑIGUEZ
ERNESTO GOMEZ CRUZ y
ROXANNA BONILLA-GIANNINI
como Lupe Carrillo

Pepe Serna · Malena Doria · Adriana Rojo

Cinematografía ROSALIO SOLANO · Música SERGIO GUERRERO
Editor JOAQUIN CEBALLOS · Canción 'Raíces de Sangre' DANIEL VALDEZ · Libreto y Dirección JESUS SALVADOR TREVIÑO

■ Fig. 3. The two main characters of *Raíces de sangre*, Carlos Rivera and Rosa Mejía, are shown on this movie poster. (Photograph courtesy of David Maciel.)

Harvard-educated Chicano attorney (played by Richard Yníquez) who becomes disenchanted with his career in a prosperous San Francisco law firm (see figure 3).

Rivera leaves the firm and San Francisco to return to his hometown, an unnamed town somewhere along the Texas-Mexican border. He becomes a volunteer at the town's community center, which is run by a group of socially committed Chicano activists who are campaigning to organize

Mexican and Chicano garment workers on both sides of the border against an Anglo-owned sweatshop called Morris Corporation. Rivera is initially opposed to the group's tactics and political agenda until he witnesses the death of one of them, an old high school friend, at the hands of the corporation's employees. He undergoes a political conversion and soon emerges as the leader of the activist group. He also undergoes a cultural and class conversion as he abandons his middle-class assumptions and assimilationist tendencies to embrace his cultural roots and to identify with the plight of the Chicano and Mexican underclass.

In the final scene, he leads a group of mourners to the gates of the corporation, where he implores them and the community at large to join forces against Anglo exploitation. The film foregrounds the Chicano town, its working-class barrios, and the poor working conditions that the corporation has created for its exploited workers. The film focuses on the transformations not only of Rivera but of some of the workers who rebel against their dehumanizing and repetitive tasks and begin to assert themselves within the confines of the sweatshop itself. A subplot focuses on a working-class Mexican family—a husband, wife, and three children—who cross over the border to try to improve their economic conditions. The husband and wife die in the back of a locked truck when their *coyote* (a border smuggler who crosses illegal immigrants from Mexico to the United States for a substantial fee) abandons them. Keller (1994, 208) considers *Raíces de sangre* (along with *El Norte* and *Born in East L.A.*) to be "an antithetical border immigration film" in that the United States is not viewed as a place to which Mexicans come to improve their lot.

In *Raíces de sangre,* Mexicans who come to the United States experience exploitation, suffering, and even death; in traditional Hollywood border films, Mexicans find financial security and happiness in the United States. As one film critic has pointed out, in *Raíces de sangre* we are shown a "web of corruption that extends between both borders" (List 1996, 99). Morris Corporation and other companies along the border resort to an old corporate tactic of hiring *mojados* (undocumented Mexican workers or "wetbacks") to replace Chicano workers who threaten to strike, thus pitting Chicano and Mexican workers against each other as each group struggles to earn a slightly higher wage than the other. This disparity in wages is particularly sharp when the wages of Mexican workers in Mexico-based *maquiladoras* (assembly plants) are compared to those of Chicano workers on the U.S. side of the border. This film vividly presents this inequitable situation. Treviño thus shows that "immigration at the Mexican border is the result of an oppressive capitalist economic structure which is international in scope" (List 1996, 100).

Alambrista! (1979)

Hollywood has produced feature-length films, such as *The Border* and *Borderline,* that deal with U.S.–Mexican border issues such as illegal or undocumented immigration but not in an honest or forthright way. One film critic calls these films "exploitation potboilers that employ Latino actors in secondary roles but are little more than 'Cowboys and Indians' dressed in farm worker's drag" (Barrios 1985, 163). The Mexican movie industry has also made several recent films about the border: *La ilegal* (The Illegal Woman), *Carta verde* (Green Card), *Mojados* (Wetbacks), and *De sangre chicana* (Of Chicano Blood); but like their Hollywood counterparts, these films seem designed to appeal to the emotions of a mass audience and generally avoid serious consideration of the complexity of border problems and issues.

Alambrista! (produced by Robert Young) tells the tale of Roberto Ramírez (played by Texan actor Domingo Ambriz), a young man who treks back and forth across the border from his native Mexico to the United States seeking work in the fields of California's agriculturally rich central valleys. The opening and closing sequences were shot on location in Mexico, and leave viewers with a sense of authenticity, a characteristic that both Noriega (1992) and Keller (1994) associate with independent Chicano film-making. Other features lending authenticity to the film are the on-location scenes shot in small agricultural towns in California, the use of realistic dialogue, and the narration of the story in Spanish. English is spoken only when Ramírez encounters English-speaking characters, and the viewer immediately senses his cultural discomfort and disorientation in these scenes. Roberto has come to the United States (as his father did before him) to better the quality of his life and that of his young wife and child. He meets Joe, a Chicano, who identifies with him and gives him a quick primer on how to survive as an undocumented worker in the United States. Joe takes Roberto under his wing but is soon crushed under a train they have hitched from San Diego to Stockton, California. Despite Roberto's initial optimism that eventually he will succeed, he soon loses hope due to his new friend's untimely death and other mishaps. For a fee, a *contratista* (labor contractor) transports him to Colorado, where he seeks work. In a memorable scene in a junkyard, Roberto vents his frustration and loss of dignity as a proud Mexican male, lashing out at the junk around him while crying that he does not want to be there. He soon discovers that his long-lost father has recently died in an agricultural accident in Colorado and has a second family, whom he visits. Disillusioned and beaten down by frustration, Roberto decides to return to Mexico, presumably to avoid repeating the mistakes his father—and previous generations—had made years before. *Alambrista!* is one of the earliest and best portrayals of the undocumented Mexican immigrant experience. The film afforded new and largely inexperienced Chicano actors opportunities to develop their careers (e.g., Edward James Olmos has a minor role as a crazed wino, and Félix Alvarez and Lilly Alvárez of El Teatro Campesino play secondary roles as well).

Seguín (1981)

Seguín is not strictly speaking a full-length feature film; it was originally produced for a sixty-minute broadcast segment on the Public Broadcasting Service (PBS) drama series *American Playhouse.* Nonetheless, despite its relatively short length, it is a complete narrative work that deserves to be included in the Chicano feature-length category primarily because it provides a non-Hollywood view of the events surrounding the battle of the Alamo. The film was to be the first episode in a six-part series that was canceled by the NEH because it became politically controversial. Chicano director Jesús Treviño spent several years researching Chicano history as part of the development of the entire project. He also put together a panel of experts with whom he consulted on a regular basis. Treviño used the same set outside of San Antonio that John Wayne had constructed in 1960 to film *The Alamo,* his version of the historic battle. The use of the same set allowed Treviño to vividly contrast his version and interpretation of history with those of Wayne. He comments, "[In Wayne's version] there are sins of omission, sins of distortion, and sins of commission in his portrayal of Hispanic realities. Using the same sets for *Seguín* that were used to promulgate a mythical version of American history gave me a sense that justice was finally being done" (Levine 1982, 47–48).

The film is a fictionalized documentary based on the life of Juan Nepomuceno Seguín (1806–1889), an important figure in Texas history who was born to a Mexican landowner near San Antonio. The historical period covered by the film is roughly the ten years between the Texas revolution against Mexico in 1836 and the Mexican War that ended with the Treaty of Guadalupe Hidalgo in 1848. One very controversial but historically accurate aspect of the film is Seguín's support for the Americans in Texas against an oppressive Mexican government led by the notoriously incompetent, corrupt, and tyrannical General Santa Anna.

Many Mexican Tejanos, like Seguín and his family, found themselves caught between a Mexican government that ignored their plight and the Anglo American colonists who had begun settling in Texas around 1830 and had quickly begun oppressing them. When Mexico refused to grant Mexican statehood to Texas in 1835, Juan Seguín joined Stephen Austin, the acknowledged leader of the Anglo settlers, in a revolt against Mexico that resulted in the 1836 independence of Texas from its mother country and the establishment of the Republic of Texas. Seguín was largely responsible for recruiting other Tejanos to join the Anglo Texans in their revolutionary struggle. Seguín, who was almost killed at the battle of the Alamo, went on to become a senator in the government of the Republic and was twice elected mayor of San Antonio. He and his family soon became the victims of racism and violence and fled to Mexico. He joined the Mexican forces that fought against the United States (and Texas) in the Mexican War (1846–1848). After the war he received an official pardon from the United States, and he and his family returned to their ranch in Texas.

Soon after the showing of the film on PBS, Treviño came under fire, mainly from Chicano historians and social critics, for his presumed endorsement of a Mexican Texan who had defended the Alamo against Mexican troops. Film critic Alejandro Morales believes that the criticism Treviño received is partly justified. He argues that Treviño does not totally grasp the historical Seguín's changing role or his character. For example, Morales observes that although Seguín at the beginning of the film is portrayed as condemning the slavery the Anglo colonists had brought with them to Texas, his opposition is compromised and not even addressed later in the film when he sides with these very colonists against Mexico (Morales 1985, 134). Treviño was also criticized for selecting Seguín to represent an early phase of Chicano opposition and resistance to Anglo domination in Texas. In response, Treviño has maintained that he has tried to capture a very complex historical situation that was characterized by contradiction and inconsistency.

As already mentioned, the NEH succumbed to both internal and external political pressure and canceled the entire series of which *Seguín* was the first segment. One can only assume that the federal powers felt threatened by an independent Chicano filmmaker who had attempted to present at least a partial alternative view of Texas history and the American myth perpetuated for more than 150 years of the Alamo as an epic battle between good and brave Anglo Texans against evil and treacherous Tejanos and Mexican troops under the command of Santa Anna. Despite the criticism he has received from Chicano brothers and sisters, Treviño certainly has presented in his film a nuanced and complex view of history and has succeeded in dispelling the Hollywood characterization of Mexican males as either bandits or drunks and of Mexican females as temptresses.

The Ballad of Gregorio Cortez (1982)

The Ballad of Gregorio Cortez is based on Américo Paredes's groundbreaking book-length study, *With His Pistol in His Hand: A Border Ballad and Its Hero,* discussed in chapter 1. The title of the film takes its departure from the English translation of the versions of the corrido that Paredes had so carefully analyzed in his book and, like the ballad, the film is grounded in the intense animosity that existed between Mexicans and Mexican Americans on one hand and Anglos and law enforcement officials on the other during the latter part of the nineteenth and the beginning of the twentieth century. As historians have documented, the Texas Rangers, a state-sponsored force that patrolled the Texas-Mexico border, were particularly abusive in their treatment of Mexican nationals and Americans of Mexican descent, and were therefore viewed with a mixture of fear and hatred.

In the film, Cortez (played by Edward James Olmos) is portrayed as a victim of circumstance. He is visited at his ranch by the local sheriff and his deputy, who question him about a recently acquired horse. Cortez explains he has recently received the horse from a man named Villarreal in exchange for a mare. The sheriff, speaking in broken Spanish, implies that Cortez is lying and that he has stolen the horse. Cortez is affronted, words are exchanged, the sheriff draws his gun, Cortez does likewise, they exchange shots, and the sheriff and Cortez's brother Romaldo are fatally wounded. Cortez flees his ranch, leaving behind his wife and young children, as well as the body of his brother (see figure 4). The deputy returns to town, a posse of Texas Rangers and local Anglo ranchers and townspeople is organized, and a chase ensues. Cortez eludes the posse—many small groups and a larger group of three hundred men—for several weeks due to

■ Fig. 4. In *The Ballad of Gregorio Cortez*, Gregorio Cortez takes flight on horseback after the shoot-out with Sheriff Frank Fly at the Cortez Ranch. (From the 1983 Embassy Pictures movie poster; reprinted courtesy of David Maciel.)

his knowledge of the terrain and his expert horsemanship. Eventually, however, he is captured, tried, and convicted of murdering the sheriff. He serves several years of his sentence before eventually being pardoned by the governor of Texas.

As in the ballad, Cortez is portrayed as both a victim and a heroic figure. Through his actions he represents the resistance of his people against Anglo tyranny and oppression so prevalent in Texas during the historical period that serves as the setting of the film. Most of the Anglos, particularly the lawmen, are characterized as at best calloused and at worst cruel racists. The film shows how Mexican Americans in the border region where the events take place attribute to Cortez the qualities of an epic hero who embodies their deepest sentiments of fear, defiance, and hope for a better life free of injustice.

The screenplay was adapted by the Chicano writer Víctor Villaseñor and Robert M. Young who, although they were not always faithful to the factual record, did not engage in exaggeration or distortion. Olmos and the actors who play his wife, the sheriff, the defense lawyer, and the court interpreter turn in excellent performances.

The NCLR and the NEH provided funding for the planning, scripting, and final production of the film. It was the pilot program for the SOMOS project, which was planning to produce a five-part series of dramatic presentations for public television. This film was, in fact, aired in 1982 on PBS stations across the United States and then distributed in movie theaters by Embassy Pictures. Most of the other films that were to be part of the project were never produced due to a lack of financial support.

El Norte (1983)

Chicano Gregory Nava directed this film, which he and his wife, Anna Thomas, cowrote. Thomas also served as producer. Although the film does not revolve around Chicano characters or deal specifically with a Chicano or even Mexican reality, it does raise a number of social issues that Chicanos and other Latinos confront.

The story, which has a strong basis in contemporary Guatemalan history, is about two adolescent Guatemalan Indians who are forced to leave their native Maya-Quiché village after government death squads threaten to kill them and all the village inhabitants. Their father Arturo is killed because he is the leader of a peasant group that tries to oppose greedy landowners who are supported by the local as well as the national power structure.

The film traces Rosa and Enrique (brother and sister), the protagonists, as they depart their village and country to journey north—the title of the movie—through Mexico with the intent of crossing the U.S.–Mexican border at Tijuana. Rather than finding political refuge and safety, they encounter continuous hardship and hostility on their trek. Rosa dies tragically of typhus in her brother's arms at the end of the film. There are references throughout the movie to the protagonists' Maya-Quiché culture, an aspect of the film that strongly links it to the strong indigenous identification of its Chicano audience.

The plight of Rosa and Enrique is also implicitly associated in the film to that of thousands of Mexican youth who have come north to the United

States over the past several decades to escape not only financial depression but political repression as well. On the other hand, the protagonists—whose second language is Spanish and who come from a rural indigenous setting in Guatemala—find Mexicans bewildering and not always willing to help them get to Mexico's northern border. As List (1996) has pointed out, the Spanish language in this film is actually the language of the oppressor (the Guatemalan landowner, the death squads, and even some Mexicans they encounter) whereas in most Chicano films Spanish is coded as a marker "of an unproblematic Pan-Latin identity" (List 1996, 107). Although Noriega would consider the use of Spanish in films to be a sign of Chicano authenticity, in this film it functions quite differently. Chicano characters in this film are not treated kindly. For example, Rosa and Enrique are brought by their Mexican coyote to Don Mocte, a Chicano labor broker who is portrayed as dishonest and ruthless. He also speaks mainly English to them thus contributing significantly to their distress and feeling of isolation in a foreign country. Enrique, who is appointed to a head waiter position in a San Diego restaurant, is turned in to the Immigration and Naturalization Service (INS) by a Chicano coworker who believes he is more deserving of the position. Mexican illegals that Rosa and Enrique meet in the United States are far more supportive and open to the Guatemalan pair.

Break of Dawn (1988)

In 1983, Paul Espinosa and Isaac Artenstein produced a biographical documentary about Pedro J. González, a legendary radio personality who produced and hosted one of the first Spanish-language radio programs in the United States. *Break of Dawn,* directed by Artenstein, is an expanded, feature-length version of the documentary. Artenstein was born in Mexico and grew up in southern California, where he completed a degree in filmmaking at UCLA. He is one of the original members of the Border Arts Workshop, where he collaborated with performance artist Guillermo Gómez-Peña to produce *Border Brujo* (1990) (List 1996, 86–87).

González, an immigrant from Mexico who came to the United States and launched a successful broadcasting career, was indicted and convicted on trumped-up charges. The film's opening sequence is a confrontation between González and the Anglo warden of San Quentin prison where González was sent to serve his term. He is portrayed as proud and defiant

■ Fig. 5. Pedro J. González plays guitar on his radio program in the movie *Break of Dawn*. (Photograph courtesy of David Maciel.)

before the warden, who accuses him of trying to create unrest among the Spanish-speaking prison population. Then, through a series of flashbacks, Artenstein portrays some major moments in González's life up to the point of the 1938 prison scene. We see him prepare himself to apply for a job as a program host, his eventual hiring by KMPC to do his own show, the show's immediate success, and his burgeoning popularity in southern California and across the Southwest (see figure 5). At one point, the Mexican consul asks González to use his popularity with Mexican and Mexican American listeners to help unionize Mexican immigrant workers in the United States. He agrees to do so but incurs the wrath of the Los Angeles district attorney and even a Chicano police captain.

The film strongly suggests that González's growing political influence and particularly his pro-union views quickly lead to attempts to destroy him. The film portrays the rape charges against him as bogus and, when he refuses to confess to them in exchange for probation, he is convicted and sent to San Quentin. He remains defiant to pressure even in prison, and his insistence on using Spanish to communicate with other Chicano and Mexican prisoners is his way of maintaining his dignity. His insistent use of Spanish even when speaking to the warden in the film's first sequence is consistent with his lifetime ethic of resisting control and domination by the Anglo power structure. The use of language as power was a guiding principle of González's life and career in Spanish-language radio, and is thus one of the film's central themes.

El mariachi (1993)

Robert Rodríguez made his film *El mariachi* for less than $10,000, an incredible feat. He had already enjoyed some success with his 1990 award-winning student film *Bedhead* before he set out to make a low-budget mainstream hit. *Bedhead* is a variant of the teen coming-of-age movie whereas *El mariachi* is a somewhat whimsical Spanish-language movie about a wandering Mexican minstrel (played by Carlos Gallardo). In the opening sequence he comes to a small Mexican border town carrying only his guitar (in a case) and hoping to find a job as a singer in one of the town's cantinas (bars). He is mistakenly identified as Azul (Reinol Martínez), a much-feared hit man who carries his weapons in a guitar case. Much of the film revolves around El Mariachi's attempts to avoid trouble. Finally, however, he is forced to trade his guitar for a pistol in order to confront and defeat not Azul, who has been killed, but an Anglo drug racketeer named Moco (Peter Marquand).

Charles Ramírez Berg (1996) has observed that the film brings together two film genres: the Mexican *narcotraficante* (drug trafficker) film and the transnational warrior-adventure film—in interesting ways. Rodríguez modeled his mode of low-cost production on the former genre, and adapted the narrative strategies and highly charged style of the latter in an attempt to make an affordable film that would appeal to the Spanish-language video market on both sides of the U.S.–Mexican border. Adhering to the best practices of the well-established, low-overhead Mexican filmmaking tradition, he shot his streamlined and lean film in less than four weeks using very efficient production methods: he served as a one-person movie company and fulfilled various artistic roles as writer, director, director of photography, sound recordist, and editor, as well as the labor-intensive roles of grip, gaffer, property master, and co-producer.

In the tradition of the warrior-adventure narrative, *El mariachi* centers on a lone male protagonist who has exceptional physical skills and a strong code of justice and morality that leads him to achieve highly altruistic ends. Following this tradition, the character of El Mariachi undergoes a severe test of loss—he loses his friend Domino who works in the bar owned by Moco—only to recover and confront and defeat the evildoer—Moco—who has caused his loss. One of the film's very positive features is that it attempts to redefine male heroism and masculinity. Rather than being a Mexican or Chicano male hero endowed with great physical prowess, El Mariachi is an antimacho, a male who identifies himself primarily as an artist and who overcomes adversity by relying on his spirituality and strong sense of self-identity.

. . . And the Earth Did Not Swallow Him (1995)

This film is based on the 1971 award-winning novel . . . *Y no se lo tragó la tierra* / . . . *And the Earth Did Not Part* by Chicano author Tomás Rivera (see chapter 5 for a discussion of this novel). The film was produced by Paul Espinosa and written and directed by Severo Pérez, an independent Los Angeles filmmaker who has created programming for the Disney Channel, HBO, and CBS. Espinosa and Pérez struggled to find a national distributor for their film, which had been backed by multiple grants from the NEH, *American Playhouse,* and the Corporation for Public Broadcasting. Finally, Kino International, a New York distributor, agreed to distribute the film.

The film's narrator, Marcos González (played by José Alcalá), is a young boy, the son of Tejano migrant workers. Annually the family joins the migrant stream with thousands of other families, traveling to the Northwest and Midwest to harvest fruit, lettuce, apples, and many other crops. Marcos reminisces over the past twelve months in his family's difficult and sometimes tragic life at home in Texas and on the road. During the course of the film, he remembers terrible scenes and episodes of murder, theft, suicide, racial bigotry, fraud, adultery, illness, poverty, and religious hypocrisy. Like the novel, the film revolves around the young boy's awakening to his own identity and the harsh conditions under which his people are forced to live. Marcos's thoughts, memories, and sensibility make up the unifying device that pulls together the disparate threads of the plot.

The defining moment in the film comes when Marcos, a quiet but intensely curious and intelligent young boy, curses his God for his family's suffering and is not punished for his act; that is, the earth does not swallow him. Chicano actors Marco Rodríguez and Rose Portillo play the young boy's parents, Joaquín and Florentina. They love him but ultimately cannot protect him from the terrible conditions he experiences as a migrant worker and his disillusionment that a bountiful God has not rescued him, his family, and other migrant workers from a virtual hell on earth.

The film won many awards including the Santa Barbara International Film Festival Best of the Festival Audience Award, the Minneapolis International Film Festival Best of the Festival prize, the San Antonio Cine-Festival Best Feature award, the Viña del Mar Festival (Chile) Jury Award, and the Cairo International Film Festival Jury Award—Artistic Achievement by Director. The film was also screened at several other U.S. festivals and at international film festivals in Russia, Italy, and France.

Selena (1997)

Gregory Nava and Moctezuma Esparza co-produced this film, which is based on the life of the famous Tejana singer Selena Quintanilla Pérez, who died tragically in 1995 (see chapter 2 for a discussion of her music). Abraham Quintanilla Jr., Selena's father, asked Nava to direct the film, possibly because he wanted his daughter's family orientation to emerge and Nava had already directed a couple of family-centered films (*El Norte* and *Mi familia/My Family*).

Selena spent most of her young career on the road with the Quintanilla family act, and when she married, she and her husband (the band's lead guitarist) moved into a house next to her parents. Selena never left home but integrated the family into her very successful, albeit truncated, career. Nava respects this family orientation in the film, which emphasizes positive family values and depicts Selena (Jennifer López plays the adult Selena) as a woman of high moral character who often put her family before herself and her career, just as an ideal Chicana daughter should. Her fictional father Abraham (played by Edward James Olmos) is portrayed as guiding Selena from the time she exhibited singing talent as a young girl through her adolescence with a firm but caring hand. Selena eventually asserts a degree of independence from her father, especially when he objects to the increasingly provocative costumes she insists on wearing during performances. The father is depicted as somewhat authoritarian, patriarchal, and stubborn, given to emotional outbursts but also willing to laugh at himself and to relent at least a little to Selena's growing independence. Selena's mother, brother, and sister are characterized as loving, understanding, and supportive, sometimes acting to take the sting out of her father's tirades.

Although the film does not create a perfect Chicano family, it does leave a very positive image of one, an image that audiences will find very comforting. At the same time, it also portrays Selena as a young woman who begins to take control of her own destiny, especially her romantic life. She initiates the romance with her future husband Chris (played by Jon Seda) by proposing the first date and eventually elopes, marrying against her family's wishes. *Selena* is simultaneously a film about family, Chicano pride, an American success story, coming of age, and a music star grounded in Tejano music who struggles to gain a wider crossover audience.

◼ Hollywood Hispanic Films

Unlike the films just discussed, films in the Hollywood Hispanic category combine Chicano expertise and sometimes even control with rigorous adherence to Hollywood production values and distribution. It is important to emphasize that these films are not typical Hollywood high-budget films designed for the largest possible viewing audiences. The very nature of the material rooted in Chicano culture and history necessarily—although unfortunately—limits the audience.

Zoot Suit (1981)

Zoot Suit is basically a filmed version of a Luis Valdez/Teatro Campesino play. Luis Valdez directed the film. Both the movie and the play revolve around the murder of a young boy at a place called Sleepy Lagoon in Los Angeles in 1942. Twenty-two young Chicano males were arrested and four were eventually brought to trial as the alleged murderers. Henry "Hank" Reyna (played by Daniel Valdez, Luis Valdez's brother), the leader of the 38th Street Gang and one of the four brought to trial, plays a central role in the film. The arrest and trial force Henry to confront questions of his own identity as well as his commitment to individuals and Chicanos in general.

Although the film is based on a historical episode, it has a strong mythical and archetypal dimension in the figure of El Pachuco (played brilliantly by Edward James Olmos), a flamboyant, supremely confident, and savvy larger-than-life individual based on the proud and cynical *pachuco* social type that other Chicano filmmakers and creative writers draw on for inspiration. In the film, El Pachuco functions as a kind of Greek chorus who comments on the main action from his position stage left or stage right. He is depicted as a supremely cool and hip outsider. Valdez presents him to us as a kind of intellectual and spiritual guide to the film (List 1996, 63). His role is to comment on and undermine the motives of the Anglo characters (the newspaper reporter who covers the Sleepy Lagoon incident and the trial, the liberal Anglo lawyer who defends the four young Chicanos, the trial judge, and even Alice Bloomfield, the woman who organizes a defense committee) as well as to mock and goad Hank Reyna when he appears to weaken in the face of the justice system. Reyna is sentenced to life in prison, falls in love with Bloomfield (who does not reciprocate his love), and is eventually released from prison when his conviction is overturned on appeal to a higher court.

One of the film's best qualities is that it provides biting and unrelenting social commentary and at the same time is entertaining. Noriega (1992, 171) has high praise for the film because it fits comfortably in his signification category as a work that is based solidly in Chicano history and "draws upon culture-based alternative forms of history telling" (i.e., teatro [theater]). Keller (1994) views the film as Chicano cinema's answer to Hollywood musicals and gang pictures that distort history and portray Chicano characters in decidedly negative or superficial ways.

American Me (1992)

Edward James Olmos directed and starred in this bleak but brutally realistic film about urban gangs and prison life. Based on a screenplay written by Floyd Mutrux in the early 1970s, the film takes its title from Beatrice Griffith's 1948 book with the same title about Chicano gangs. Olmos and filmmaker Robert Young secured the rights to the screenplay, and Olmos participated in the rewrite of it although his name does not appear among the screenwriting credits. Olmos plays the lead part of Santana, a role inspired by Cheyenne, who was an actual Chicano gang leader who died in prison in 1972. Santana is an East Los Angeles Chicano who as a juvenile kills a fellow detainee in jail and is given a long-term sentence in California's Folsom State Prison. He soon becomes a very tough and insensitive leader who sets up an underground drug trafficking operation at Folsom.

The film begins in the final moments of Santana's life as a prison warlord and head of the prison's Mexican Mafia. Through a series of flashbacks and flash-forwards, we are given glimpses of his life at home and on the mean streets of East Los Angeles, his first petty crimes, the violent murder of an Anglo detainee who had raped him in jail, his life in prison, and his brief and violent relationship with his girlfriend. Santana is brutally executed in prison by members of his own mafia. We also learn that his father was beaten and his mother raped by Anglo servicemen during the infamous Los Angeles Zoot Suit Riots of 1943.

In his original screenplay, Mutrux had characterized Santana as a romantic hero in the mold of Mexican revolutionary hero Emiliano Zapata.

Olmos changed this characterization to an image of "a cold and calculating prison lord" (Fregoso 1993, 123). Olmos comments on the character he created and his mission in directing and acting in *American Me,* "I want to show that there's a cancer in this subculture of gangs. . . . They'll say, 'You've taken away our manhood with this movie.' I say to them, 'Either you treat the cancer or it'll eat you alive' " (Fregoso 1993, 123). Olmos's apparent intent is to shock young Chicanos and their communities rather than to attract a wide audience.

Film critic Linda Fregoso (1993, 123) has said that what she likes best about the movie "is precisely its novel, unflinching treatment of Chicano masculinities, its shrewdly oblique refusal to romanticize the defiance of the masculine heroic figure." She contrasts the depiction of the male in this film to that in other films such as *Zoot Suit.* She also believes that the graphic violence and the gruesome details of Chicano prison life—the film was shot on location at Folsom State Prison—are not gratuitous. Instead, Fregoso and other critics have criticized Olmos for making the dysfunction and disintegration of the Chicano family—Santana's mother and father—responsible for their sons and daughters turning to crime, violence, and gangs. They would argue that societal factors such as the material conditions of poverty and unemployment among young Chicanos in the barrio are the cause.

La Bamba (1987)

La Bamba, which was directed by Luis Valdez, was released in both English and Spanish versions and has grossed more than $50 million. It is based on the life of Ritchie Valens (Richard Valenzuela), the Chicano rock and roll singer (see chapter 2). The content is undeniably Chicano: Valens's humble beginnings and life as a child and adolescent in a Chicano section of Los Angeles, his working in the fields, his devotion to his mother and siblings, and his discovery of his Indo-Mexican roots. Yet there is a tension in the film as the music industry transforms him into a nondescript and nonthreatening singer who apparently is all too willing to assimilate into Anglo culture in order to enhance his career as a singer. In the film, he readily agrees to anglicize his name in order to become more acceptable to the young, middle-class Anglo fans who made up most of the rock and roll audience of the late 1950s.

Director Luis Valdez has received criticism for several aspects of the film, including the selection of a non-Chicano (Lou Diamond Phillips) to play the lead role of Ritchie. In Valdez's defense, several other roles are played by Chicano and Chicana actors. There are those who have questioned Valdez's judgment in having directed a film that seems to send an assimilationist message, at least to a Chicano audience. Since Ritchie Valens chose an assimilationist route to success, critics argue that the director should have chosen another Chicano figure whose personal history was more exemplary to a Chicano audience and more representative of the Chicano experience in the United States. In Valdez's defense, however, he has succeeded in educating a broad spectrum of the moviegoing audience in the United States and Mexico that Valens was a Chicano. Perhaps one can also praise Valdez for highlighting the difficult decisions that Valens had to make (e.g., the anglicization of his name) in order to succeed.

Valdez may have meant to use the life of this particular young Chicano to criticize the recording industry and society at large for requiring that a minority deny his ethnicity in order to be successful. Valdez himself stated in interviews after the release of the movie that he was simply trying to make an "American movie" (Lubenow 1987, 79). What he meant by this statement is open to speculation, but it is at least clear that he was not trying to make an explicitly Chicano movie. *La Bamba* therefore fits very comfortably in the Hollywood Hispanic category.

Born in East L.A. (1987)

Before directing this film, Cheech Marin had partnered with his associate Thomas Chong to co-direct several hilarious comedies: *Up in Smoke* (1978; the highest-grossing comedy of that year), *Cheech and Chong's Next Movie* (1980), *Cheech and Chong's Nice Dreams* (1981), *Cheech and Chong Still Smokin'* (1983), *Things Are Tough All Over* (1982), and *The Corsican Brothers* (1984). At the time of their release, these films did not receive serious attention from Chicano film scholars and historians, probably because the image of Chicanos they portrayed was considered generally negative and not in keeping with the cultural nationalist, artistic, or social agendas that were the legacy of the Chicano Movement of the 1960s and 1970s. The character Marin played in these movies was slapstick and one-dimensional; that is, quite different from the lead characters in the Chicano films I have already discussed, as well as many others that depict men and women with complex psychological makeups. It is no wonder, then, that Cheech and Chong's movies, although highly entertaining and comical, were considered to be light in comparison to more serious Chicano film projects. These films also seemed directed at a young, mainstream audience that could readily identify with the counterculture topics of recreational drug use and explicit sexual material presented in a humorous fashion.

Born in East L.A. is the first movie that Cheech Marin directed on his own. He has said that he got the idea for the film while reading a newspaper account of a Chicano, a U.S. citizen, who was deported to Mexico and also while listening to Bruce Springsteen's very popular hit, "Born in the USA." He first wrote and produced a music video and then the film, both of which parody the song (List 1992). Although the intent of Springsteen's song might have been to portray harsh realities of working-class life, it came to be associated with the narrowly defined American patriotism of the time. Marin's intent was to write and direct a film that would parody the song and thereby challenge the underlying assumption that had been attributed to it as the result of ideological manipulation by conservative political interests of the late 1980s. " 'Born in the USA' came to signify 'US for non-others (white Anglo Americans)' and, with that, 'foreigners, non-whites, go home' " (Fregoso 1990, 271). The film is a critique of white racism, particularly white racism directed toward ethnic minorities and immigrant groups that are considered to be foreigners and therefore unwelcome in Anglo America.

The film's plot is simple. Rudy (played by Marin) goes to a toy factory in downtown Los Angeles to meet his mother's cousin Javier (played by Paul Rodríguez), an undocumented Mexican immigrant. He is rounded up in an INS raid on the factory. Despite his protestations, the arresting officials will not believe that he is a U.S. citizen, mainly because he looks foreign, and he is deported. In Mexico he is lost and confused because he speaks Chicano Spanish and does not fully understand the culture. In other words, the film focuses on differing and contested definitions of foreignness and thereby captures some of the U.S. political xenophobia, which in its most extreme and virulent form would seek to rid the United States of all foreigners, including Chicanos and Asian Americans who were also considered to be foreign (i.e., nonwhite).

Much of the rest of the film revolves around Rudy's attempts to return to the United States. He succeeds in doing so when he crosses the border with a group of foreign-born Asians he has trained in Mexico to behave like East L.A. Chicanos in order to disguise their true identities and allow them to merge unnoticed into the workforce of multiethnic Los Angeles. The film has many humorous and parodic scenes, but throughout it maintains an underlying critical view of the politically reactionary climate of the time. With this film, Cheech Marin demonstrated to critics that parody and humor could be effective instruments for social criticism and that an entertaining film could also have a serious message.

The Current State of Chicanos in U.S. Cinema

Chicanos have made modest advances in the film industry over the past thirty years, and at the dawn of the twenty-first century Chicano filmmaking has promise. Yet a recent research project and report commissioned by the Screen Actors Guild (SAG) at the suggestion of its Latino/Hispanic Subcommittee paints a depressing picture of the status quo. The media and cinema experts at the Tomás Rivera Policy Institute (TRPI) examined Latino audience trends, Latinos and the cinema market, actors' attitudes about the employment and depiction of Latinos in the entertainment industry, and the state of the film industry vis-à-vis Latinos. Their findings and recommendations are contained in the report, *Missing in Action: Latinos in and out of Hollywood* (TRPI 1999).

Although the findings and recommendations apply to all Latinos, we can reasonably extrapolate them to Chicanos. The TRPI found that the Latino audience for movies is split. U.S.–born Latinos are avid consumers of movies, whereas foreign-born Latinos are less likely to go. Therefore, the film industry has a great opportunity to expand its audience by attracting larger numbers of foreign-born Latinos. To achieve this, the industry must find the content and language in films that will appeal to this portion of the community.

The TRPI experts also found that Latinos are more likely to see films that star Latino/Latina actors than they are to see equally popular films that do not star Latinos. Although Latinos do not place ethnicity at the top of the list of reasons to see a film, it clearly plays a role. A slight majority of Latinos reports that, overall, Latinos are presented in a positive light in movies and on television, but they also report that the most common image of Latinos and Latinas is negative. Many also see stereotypes in the presentation of Latinos.

According to the TRPI researchers, Latino/Latina actors comprised just 4 percent of SAG membership and received only 3.5 percent of guild roles in 1998. Latinos also account for less than 2 percent of the membership of the Writers Guild of America. Guild figures released in 1999 show significant declines in Latino membership in specific categories compared to 1998: from 4 percent to 3.5 percent for actors, and from 3.1 percent to 2.3 percent for directors. Latinos make up a scant 1.3 percent of the writers for prime-time television. Moreover, Spanish-surnamed employees account for just 1.9 percent of executive positions at major film studios and television networks. There is no Latino executive who occupies a creative decision-making position.

TRPI's recommendations to the SAG and the industry in general are hard-hitting and sweeping:

1. Promote color-blind casting.
2. Inform behind-the-camera decision makers.
3. Show the real American scene and increase Latino programming.
4. Address pay and non-union work issues specific to Spanish-language television.
5. Play a more aggressive role in promoting Latino inclusiveness in the entertainment industry.

Appendix: Chicano Cinema of the Late 1960s through the 1990s

Chicano Documentaries and Short Films of the 1960s and Early 1970s

Most Chicano filmmakers cut their teeth by producing talk shows, soap operas, and other programs for television such as *Canción de la raza* (The People's Song), *Unidos* (United), *Reflecciones* (Reflections), *Acción Chicano* (Chicano Action), and *The Siesta Is Over.* These programs were followed by a series of politically aware documentaries and short films on the Chicano experience:

■ Luis and Daniel Valdez's *Yo soy Joaquín/I Am Joaquín* (1967), a film adaptation of Rodolfo "Corky" Gonzales's poem

■ David García's *Requiem-29* (1971), about the East Los Angeles riots of that year and the death of Chicano reporter Rubén Salazar

■ Jesús Treviño's *América tropical* (1971), about the events surrounding the destruction of Mexican muralist David Siqueiros's mural in Los Angeles

Treviño's *La Raza Unida* (1972), about the 1972 national convention of the newly formed La Raza Unida Party

Treviño's nationally televised *Yo soy chicano* (1972), about the history of Chicano protest including the Chicano Movement and its identification with Mexican Indian culture

The Valdezes' *Los vendidos* (1972), a film adaptation of a Teatro Campesino acto

Ricardo Soto's *A la brava* (1973), about the conditions for Chicano prisoners in California's Soledad penitentiary

Rick Tejada-Flores's *Sí se puede* (1973), documenting César Chávez's twenty-four-day fast in Arizona to protest proposed anti-strike legislation by the Arizona legislature

■ Soto's *A Political Renaissance* (1974), about the emergence of Chicano political power

■ José Luis Ruiz's *The Unwanted* (1974), about the trials and tribulations of Mexican undocumented workers in the United States

Documentaries, Short Films, and Videos Since the Mid-1970s

The pace of production of Chicano documentaries, short films, and videos during the past twenty years has been steady. I will list and briefly comment on those that film scholars and critics seem to consider the most representative and the best of the numerous films produced and shown at festivals, on television, or in movie houses (Keller 1994, 199–206).

Anthropological or Folkloric Themes

■ Les Blank's *Chulas fronteras* (1976) and its sequel *Del mero corazón* (1979), documenting popular music along the Texas-Mexican border

Esperanza Vásquez and Moctezuma Esparza's *Agueda Martínez* (1977), chronicling the lifestyle of an elderly woman in northern New Mexico

Daniel Salazar's *La tierra* (1981), presenting life in Chicano communities in southern Colorado's San Luis Valley

Alicia Maldonado and Andrew Valles's *The Ups and Downs of Lowriding* (1981), examining the lives of low riders through the eyes of the owners/artists

- Paul Espinosa's *The Trail North* (1983), reenacting the trek north to California of a Mexican family from Baja California

Political Discontent and Reform Themes

- Severo Pérez's *Cristal* (1975), documenting the founding of La Raza Unida Party in Crystal City, Texas, by José Angel Gutiérrez
- Paul Espinosa and Isaac Artenstein's *Ballad of an Unsung Hero* (1983), chronicling the life of Pedro J. González, a pioneering radio figure and recording star
- Ricardo Trujillo's *Tixerina: Through the Eyes of the Tiger* (1983), an interview with Reies López Tijerina
- Jesús Treviño and José Luis Ruiz's *Yo soy/I Am* (1985), reviewing the progress that Chicanos have made since the Chicano Movement
- Carlos Avila's *Distant Water* (1990), focusing on the challenges of growing up in Los Angeles in the 1940s and 1950s
- Héctor Galán's *Los mineros* (1990), documenting the struggles of Chicano miners in Arizona between 1903 and 1946
- Cheche Martínez and Colin Jessop's *Sin fronteras* (1991), denouncing police brutality against Chicanos and Mexicans living in border communities
- José Luis Ruiz and Jesús Treviño's *Chicano! History of the Mexican American Civil Rights Movement* (1996), a four-part video series presenting a panoramic view of the Chicano struggle for justice and equal rights

Literary, Musical, and Artistic Themes

- Jeff and Carlos Penichet's *El Pueblo Chicano: The Beginnings* (1979) and *El Pueblo Chicano: The Twentieth Century* (1979), which give an overview of Chicano cultural roots and contemporary issues
- Joe Camacho's *Pachuco* (1980), about the 1941 Zoot Suit Riots in Los Angeles
- Efraín Gutiérrez's *La onda chicana* (1981), about a 1976 concert performed by Little Joe y la Familia and other Tejano groups
- Paul Venema's *Barrio Murals* (1983), documenting the creation of the Cassiano Homes murals on San Antonio's west side

Beverly Sánchez-Padilla's *In the Company of José Rodríguez* (1983), about La Compañía de Teatro de Albuquerque

■ Jesús Treviño's *A Spirit Against All Odds* (1985), featuring one of San Antonio's best-known Chicano artists

Abe Cortez's *Hip Hop: The Style of the 80s* (1987), dealing with break dancing, graffiti, art, and rap music

Isaac Artenstein's *Border Brujo* (1990), about Mexican-born performance artist Guillermo Gómez-Peña

Jorge Sandoval's *Las tandas de San Cuilmas (los carperos)* (1990), a filmic version of a contemporary Chicano play

Luis Valdez's *The Pastorela: A Shepherd's Play* (1991), a traditional Christmas-season play

Roy Flores's *Tejano State of Art* (1992), an overview of the history of Tejano music

■ Daniel Jacobo's *The Aztlán Chronicles* (1992), a documentary in which Luis Valdez discusses important aspects of Mexican Indian culture

■ Jacobo's *The Texas Tornados* (1992), filming a live concert by the musical group of the same name

Juan Garza's *Fascinating Slippers* (1992–93), documenting the creation of an art piece by Gluglio "Gronk" Nicandro

■ David Zamora Casas's *Dos por dos* (1993), about his own work as a performance artist

Undocumented Workers, Farmworkers, and Migrant Workers

Ricardo Soto's *Cosecha* (1976), about migrant labor

■ Soto's *Migra* (1976), about the arrest of undocumented workers

Soto's *Al otro paso* (1976), on the economy of the border

Soto's *Borderlands* (1983), on complex interrelations along the U.S.–Mexican border

Jesús Carbajal and Todd Darling's *Año Nuevo* (1984), tracing the court case brought by twenty-two undocumented Mexican workers against their employer, the Año Nuevo Flower Ranch

The United Farm Workers Union's *The Wrath of Grapes* (1986), documenting the struggle of California farmworkers

- Severo Pérez's *There Goes the Neighborhood* (1987), about how established Latino communities react to recently arrived immigrants from Latin America and elsewhere

- Paul Espinosa's *Vecinos desconfiados/Uneasy Neighbors* (1989), exploring the strong feelings and growing tensions between migrant workers and affluent San Diego homeowners

- Leopoldo Blest Guzmán's *Un cielo cruel y una tierra colorada* (1991), about three friends who come to California from Mexico to seek a better life

- Adán Medrano's *Yo trabajo la tierra* (1991), about the day-to-day lives of farmworkers' families

The Liberated Male

- Daniel Jacobo's *Pain of the Macho* (1991), satirizing *machismo* and other myths of the stereotypical Latin lover

- Gary Soto's *The Bike* (1991), a coming-of-age film

- Harry Gamboa Jr.'s *In Living Color. El Mundo L.A.: Humberto Sandoval, Actor* (1992), a documentary/performance project that explores the consciousness and attitudes of a Chicano male

- Luis Avalos's *El regalo de Paquito* (1993), which explores how a young boy learns the lesson of commitment to family

Documentaries, Short Films, and Videos by Chicanas

- Conchita Ibarra Reyes's *Viva: Hispanic Women on the Move* (1979), about the successes and struggles of Chicanas

- Sylvia Morales's *Chicana* (1979), a panoramic view of the development of women's roles

- Mercedes Sabio's *Wealth of a Nation—Hispanic Merchants* (two parts, 1981), dealing with Hispanic businesses both inside and outside of Latino barrios

- Elvia M. Alvarado's *Una mujer* (1984), dealing with rape and sexual assault

- Morales's *Los Lobos: And a Time to Dance* (1984), about the musical group of the same name

- Betty Maldonado's *Hispanic Art in the U.S.A.: The Texas Connection* (1988), focusing on seven Texas artists
- Lourdes Portillo and Susana Muñoz's *La Ofrenda: The Days of the Dead* (1989), which explores the pre-Hispanic roots of this religious celebration and the social dimensions of death
- Patricia Díaz's *My Filmmaking, My Life* (1990), which explores the life of Mexican filmmaker Matilde Landeta
- Betty Maldonado's *Las nuevas tamaleras* (1991), about the tradition of making tamales at Christmas time
- Frances Salomé España's *El espejo/The Mirror* (1991), a highly experimental presentation of the director's own life in East Los Angeles

Discussion Questions

1. Describe some of the racial and cultural stereotypes prevalent in early Hollywood films.

2. How do the films *The Lawless* and *Salt of the Earth* differ from most of the Hollywood films produced through the 1950s?

3. Summarize the major categories of Chicano documentaries, short films, and videos made during the past thirty years.

4. Discuss what Chon Noriega and Gary Keller mean by the "authenticity" of Chicano films.

5. Why can *Raíces de sangre* be considered "an antithetical border immigration film"?

6. How is *Alambrista!* different from many American and Mexican films about the border?

7. In what sense does *Seguín* present a view of the battle of the Alamo that is counter to the Hollywood portrayal of the battle in films such as *The Alamo*? Why did the film director come under fire?

8. Does *El norte* meet Noriega's standards as an authentic Chicano film?

9. What is unusual about the way in which *El mariachi* was produced?

10. How do Hollywood Hispanic films differ from independent Chicano films?

11. Why have *American Me* and *La Bamba* received criticism from Chicanos?

12. Discuss the current state of Latinos in U.S. cinema.

■ Suggested Readings

Fregoso, Rosa Linda. 1993. *The Bronze Screen: Chicana and Chicano Film Culture.* Minneapolis: University of Minnesota Press.

Kanellos, Nicolás. 1994. *The Hispanic Almanac.* Detroit: Visible Ink.

Keller, Gary D. 1985. *Chicano Cinema: Research, Reviews, and Resources.* Tempe, Ariz.: Bilingual Review/Press.

———. 1994. *Hispanics and United States Film: An Overview and Handbook.* Tempe, Ariz.: Bilingual Review/Press.

Noriega, Chon A., ed. 1992. *Chicanos and Film: Essays on Chicano Representation and Resistance.* Minneapolis: University of Minnesota Press.

Noriega, Chon A., and Ana M. López, eds. 1996. *The Ethnic Eye: Latino Media Arts.* Minneapolis: University of Minnesota Press.

4

Newspapers, Radio, and Television

Whether we scan the radio dial, surf the television channels, review the listings in our local newspaper, or visit the newsstand, we are likely to come across Spanish-language music, entertainment, news, and information about a wide variety of topics of interest to Latinos. The presence today of Spanish-language newspapers, radio, and television has resulted from a long and somewhat conflicted history in each of these media. In this chapter, I will give an overview of the development of these media in the Southwest and elsewhere where there are large concentrations of Americans of Mexican descent. I will also describe the status of each at the beginning of the twenty-first century.

▪ Newspapers

Spanish-language newspapers in the Southwest have been at the forefront nationally in helping to preserve the Spanish language and Mexican and Mexican American cultural identity in the face of an Anglo culture that became more aggressive after 1848 in imposing its own values, identity, and language on a militarily conquered people. Particularly from about the mid-1850s to the mid-1900s, the Spanish-language press has been an important institution in providing leadership to bring communities together politically and socially for the sponsorship of patriotic and cultural celebrations, the organization of Spanish-language schools and medical clinics, and similar efforts. Newspapers have been leaders in fighting discrimination and racism, especially through the editorial pages and letters to the editor. They have also functioned to promote cultural events in the Spanish-speaking communities and to encourage artistic expression by publishing original poetry and fiction or by reprinting poetry or excerpts of works by established Mexican, Spanish, and Latin American authors (Kanellos 1990, 107–8). As Luis Leal (1989, 158) has pointed out, Spanish-language newspapers also were carrying out and promoting political activities even before 1848. For example, *El crepúsculo de la libertad* (The Dawn of Liberty) led a campaign in 1834 for the election of representatives to the Mexican Congress.

The State of Spanish-Language Newspapers During the Nineteenth and Early Twentieth Centuries

La gaceta de Texas (The Texas Gazette) and *El mexicano* (The Mexican) were founded in 1813, and Santa Fe's *El crepúsculo de la libertad* in 1834. These three newspapers were but the first of numerous Spanish-language newspapers that were founded during the nineteenth century and that offered new Americans of Mexican descent an alternative to the flow of information from English-language sources. Los Angeles supported several newspapers, including *La estrella de Los Angeles* (The Los Angeles Star) and *El clamor público* (The Public Clamor) during the 1850s, and *La crónica* (The Chronicle) from the 1870s to the 1890s. San Francisco newspapers included *La voz de México* (The Voice of Mexico) from the 1860s to the 1890s, *La república* (The Republic) from the 1870s to the 1890s, and *La voz del nuevo mundo* (The Voice of the New World) in the 1870s and 1880s.

It is estimated that many hundreds of newspapers were published throughout the Southwest from the 1850s to the 1950s not only in the commercial port cities of Los Angeles and San Francisco but in cities such as Brownsville, San Antonio, and El Paso, Texas; Las Cruces and Santa Fe, New Mexico; Tucson, Arizona; and Santa Barbara, California (Ríos 1973).

In the twentieth century, it was the elite, educated, upper-class Mexican exile community that was largely responsible for continuing many of the newspapers started decades earlier and for setting up larger and more sophisticated publishing enterprises. Many exile and expatriate Mexican intellectuals and entrepreneurs were also intent on promoting the interests of the Mexican community in exile and on creating a *México de afuera* (the other Mexico) by duplicating in the United States the elite and educated culture they had temporarily left behind.

Ignacio Lozano was one of the most powerful and influential business, intellectual, and political figures in the exile community. In 1913, several years after his exile to the United States, he founded *La prensa* (The Press) in San Antonio, where he had settled; in 1926, he founded *La opinión* in Los Angeles. He brought savvy business practices and high professional journalistic standards to these newspapers, which accounts for their consistent quality and longevity (*La opinión* is still owned and published by the Lozano family in Los Angeles today).

In their news stories, cultural features, and advertising these newspapers catered primarily to the educated exile and immigrant Mexican community, and increasingly also to the native-born Spanish-speaking population of not only San Antonio and Los Angeles but wherever the newspapers' extensive distribution systems could reach readers. At least in the beginning, most of the editors, journalists, and writers were drawn from the Mexican exile community, but Lozano also employed Spaniards and Latin Americans to write for his newspapers. Mexican moralists, or *cronistas,* such as Julio G. Arce and Benjamín Padilla assumed pseudonyms and wrote sometimes scathing short satirical pieces promoting a México de afuera mentality that was critical of working-class and rural Mexican immigrants as well as of less-educated native-born Chicanos (Kanellos 1993, 110–117).

The Content of Spanish-Language Newspapers

Both the small local newspapers and the larger ones founded by Lozano and other exile families in the nineteenth and twentieth centuries are rich sources of political expression in the form of editorials, letters to the editor, news stories, advertisements, and announcements. These newspapers are also repositories of artistic expression in the form of poetry, short fiction, and satirical vignettes. Like editorials, letters to the editor, and news stories, these forms of popular literature express concerns about societal norms and practices, but they also reveal very personal sentiments about a variety of subjects such as love, spirituality, and death. Some of the newspapers published occasional literary pieces; others such as *El cronista del valle* from Brownsville and *América hispano* and *La crónica* from San Francisco published poetry or short fiction in almost every issue. These newspapers together published thousands of examples of poetry and prose fiction over their composite history of almost 150 years (Tatum 1982, 23).

PROSE Sometimes the writers of prose pieces were identified and at other times they remained anonymous. An example of the latter is a late-nineteenth-century account of the life and times of Joaquín Murieta, a legendary social rebel, that appeared in serialized form in the Santa Barbara Spanish-language newspaper *La gaceta* (The Gazette). This fictionalized version gives the reader a vivid description of Murieta's boyhood in Sonora, his 1850 journey to California as a young man, the assassination of his brother by U.S. authorities, his first encounters with Anglo law, and his life as a fugitive from justice. Some of the more vivid and entertaining episodes include his relationship with a notorious bandit Three-Fingered

Jack, the knifing of an officer of the law near San Jose, California, in 1851, Murieta's encounter with and shooting of a Mr. Clark in 1852, and his flight to the rugged mountain terrain around Mt. Shasta after a shoot-out with R. B. Buchanan, the sheriff of Yuba County (California). The anonymous author crafts these and other episodes in Murieta's life to characterize him as a brave and fierce defender of his people, a much-admired leader of his band of social rebels, but also as a hapless victim of circumstance and outright prejudice.

As mentioned previously, moralists Benjamín Padilla and Julio G. Arce published extensively in Spanish-language newspapers. Although certainly biased toward the educated Mexican exile community, both offer an informative and interesting perspective on the socio-historical and cultural aspects of their era. Padilla was best known by his pseudonym "Kaskabel" (a play on *cascabel* [rattlesnake]), an appropriate name for a journalist famous among his Mexican American readers for his biting wit. Widely published in several newspapers from Texas to California between 1925 and 1930, he wrote short humorous pieces mainly satirizing social customs. He often ended his pieces with mordant and didactic comments. Padilla was a perceptive observer of human foibles as well as social institutions such as the medical profession, marriage, and the Catholic Church. In "Los ricos sin cuartilla" (Rich People Who Don't Own a Shred), he pokes fun at the pretensions of the supposedly wealthy who strut about publicly putting on airs and lording it over their perceived social inferiors while hiding their own poverty. In "Memento homo" (Remember Man), Padilla uses his pen to satirize Catholics who use the practice of receiving ashes on their forehead on Ash Wednesday to publicly demonstrate their saintliness. He portrays young women as being more concerned that they will receive a pretty ash cross than with the symbolic meaning of the ashes, whereas old women go to great lengths to have their ash crosses last as long as possible. Padilla takes on the institutional Catholic Church in "Carta de una muchacha tapatía a su Santidad Pío J . . ." (A letter from a young woman from Jalisco to His Holiness Pope J . . ."). The young woman implores the pope to intercede on her behalf because she and her boyfriend cannot afford to marry due to the high fee their local parish priest charges for the marriage ceremony.

Like Benjamín Padilla, Julio G. Arce, better known by his pseudonym Jorge Ulica, was widely published in Spanish-language newspapers during the 1920s. Called *Crónicas diabólicas* (Diabolical Chronicles), his short satirical prose pieces are even more biting than Padilla's. One scholar has pointed out that Arce maintains an ambivalent position in the cultural battle that was being waged between Mexican Americans and Anglos at the beginning of the twentieth century. Although he is openly critical of certain Anglo institutions and customs, he maintains an elitist's distance from his fellow Mexicans—he was born in Mexico and moved to San Francisco as an established journalist—and from Chicanos (Lomas 1978, 48).

Among the aspects of Anglo culture that Arce satirizes are elections, Prohibition, a worsening economic situation, and social practices such as public dances and football games. In "No voté pero me botaron" (I Didn't Vote but They Threw Me Out), he criticizes the American political process. A bewildered Mexican national is visited by a strange array of political pressure groups who try to persuade him to vote for or against a proposition he does not fully understand. In "Quién arrebató mi paleto?" (Who Stole My Overcoat?), he is critical of the fanaticism of police agents who try to enforce the arcane laws of Prohibition at a time when U.S. citizens could freely and frequently cross the border into Mexico to drink alcoholic beverages without restriction. Arce's "Sanatarios para bailadores" (Hospitals for Dancers) is a humorous description of well-equipped hospitals and their well-trained professional staffs supposedly set up in large U.S. cities to receive the victims injured in dance hall brawls. In "Touchdown extraordinario" (Extraordinary Touchdown), Arce pokes fun at the popular sport of American football and the propensity of its fanatical fans to become overly involved in its competitive aspects.

As an educated Mexican national and a member of Mexico's elite class who came to the United States as an exile to escape political persecution, Arce is critical not only of U.S. institutions, customs, and cultural practices but of Mexican immigrants and resident Mexican American citizens. He is obviously displeased that both groups have abandoned their Mexican culture and language to ape Anglo ways. At the same time, however, he attacks them for not adapting to the culture of the United States. For example, in "No estamos bastante aptos" (We Aren't Competent Enough), he satirizes Mexican immigrants whom he believes have inadequate educational preparation for their souls to become U.S. citizens after the death of the body.

Women also stand out as popular newspaper writers. Two, Laura de

Pereda and María Esperanza Pardo, are representative of an important group of Mexican American writers who published their prose and poetry in newspapers from about 1850 to 1950. Laura de Pereda, whose style is highly evocative and lyrical, published several short stories reflective of the nineteenth-century romantic sentimentality that characterized much of Mexican and American literature of that era. "Bucólica" (Bucolic), perhaps her best work, is a beautifully rendered tale about a shepherd's discovery of his love for another. "Más muerto que la muerte" (More Dead than Death) is an allegory about the triumph of life over death. Pereda presents the same struggle in "Víctimas del deber" (Victims of Duty), in which a railroad switchman must choose between the lives of his young wife and son and those of a trainload of people.

Like Pereda's stories, those by María Esperanza Pardo are tinged with sadness. Most of the protagonists are women who have suffered some form of personal tragedy—usually at the hands of men—with which they are barely able to cope. For example, in "El perfume de la otra" (Another Woman's Perfume) a young woman who has lost the will to live after discovering her lover's deception struggles unsuccessfully to overcome her depression.

POETRY   In addition to prose fiction, a substantive body of Mexican American poetry was published in Spanish-language newspapers in the Southwest between the 1850s and the 1950s. Much of the poetry that appears in the 1850s and 1860s is anonymous, but by the 1870s, several named poets began to establish themselves by publishing in different newspapers. These anonymous and identified poets composed poetry on a wide range of topics including protests against social injustice, patriotism, love, religion and spirituality, death, and commemorative and elegiac themes. Social protest and love poetry constitute by far the most common topics.

The Mexican American population suddenly found itself politically disenfranchised after the 1848 Treaty of Guadalupe Hidalgo. Poets often spoke collectively for these second-class citizens by protesting against the gross abuses of their civil rights, the denigration of their culture, and the questioning of their patriotism. They also protested the threats against the Spanish language in public schools and elsewhere.

The social poetry published in Spanish-language newspapers falls into three general categories:

1. Poetry that addresses specific political issues or historical occurrences
2. Poetry that affirms the positive cultural traditions and practices—including linguistic traditions—of Hispanics in general and Mexican Americans in particular
3. Patriotic poetry that attempts to combat prevailing negative stereotypes of Mexican Americans as disloyal to the United States, cowardly, and generally unpatriotic

As early as 1856, an anonymous poem published in the Los Angeles newspaper *El clamor público* protests the double standard of the U.S. Supreme Court in its treatment of Americans of Mexican descent. The poet observes that this institution, which should represent the highest standard of the U.S. court system, is in reality part of a hierarchical system that is far too arbitrary and powerful (Tatum 1982, 42).

Poems that express cultural pride are also common. A good example is López de Ayllón's 1927 short poem "Mi raza" (My People) published in the Brownsville newspaper *El cronista del valle*. It is typical of the efforts of Chicano poets early in the twentieth century to combat racist attacks in the English-language press and elsewhere. I quote the entire poem in order to illustrate the determination with which Ayllón and other Mexican Americans have responded to negative stereotyping (*El cronista del valle*, 14 June 1927, 2; English translation mine).

Mi raza es una raza de espíritu guerrero
valiente hasta la audacia, tenaz hasta morir,
de nobles sentimientos, de genio aventurero
que supo un nuevo mundo llegar a descubrir.

Es una raza fuerte que lucha con firmeza
por conseguir los fines que tiene su ideal . . .
antes buscaba guerras, por su ansia de grandeza
y ahora tan sólo anhela la paz universal

Es una raza noble que vive de ideales
y lleva enarbolada, en sus marchas triunfales,
una bandera blanca que es símbolo de unión . . .

Y en su escudo de guerra ostenta como mote
"el espíritu noble que tuvo don Quijote
y el ansia de conquista de Cristóbal Colón."

My race is one with a warlike spirit
valiant even unto daring, tenacious unto death,
of noble sentiments, of an adventuresome nature
a race that knew how to discover a new world.

It is a strong race that struggles firmly
to obtain the goals of its ideals . . .
whereas before it sought war in order to enhance its greatness,
now it desires only universal peace.

It is a noble race that lives according to its ideals
and carries high on its triumphant marches
a white flag that is a symbol of unity . . .

And on its shield of war it brandishes as its emblem
"the noble spirit that Don Quixote possessed
and the eagerness of conquest of Christopher Columbus."

Social societies, predecessors of the American GI Forum and LULAC, were founded in many Mexican American communities in the late nineteenth and early twentieth centuries. One of their main objectives was to give the Spanish-speaking population a sense of social and cultural cohesiveness in order to preserve cultural traditions and practices and use of the Spanish language. M. Padilla Mondragón's 1914 poem, "Salutación a la sociedad Hispano-Americana" (Salutation to the Hispanic-American Society), published in *La estrella,* praises the social society as a refuge in times of difficulty.

World War I (1914–1918) occasioned the outpouring of patriotic sentiments on the part of many Mexican American poets. For example, in "Patria querida" (Beloved Country), the poet Alfredo Lobato praises the United States as he sails off to fight in Germany. In this poem, he views Germany as an imminent threat to the United States and to the American way of government.

Several of the better-known poets who published in Spanish-language newspapers wrote of love. Felipe Maximiliano Chacón, one of the most prolific Mexican American writers of the first part of the twentieth century, devotes several poems to this theme. In a 1906 poem, "Desengaños" (Deceits), published in the Albuquerque paper *El eco del valle* (The Valley Echo), he complains bitterly that the woman he loved rejected his affection when they were young, innocent, and pure. Now, years later, he confesses that he still loves her even though no one else will accept her.

Chicano Movement Era Newspapers

The Chicano Movement of the 1960s and 1970s spawned more than fifty newspapers—some in Spanish only, others in English, and still others in both languages. Chicano community and student groups, unions, and political and social organizations published these papers in communities and on college campuses throughout the Southwest and elsewhere. These publications, of varying length, reported political and cultural activities and promoted the different political agendas of their sponsors. Some of the newspapers appeared on a regular basis, others sporadically, depending on the ability of sponsoring groups to finance and staff their production; a few lasted for several years.

Tomás Ybarra-Frausto (1977, 84) has associated the publication of literature in these newspapers with the emergence of a Chicano poetic consciousness in the mid-1960s. He observes that *El malcriado* (The Brat), the official publication of the United Farm Workers Union at Delano, California, published children's fiction, short stories, and sketches in addition to *corridos* and *décimas,* many of them authored anonymously by what he describes as "unsophisticated working people" who, perhaps for the first time in their lives, were given the opportunity to express themselves in writing. Some anonymous poems deal with a broad range of human concerns and experiences such as love, desire, and death but the most striking often "encompass not an individual drama but the experiences of a collective protagonist: the rural working class."

Although often crudely crafted, much of the poetry is poignant and lyrically honest and draws on the concrete life experiences of its unknown authors. On the other hand, many poems are highly crafted, "reflecting a range of temperament encompassing the lyrical, the sentimental, the ironic, the apocalyptic and the prophetic. Most exhibit a social breadth with the most persistent theme stressing a fervor for social change" (Ybarra-Frausto 1977, 84). The tone of this poetry is often triumphant and optimistic, conveying utopian desires that the organization it represents will eventually win the struggle for a better life for Chicanos everywhere.

Unity is a theme that runs through much of the poetry, corridos, and other popular literature published in *El malcriado.* The compositions urge the newspaper's readers to join the struggle under the common flag of the union to support the *campesinos* in their valiant efforts to win for themselves a living wage, acceptable working conditions, and above all else, their human dignity as workers.

El grito del norte (The Northern Outcry), published in Española, New Mexico, beginning in 1968, played a similar role in supporting Reies López Tijerina and his Alianaza political organization as *El malcriado* did in supporting César Chávez and the United Farm Workers except that the former newspaper was not in any sense an official publication of the Alianza. Like its California counterpart, *El grito del norte* regularly published poetry and song forms such as corridos, *canciones,* and *coplas* in its pages, with the corrido being the most common form of poetic expression. Reflected in an early statement of purpose, the newspaper placed a major emphasis on preserving the cultural traditions of the rural agrarian class in the Southwest: "Su propósito es cooperar en el desarrollo de la causa de la justicia de la gente pobre y ayudar a conservar la rica herencia cultural de La Raza" (The purpose [of the newspaper] is to cooperate in the poor people's development of their cause for justice and to assist in the preservation of the people's rich cultural heritage; Ybarra-Frausto 1977, 90).

The urban equivalent of *El malcriado* and *El grito del norte* was the newspaper *Con safos* (slang for "The Same to You"), founded in Los Angeles in the early 1970s. Ybarra-Frausto (1977, 98) has described this publication as "a feisty compendium of literature, art, and documentary reporting." The editors spurned what they perceived as escapist, non-committed literature to focus on creative work that focused narrowly on the history, language, and lifestyle of the barrio whence many of its founders and contributing writers had come. The name itself was meant to appeal to a sense of defiance, insularity, and rebelliousness in the face of a dominant society that through City Hall and the Los Angeles Police Force had too long taken the plight of the poor Los Angeles barrios for granted and had treated its inhabitants like second-class citizens with little power and few rights as citizens. The creative thrust of the poetry and other literature published by *Con safos* was to demonstrate that "the actual Chicano experience has its own distinct vitality and dynamics" (Ybarra-Frausto 1977, 99).

All artists (creative writers as well as visual artists) who contributed to the newspaper were urged to create art that expressed and validated their own experiences and were discouraged from adhering to the aesthetic norms of either Anglo American or Mexican literature and art. The poetry published in the paper during the early 1970s generally emphasized the collective persona of the urban proletariat, "explored the pulsating, squalid turf of the barrio, and evoked the mutilated existence of the wino, the junkie, and the pachuco" (Ybarra-Frausto 1977, 100). The warmth of relationships, or *carnalismo,* among all Los Angeles barrio dwellers and solidarity with their brothers and sisters in other urban ghettos was expressed in many poems.

The northern California Chicano Movement publication *El pocho Che* (The Gringoized Che) had a very different emphasis and focus than *Con safos.* The very name of the literary collective that founded and supported the publication was taken in part from Che Guevarra, the celebrated Argentinean revolutionary who had fought alongside Fidel Castro in Cuba and had tried to spread his revolutionary zeal throughout Latin America. This association of mainly Chicano writers, poets, and artists was militant to the core, a commitment reflected in the literature it published. The members of the collective saw themselves as part of an international struggle for freedom and justice, and they identified themselves with "cultural workers" everywhere, especially in Latin America. *El pocho Che* ceased publication in 1971 and evolved into a series of poetry and art books by some of northern California's most important writers and visual artists.

Post–Chicano Movement Era Newspapers

Most of the newspapers that grew out of the ferment of the Chicano Movement had disappeared by the mid-1970s. What have persisted to this day are large urban newspapers with a constant readership and source of revenues from advertising. *La opinión* is the best example of such a newspaper. Although it has been a vehicle for political protest and the champion of social causes since its founding in 1926, it was never as radical as most of the local and regional activist newspapers just discussed, and its readership has continued to be middle class and educated. Founder Ignacio Lozano turned over the operation and management of the paper to his son in 1950. When Ignacio Lozano Jr. was named U.S. Ambassador to El Salvador in 1976, he left his son José and his daughter Mónica as co-publishers. The circulation of the newspaper increased under their leadership. A 1990 survey revealed that most of its readership consists of Mexicans and Chicanos (66 percent), but significant percentages are Central Americans and South Americans as well as second- and third-generation Latinos interested in preserving their cultural identity. (By now the percentage of South and Central American readers is likely to have increased.) The paper's circulation exceeds 150,000 and is growing rapidly every year. Most of the advertising is bought by local merchants hoping to appeal to a Chicano/Latino clientele but advertising by national companies is increasing.

The paper's daily coverage includes news, sports, and entertainment. The front page tends to emphasize Latin America, but a local news story that involves or somehow affects Latinos will occasionally be carried on it. The daily "Panorama" section is an excellent source of information about the Anglo and Latino music, entertainment, and artistic worlds. The sports section carries a broad range of U.S. sports news but also consistently covers sports events in Latin America, especially soccer news. The editors do not shy away from expressing strong opinions and stances on both local and national issues, including those that may affect their readership.

La opinión is by far the largest Spanish-language newspaper today that appeals to a Chicano readership, but there are important smaller-circulation newspapers that have established a niche in their respective communities. *The Laredo Morning Times* has published a Spanish-language news page seven days a week continuously since 1926. *El heraldo de Brownsville,* published seven days a week by *The Brownsville Herald,* has been in continuous existence since 1934 as a six-page broadsheet edition. It serves the Texas Rio Grande Valley region. The Compañía Periodística del Sol de Ciudad Juárez (The Juárez Sun Newspaper Company) has published three newspapers since about 1943: *El fronterizo* (The Border Newspaper), the morning edition; *El mexicano* (The Mexican Newspaper), the afternoon edition; and *El continental,* the evening edition. The three newspapers serve a largely Mexican and Chicano Spanish-speaking readership on both sides of the U.S.–Mexican border from Ciudad Juárez–El Paso to Tijuana–San Diego. In addition to these dailies are numerous other newspapers that publish from twice per week to twice per month. Many of these publications serve small cities or clusters of towns throughout the Southwest and are, like their mid-nineteenth to mid-twentieth-century counterparts, important vehicles of information about major community events, local cultural and social events, and other information of interest to their readerships.

■ Radio

Commercial radio broadcasting began in the United States early in the twentieth century. Spanish-language radio programs transmitted within the United States soon followed. By the mid-1920s, some stations owned and operated mainly by non–Mexican Americans began devoting a few hours per day to music, news, and other programs of interest to Spanish-speaking listeners.

The Early Years: Brokers and Broadcasters

Spanish-language brokers negotiated with radio stations directly or through agents to buy airtime for a flat rate. Stations would sell only time slots that were unprofitable for English-language programs, such as early mornings and weekends. The brokers in turn sold advertisements to local businesses and programmed the broadcasts themselves. The brokers' profit was the difference between the flat rate they paid the stations and the money they took in from selling advertisements. Many of the brokers had had previous experience in Mexican broadcasting or theater (Gutiérrez and Schement 1979, 5–6).

One of the early Mexican American figures to pioneer original Spanish-language programming in California was Pedro J. González. Between 1924 and 1934, he was responsible for, among other shows, *Los madrugadores* (The Early Risers), which was broadcast between 4 and 6 a.m. primarily on Los Angeles station KMPC. This particularly powerful, 100,000 watt station could be heard as far away as Texas and was a favorite of Chicanos throughout the Southwest as they began their day. As described in chapter 3, two films have been made about González: the documentary *Ballad of an Unsung Hero* (1984) and a full-length feature film *Break of Dawn* (1988). Both films document his troubles with established authority due mainly to his progressive political views and his willingness to express them on radio and elsewhere. He was convicted on trumped-up rape charges and served six years in prison before he was deported to Mexico in 1940. He continued his radio career across the border in Tijuana and eventually returned to the United States to retire in the 1970s (Subervi-Vélez et al. 1997).

Through the brokerage system, Spanish-language radio continued to grow across the Southwest in the 1930s and 1940s. By the late 1930s a solid number of European American–owned stations were airing programs, some having only short runs and others running as daily programs for years. Due to increasing demand, in 1939 the International Broadcasting Company, based in El Paso, began to produce and sell Spanish-language programs to stations throughout the United States. Many of these programs featured Mexican radio personalities such as José Samaniego and Fernando Navarro (Gutiérrez and Schement 1979, 6–7).

During the Second World War (1939–1945), the U.S. government imposed tight restrictions on English radio broadcasters and even more stringent regulations on foreign-language broadcasters, particularly Japanese, German, Polish, and Italian broadcasters. Although Spanish-language broadcasters were not singled out as potentially subversive, the U.S. Office of Censorship imposed the same restrictive measures on them. During the war San Antonio broker Raúl Cortez applied to the Federal Communications Commission (FCC) for approval of a new radio station, with the rationale that he would use his radio programs to rally Mexican Americans to the war effort. He received approval but by the time his station, KCOR, went on the air, the war had ended.

The founding of KCOR was momentous in the history of Spanish-language broadcasting in the Southwest because it was the first station fully owned and operated by a Mexican American. The extension of the AM band in the late 1940s opened up some opportunities for other entrepreneurial Mexican American businessmen (sadly, they were all men) and brokers. Paco Sánchez in Denver also bought and operated a station, but unfortunately, the vast majority of Spanish-language stations simply hired Mexican American brokers and other employees on salary or commission. Thus Mexican American ownership of radio stations was then—and is now—uncommon (Gutiérrez and Schement 1979, 9).

The Transition Years: The 1950s to 1970s

Spanish-language radio underwent a period of transition during the 1950s. Some stations made employees of their Mexican American announcers while other stations continued to sell to brokers and to hire announcers on a part-time basis. "Personality radio" became the pattern as on-air personalities—brokers and announcers—were heavily invested financially in attracting and retaining a large listening audience; the larger the audience, the greater the revenues from advertising. (This is, of course, even truer today in both radio and television, where a minute of commercial time on widely broadcast programs, such as the Super Bowl or certain events at the Summer Olympics, can sell for more than a million dollars.) The goal was to make listeners loyal to a radio personality such as an announcer, a newsperson, or a performer.

Radio personalities often dispensed commentary on current affairs in addition to their regular roles; that is, they became informal editorialists who issued opinions on political candidates and municipal issues. They would also supplement their incomes by charging listeners for *dedicaciones* (dedications), songs played on special occasions such as birthdays and anniversaries. Spanish-language radio in general became more prominent in the field of foreign-language broadcasting as Spanish supplanted Polish, Italian, and other prewar broadcast languages (Gutiérrez and Schement 1979, 10).

As Spanish-language radio in the Southwest continued to grow in the 1960s, scholars began to study the relationship of this medium to its largely Chicano audience. A 1966 report estimated that two-thirds of the Spanish-language stations in the United States were in the Southwest and called the stations "the one and only force which is now promoting the use of Spanish" (Christian and Christian 1966, 296), a dubious statement.

At this time, music and soap operas dominated the programming of these stations. Another study noted that stations broadcasting in both English and Spanish in general tended to devote a larger share of their day to programming in Spanish than did other foreign-language stations to their respective languages. Scholars have also noted that the majority of the Spanish-language announcers were not Chicano but natives of Latin American countries. Apparently, station owners—presumably Chicano owners as well as Anglo owners—preferred them because of a belief that they spoke a more standard dialect of Spanish, one that was not too *pocho* (gringoized) or too "peasanty" (i.e., the Spanish of rural Chicanos and Mexicans; Grebler, Moore, and Guzmán 1970, 431–32).

Although "personality radio" continued as a strong trend in the 1960s, a fixed format began to replace it, especially in larger stations where management, rather than an individual disk jockey, would select music consistent with the station's image. The disc jockey's personal touch in terms of advertisements and announcements diminished as his or her role became that of plugging in prerecorded commercials and public-service announcements (Gutiérrez and Schement 1979, 12).

Spanish-language television grew in popularity in the late 1960s and

1970s, challenging the monopoly that radio had enjoyed with Spanish-language audiences in the Southwest. The established radio audience had aged, forcing stations to resort to more sophisticated forms of marketing and advertising and programming to attract and hold new listeners. Stations became more dependent on audience demographics, rating services, and census figures. Some advertising agencies even began specializing in Spanish-language radio and television markets.

Radio was seen to have certain benefits over television in reaching Chicanos and Mexican immigrants alike. For one thing, it was not as expensive to produce advertisements and programs for radio as for television. For another, radio was more versatile in its ability to adapt language to its target audience. Bilingual programming could be developed and directed to a bilingual audience while Spanish-dominant programming could be designed for the recently arrived Mexican immigrant or seasonal worker. Even Chicanos educated in English and totally fluent in English would continue listening to Spanish-language radio programs while at the same time preferring English-language television (Gutiérrez and Schement 1979, 13). As Gutiérrez and Schement commented in 1979, Spanish-language radio "continues to be a strong medium of communication for Chicanos, but it is also a medium that appears to be most heavily used by members of the Chicano community who are the weakest economically and politically," a statement that probably remains very true today.

Radio in the Last Twenty Years

As the Chicano population has increased in proportion to the Anglo population in cities throughout the Southwest as well as in Chicago, New York City, Seattle, and Kansas City, the number and presence of Spanish-language radio stations has grown as well. Profits realized from increased advertising and audience position vis-à-vis English-language radio stations have been the primary reason for this growth. In fact, in some cities such as Los Angeles and San Antonio Spanish-language stations rank as high as English-language stations in audience share.

In 1991 there were 185 AM and 203 FM stations transmitting full-time in Spanish, the majority of them in the Southwest. An additional 197 AM and 203 FM stations were airing Spanish-language programs at least a few hours per week (Subervi-Vélez et al. 1997, 231). By 1996, 461 radio stations across the United States (again, the majority in the Southwest) offered a wide variety of programs in Spanish. This growth trend is likely to continue.

Growth in Spanish-language radio broadcasting is indeed good news for Chicanos, recent Mexican immigrants, and other Latinos. Latino/Chicano ownership of radio stations, however, presents a less positive picture of the industry. In 1980, in the top ten markets that included New York, Los Angeles, Chicago, and San Antonio, only 10 percent of the stations were owned by Latinos or Chicanos.

Another disturbing trend prevalent in the past decade is the concentration of stations, particularly the most profitable ones, under the ownership of major corporate groups such as Tichenor Media System of Dallas, the Spanish Radio Network in partnership with SRN Texas, Inc. (a wholly owned subsidiary of Tichenor Media System), the Spanish Broadcasting Systems (SBS), Lotus Communications, and Radio América (Subervi-Vélez et al. 1997, 232).

A very different ownership model is represented by the nonprofit Radio Bilingüe network in California. Hugo Morales, a Chicano Harvard Law School graduate, partnered with Lupe Ortiz and Roberto Páramo in 1976 to found a radio network that sought to improve the lives and sustain the cultural identity of farmworkers in California's San Joaquin Valley. One of its stations, KSIV-FM in Fresno, transmits "a variety of music programs plus a diversity of information related to health, education, immigration, civic action, and the arts" (Corwin 1989, 3). It is supported primarily by donations from community members, local businesses, and some foundations. KSIV uses a two-satellite system to beam its programs twenty-four hours a day to four hundred public radio stations across the United States and Puerto Rico. Programs are also made available to commercial stations. The network has a professional staff but also a large volunteer force that helps it maintain programming variety and independence from commercial interests (Corwin 1989, 3, 33).

The Changing Shape of Spanish-Language Radio

Although statistics on Spanish-language radio cannot be disaggregated by group (Chicano, Cuban, Puerto Rican, etc.), *Hispanic Business* reported in a December 1998 issue that Latino consumers are increasingly prized by advertisers, who were projected to spend an estimated $440 million for radio airtime on Spanish-language radio during 1998. That revenue was expected to grow 19.7 percent over the five years from 1998 to 2003. His-panTelligence, an organization that monitors the media, projected that the revenue share of Spanish-language stations would grow from 3 percent to 6 percent by 2010 (Nordholm 1998, 62).

These promising statistics show that the increase in the Latino population is generating keen interest on the part of advertisers to attract a larger share of an expanding market. But they are mitigated by the fact that many of the Spanish-language stations and networks are not owned by Latinos. Of the ten top-billing (advertising revenues) stations in the country, only five are owned by Latinos (*Hispanic Business* 1998, 62).

One promising development in Spanish-language radio is the $250-million acquisition in 2000 of Latin Communications Group by Latino-owned Entravisión. The agreement made Entravisión one of the largest Spanish-language media corporations and included the purchase of seventeen television stations in sixteen markets and twenty-six radio stations in fourteen markets. Federico Subervi-Vélez, a professor of communications at the University of Texas at Austin and frequent critic of Anglo-dominated media in the United States, commented on the acquisition: "The same way the general market media are merging and consolidating, Spanish-language media owners are doing the same type of collaborative investment to improve their return. If this investment works, it will be because they bring in more advertisers. If they do, it will mean more capital for Latino media in general" (Higuera 2000, 26).

█ Television

In general, Spanish-language television in the United States today differs from Spanish-language radio in one important way: there are far fewer locally owned and controlled channels than radio stations, even taking into account that large corporations own most radio stations. This situation is the combined result of the financial and corporate history of television in this country as well as the relationship of the Mexican television industry to Spanish-language television in the United States.

The Spanish-Language Television Industry

The state of Spanish-language television today is very different from what it was fifty years ago. Much as in the early days of Spanish-language radio, some farsighted entrepreneurs began in the late 1940s and early 1950s to develop special Spanish-language programs for English-language television, which was just beginning to take hold as a popular electronic medium across the Southwest. These television-program brokers were as financially successful as their counterparts in radio and, in fact, several of them had been radio brokers and therefore knew the business of successful brokering.

By the 1960s, it was common for brokers to sell part-time Spanish-language programming to English-language stations in cities such as Los Angeles, Houston, Chicago, Tucson, and Phoenix where there were large Latino (mainly Chicano) populations. The 1951 program "Buscando estrellas" (Star Search) was perhaps the earliest and most successful of the brokered programs. It also established a practice that even today characterizes Spanish-language television: the importation of foreign (mainly Mexican) personalities, programs, and movies. "Buscando estrellas," hosted by Pepe del Río, brought Mexican talent to San Antonio and also offered some local talent the opportunity to begin their television careers. Between 1956 and 1961, Pepe del Río hosted "Cine en español" (Movies in Spanish), a very popular program that featured old Mexican, Spanish, and Argentinean movies (Subervi-Vélez et al. 1997, 233).

The success of brokers eventually led the way to the establishment of stations directed at Latino viewers. In 1955 KCOR-TV Channel 41 in San Antonio, the first clearly defined Spanish-language television station in the United States, began modest Spanish-language programming in the evenings. Raúl Cortez, founder and owner of radio station KCOR-AM, was also behind this effort. Approximately half of the evening programs were live variety and entertainment shows that featured talent from Mexico. Many of the shows were recorded in Cortez's radio station studios and were aired simultaneously on radio and television (today this is called *simulcasting*). KCOR-TV also imported movies and other prerecorded programs mainly from Mexico. Later, KCOR-TV changed its name to KUAL and then to KWEX in 1961 when, due to inadequate advertising revenues, Cortez was forced to sell the station to Mexican media tycoon Don Emilio Azcárraga Vidaurreta. Azcárraga owned the Mexican Telesistema media company, which later changed its name to Televisa (Kanellos 1994, 284–86).

The Spanish-language television industry in the United States began to change in the 1960s as three very large networks—Spanish International

Network (which later became Univisión), Telemundo, and Galavisión—came to dominate the ownership and operation of most channels. One very important event was the initiation and organization of the Spanish International Communications Corporation (SICC) by René Anselmo and Emilio Azcárraga Milmo, Don Emilio's son. Although the Federal Communications Act Section 310 "prohibits the issuing of broadcast licenses to aliens, representatives of aliens, or to corporations in which aliens control more than one-fifth of the stock," the corporation skirted FCC restrictions on licensing by recruiting investors who were U.S. citizens to control the majority interest in the enterprise. Don Emilio, a Mexican citizen, was then permitted to own 20 percent of the company.

Taking advantage of foreign citizens' right to hold minority stock in television companies in the United States, in 1961 Don Emilio and his son Anselmo established Spanish International Network (SIN) and began to provide programming that was produced in Azcárraga's Telesistema studios in Mexico City. SIN soon began to expand through a series of purchases, mergers, and reorganizations. It added WXTV New York (1968), WLTV Miami (1971), and KFTV Fresno/Hanford (1972) and extended its network through agreements with some stations owned by SICC/SIN, including KDTV San Francisco (1974) and KTVW Phoenix (1976). It also affiliated itself with stations in Albuquerque, Chicago, Corpus Christi, Houston, and Sacramento not owned and operated by SICC/SIN.

Televisa, the Mexican parent corporation, also broadcast television programming to U.S. border cities from its stations in Ciudad Juárez, Mexicali, Nuevo Laredo, and Tijuana. Televisa exported programming from Mexico to the United States via SIN, and by 1976 SIN became the first major U.S. television broadcasting company to distribute programming to its affiliates via domestic satellite. In 1979 SIN established another precedent in U.S. television history when it began paying cable franchise operators to carry its satellite signals. In 1980 it sought and was granted permission to establish low-power television stations whose transmission was limited to a twenty-mile radius. Thus by 1983 SICC/SIN stations were providing programming to more than 3.3 million Latino households in the United States (Kanellos 1994, 286–87).

In addition to programming from Televisa, SIN also imported programs from Brazil, Venezuela, Spain, Argentina, and Puerto Rico for broadcast to U.S. Latinos. *Telenovelas* (soap operas), game and variety shows, music festivals, comedies, and sports have continued to be the most popular programs. SIN also provided extensive coverage of U.S. presidential and municipal elections in the 1980s, as well as coverage of elections and other political events in Mexico, Central America, and South America.

After a decade-long struggle involving stockholders' infighting and several licensing and other suits in federal court, in 1987 SIN/SICC was renamed Univisión and came under the control of a group of U.S. investors including Hallmark Cards and First Capital Corporation of Chicago. In the same year the cable service Galavisión split from Univisión to remain under the control of Azcárraga's Televisa and its new U.S. enterprise, called Univisa. Hallmark Cards sold its interest in Univisión in 1991 to a wealthy U.S. investor as well as to Emilio Azcárraga Milmo and powerful Venezuelan television interests. Throughout the 1990s, Univisión continued acquiring U.S. television stations, including WGBO in Chicago and KXLN in Houston.

The giant Univisión network consists today of more than a dozen full-power stations, one low-power station, a dozen affiliated UHF stations, and more than six hundred cable carriers in all major U.S. television markets. Its continuous programming reaches approximately 92 percent of U.S. Latino households that have cable television. Telemundo is currently the second-largest U.S. Spanish-language network serving Chicano/Mexican audiences in cities such as San Francisco, Houston, Chicago, and San Antonio. Galavisión is the third major player in the U.S. Spanish-language television industry, reaching about 30 percent of Latino households via three hundred cable affiliates (Kanellos 1994, 288–90).

In addition to Univisión, Telemundo, and Galavisión, there are several other Latino-oriented television companies and program ventures in the United States today. International Telemúsica, Inc.—which produces a show featuring international music videos, entertainment news, promotions, and lifestyle segments—targets a young Latino and Latin American audience. Viva Television Network, Inc., provides Spanish-language documentaries, public affairs, music, sports, comedy, children's programming, art films, and popular movies. Its target is the eighteen- to forty-nine-year-old Latino audience. HBO en Español (Home Box Office in Spanish) provides HBO and Cinemax subscribers the option of Spanish-language audio for telecast motion pictures and sports events. Its "Selecciones en Español" currently offers Spanish-dubbed and original movies and other programming to its Spanish-speaking viewers in cities throughout the Southwest including Houston, San Antonio, El Paso, and San Diego. Other Anglo-owned and -operated television networks provide Second Audio Program (SAP) or a Spanish soundtrack for standard series such as "The Love Boat," "McMillan and Wife," "Magnum, P.I.," "Columbo," and "Knight Rider." These programs are dubbed not only for a U.S. Latino audience but for exportation to Latin America. Los Angeles television station KTLA has been a pioneer in providing this service (Kanellos 1994, 292–96).

The Viewing Audience

Current data on the number or percentage of Chicanos who view Spanish-language television are not available, but we can assume that the audience is large and growing. A mid-1980s Strategy Research Corporation report revealed that two-thirds of all U.S. Latinos watched at least some Spanish-language television and that they spent about two and one-half hours per day doing so. This report also found that Spanish-language television was less popular in Texas and southwestern markets than in New York City and Chicago. Although these figures are not current nor disaggregated for Americans of Mexican descent, we can assume that trends are probably reasonably similar today as fifteen years ago. What we do know with some certainty is that, unlike radio, most programming on Spanish-language television is not tailored for a particular segment of the general Latino population.

Local television stations—even those owned by Univisión or another conglomerate—do produce local newscasts and target some other programming to their audience. For example, television stations in cities such as San Antonio and Phoenix occasionally will run popular Mexican movies or Mexican-oriented programs that are likely to appeal to their local Chicano/Mexican audience (Veciana-Suárez 1987, 53). Given the structure of the Spanish-language television industry, however, local programming is relatively rare. Thus, a Chicano in Los Angeles is apt to view the same telenovela or comedy show as a Cuban American in Miami or a Puerto Rican in New York City. Because most of the soap operas and comedy and variety shows are imported from Latin America, it is common to hear, for example, two lovers speaking to each other in heavy Argentinean or Venezuelan accents. Chicano/Mexican immigrant viewers simply have grown accustomed to the peculiarities of a wide range of Spanish dialects and regional word usage on the programs they watch.

Chicanos on Television and in the News

As Clara E. Rodríguez, a media scholar, has pointed out, "That Hispanics are underrepresented and misrepresented in the media (newspapers, radio, television, and cinema) is supported by current and extensive historical and empirical research" (Rodríguez 1997, 5). An exhaustive 1994 report, *Out of the Picture: Hispanics in the Media* (prepared for the National Council of La Raza [NCLR] by the Center for Media and Public Affairs; summarized in Rodríguez 1997), concluded that (a) Hispanics are almost invisible in both the entertainment and news media; and (b) when Hispanics do appear, they are consistently and uniformly portrayed more negatively than other racial and ethnic groups. This report does not differentiate among Chicanos, Cuban Americans, Puerto Ricans, and other Hispanic subgroups, but its conclusions and findings of general trends are probably as applicable to specific subgroups as they are to the whole.

As the 1994 NCLR report points out, several earlier studies had focused on the underrepresentation and stereotyping of Latinos in television. For example, in a three-season (1975–1978) study of fictional commercial television series characters, a Michigan State University team of researchers concluded that, "Hispanic Americans are significantly underrepresented in the TV population." The team studied a total of 3,549 TV characters and found that only fifty-three Latinos—1.5 percent—had speaking roles. The percentage of Latina characters was even lower. A typical viewer who watched an average of twenty-one hours of English language television per week would see only five or six Latino characters (Greenberg and Baptista-Fernández 1980).

The Center for Media and Public Affairs concluded in a 1991 report, *Watching America,* an analysis of programming from 1955 to 1986, that overall Latinos represented about 2 percent of television characters. The trend had actually gotten worse over the thirty-year period studied, however, decreasing from 3 percent in the 1950s to about 1 percent in the 1980s (Lichter, Lichter, and Rothman 1991).

More recent studies have simply confirmed the trend identified in the *Watching America* report. A 1993 study focusing on children and television reported that on network television (ABC, CBS, and NBC), PBS, and cable television, "Hispanic characters are particularly absent from commercial entertainment television," and that Latino and other ethnic minorities "are particularly excluded as actors, actresses, or even caricatures in mainstream commercial programs" (Subervi-Vélez and Colsant 1993, 45).

The NCLR report is equally disturbing in its conclusions regarding Latinos and the news. It cites a 1983 Project CASA study which found "that only 18 percent of television stories and 17 percent of radio stories qualified as Hispanic-focused. Moreover, the vast majority of these stories focused on crime and other 'hard' news; less than 14% of television and 4% of radio stories dealt with minority issues" (quoted in Rodríguez 1997, 25). The NCLR report emphasized that "inadequate broadcast news coverage of Hispanics is particularly obvious when measured by the number and proportion of Latinos who appear on-screen as correspondents, anchors, and other 'newsmakers'" (quoted in Rodríguez 1997, 25). It cites a finding from a 1992 study that, of all the television stories on network newscasts in 1989, only 1 percent were by Latino reporters. A 1993 Annenberg study corroborated that Latinos make up only 1.5 percent of television network correspondents and anchors, a lower percentage than for any other ethnic minority studied (e.g., African Americans constituted 14.2 percent; Rodríguez 1997, 25).

Using a research method called "content analysis," researchers have studied the portrayal of Latino and other ethnic minority characters, especially in fictional entertainment television programs. One major study conducted for the Center for Media and Public Affairs analyzed a sample of 620 fictional entertainment programs from the 1955 through 1986 seasons, containing 7,639 individual characters with speaking roles. It found that only 32 percent of Hispanics on television in the 1955–1986 period were portrayed positively. By contrast, 41 percent of Hispanics were portrayed negatively, compared to 31 percent of whites and only 24 percent of blacks (Rodríguez 1997). The Annenberg School of Communications, known for its rigorous research, reported similar findings in a 1993 study covering the 1982–1992 period (Rodríguez 1997, 27).

Based on these and other 1990s studies, the 1994 NCLR report observed that a common media stereotype of Latinos on television is that they are poor, of low socioeconomic status, untrustworthy, and lazy. A second common stereotype is that Latinos are failures in their personal lives and their careers. A variant of this stereotype is that Latinos do not have to be taken seriously because they are deceitful, "tricksters," and predominantly criminals (Rodríguez 1997, 28). On so-called "reality-based" series such as "Cops" and syndicated series such as "Star Trek: The Next Generation,"

Latinos are portrayed even more negatively than they are on network television shows.

The conclusions in the NCLR report are devastating in terms of the role of Latinos on television: "Measured by both the number and proportion of characters, or the quality of roles portrayed, Hispanics on TV network shows appear to have made little progress since the 1950s." Further, such portrayal is especially disappointing at a time when Latinos are emerging as the largest U.S. ethnic minority group and when rapid demographic change is focusing increasing attention on multicultural themes and issues (Rodríguez 1997, 33).

In 1996 the Center for Media and Public Affairs prepared a second report for the NCLR, entitled *Don't Blink: Hispanics in Television Entertainment* (Lichter and Amundson 1996). This study, a content analysis of the 1994–1995 television season, is an update of a 1994 Center study, *Distorted Reality,* the first content analysis of how prime-time television portrays Hispanic characters. That study, based on the 1992–1993 television season, had painted a dismal picture of a group that "is barely visible on America's television screens and was all too often confined to stereotypical roles" (Lichter and Amundson 1996, 1).

The authors of *Don't Blink* observed that the 1994–1995 television season included some breakthroughs for Latinos in network television although "it did little to change longstanding patterns in television portrayals" (Lichter and Amundson 1996, 1). The proportion of Latino characters doubled from the 1992–1993 season to the 1994–1995 season, but this represented a rise from only 1 percent to 2 percent of all characters. The addition of new series such as "House of Buggin" (the first Latino sketch comedy show on the air), "Medicine Ball," "Chicago Hope," and "My So Called Life" created new opportunities for Latino characters to play either leading roles or important secondary roles.

Another promising sign was that negative roles for Latinos—including the number of Latinos shown committing crimes—fell almost half between the 1992–1993 season and the 1994–1995 season. At the same time, however, the portrayal of Latino criminality far exceeded the portrayal of either white or black criminality. Latino characters did not make any advances in terms of being portrayed as successful; in fact, the social and economic status of these characters slipped between the 1992–1993 and 1994–1995 seasons. The proportion of characters who were poor or working class increased from 28 percent to 55 percent, and the proportion of

Latinos portrayed in professional occupations or as business executives declined from 25 percent to 17 percent. The portrayal of Latinos in law enforcement occupations did increase, however (Lichter and Amundson 1996, 2–3).

Latinos played somewhat more prominent roles on 1994–1995 syndicated and "reality-based" shows when compared to their roles on network television. Examples were Lt. B'Elanna Torres (an officer of dual Klingon-Hispanic heritage) on "Star Trek: Voyager," who over two seasons became more controlled and well balanced, and Lt. Miguel Ortiz on "SeaQuest DV," who continued to be a loyal, brave, and trustworthy crew member. (Robert Beltrán, who portrays a Native American on "Star Trek: Voyager," is in fact of Mexican Indian heritage.) On "reality-based" shows such as "Cops" and "America's Most Wanted," Latinos were portrayed less often as committing crimes and more often as innocent victims than during the 1992–1993 season. They thus were portrayed upholding the law more than breaking it (Lichter and Amundson 1996, 5).

On the downside, however, network shows that reasonably should be expected to include Chicano characters in leading or supporting roles are "Baywatch" (set in southern California) and "Walker, Texas Ranger" (set in Texas), yet Latinos are strangely absent. It is not surprising that *Don't Blink* names these two shows among the worst of the 1994–1995 television season in terms of the presence of Latino characters.

Latino characters on network television continued not to be identified with a particular segment of the Latino community. It is thus difficult to associate characters such as Héctor Elizondo on "Chicago Hope," Lt. Torres, or Lt. Ortiz as, for example, Chicano or Puerto Rican. Although this is regrettable in that network television creates flat and generic Latinos without specific cultural markers, it is understandable given the goal of network television to appeal to a general audience across the United States.

Organizations such as the Center for Media and Public Affairs, the NCLR, and the Latino/Hispanic Subcommittee of SAG have performed an invaluable service in providing regular and systematic monitoring of the role of Latinos in network, syndicated, and public television. Their studies and reports document a generally discouraging picture of the U.S. television industry at the end of the twentieth century. The industry continues largely to ignore and misrepresent this country's largest ethnic minority group.

To compound this already depressing situation, at least one media scholar has identified the conservative national political agendas of the 1980s and the 1990s as a significant obstacle in the way of government-based policy providing a remedy to the problems identified in the studies and reports just cited. The deregulation of the broadcast industry and lax enforcement of pertinent laws (e.g., the Fairness Doctrine and equal employment opportunity laws) "have greatly eroded the few avenues for effective advocacy to challenge the licenses of discriminatory stations. Also, the April 1998 United States Court of Appeals decision against the FCC's rules on minority representation in radio and television inflicted another major blow against minorities in this industry" (Subervi-Vélez 1999, 137–38).

These trends were evident recently when a coalition of organizations (the National Latino Media Council, the NAACP, the Asian–Pacific American Coalition, and the American Indians in Film and Television) waged a large and effective campaign to protest the dismal number of leading and supporting roles that ethnic minorities would have in the 2000 television season. They targeted the three dominant networks (CBS, NBC, and ABC) as well as Fox and other important cable channels. At the time of this writing, the coalition was striking agreements with the networks to, for example, appoint a vice-president or a similarly senior-level executive to oversee their respective diversity efforts.

Harry P. Pachon, president of the Tomás Rivera Policy Institute, commented, "These agreements are a good first step, but it's a baby step. If we had done something like this 20 years ago we wouldn't have the problems that we have today" (*Hispanic Business,* March 2000, 20). The formation of the National Latino Media Council, a coalition of twelve distinct Hispanic organizations, should help maintain the pressure on the networks and assure that the agreements with the networks are robust and honored. The council will be interested not only in increasing the number and importance of Latinos in television roles, but also in negotiating network agreements in areas such as advertising, financial services, and procurement, thereby improving the financial status of Latino-owned businesses that deal with television networks.

Advocacy groups such as the recently formed council will have to continue systematically studying and documenting discrimination against Latinos/Chicanos in the television industry in terms not only of their portrayal on television programs, but of their employment in key artistic and executive positions as well. Statistical studies of the kind done by the Center for Media and Public Affairs have been useful in giving us a snapshot of Latino presence and participation. Perhaps in the future scholars should use content analysis in order to examine factors such as the framing, trends, interactions, and ideology of the portrayals of Latinos/Chicanos. Such studies should probably deal more specifically with genres such as drama/adventure programs, comedies, children's programs, talk shows, and soap operas and should include Spanish-language television based in the United States. The ongoing analysis of labor statistics (i.e., employment patterns) would also be useful in giving a more complete picture of Latinos/Chicanos within the U.S. television industry.

What follows from these recommendations for future study and analysis is that colleges and universities need to encourage more Chicanos to specialize in media studies at both the undergraduate and graduate levels. Chicanos should also be encouraged to major in different aspects of broadcasting in order to be ready to fill positions that we hope will become increasingly available in the television industry (Subervi-Vélez 1999, 138–41).

The brief review of newspapers, radio, and television in this chapter reveals that these forms of popular culture are not currently thriving cultural industries when Chicano financial ownership and control are taken into account. Furthermore, Chicano editors, producers, and directors are underrepresented in media industries, particularly in an area such as southern California that has a large population of Americans of Mexican descent. Chicano writers, actors, and performers are also significantly underrepresented. This depressing situation in California as well as elsewhere in the Southwest and across the United States stands in stark contrast to the net increase in Chicano readers, listeners, and viewers of media over the past several decades.

■ Discussion Questions

1. Have Spanish-language newspapers as a culture industry been manipulated by powerful economic interests at the expense of readers' concerns and interests? Why or why not?

2. What social and cultural roles have Spanish-language newspapers played in the past 150 years?

3. Characterize the writings of Benjamín Padilla and Julio G. Arce.

4. What was the function of Spanish-language newspapers during the Chicano Movement?

5. How was Pedro J. González important to the early history of Spanish-language radio?

6. In what ways did Spanish-language radio change in the 1950s?

7. Discuss how the success of television brokers led the way to the establishment of separate stations aimed at Latino audiences.

8. In what ways did the Spanish-language television industry begin to change in the 1960s?

9. Could mass cultural theorists make a case that in the Spanish-language television industry power is concentrated in the hands of a few individuals who have little interest in consumers' needs and concerns?

10. Describe the characteristics of the viewing audience for Spanish-language television in the United States.

11. What have studies revealed about the stereotyping of Latinos in mainstream television programming?

12. How have Latino groups responded to the generally negative state of participation of Latinos in mainstream television?

◼ Suggested Readings

Gutiérrez, Félix F., and Jorge Reina Schement. 1979. *Spanish-Language Radio in the Southwestern United States.* Austin: Center for Mexican American Studies.

Kanellos, Nicolás. 1993. A Socio-Historic Study of Hispanic Newspapers in the United States. In *Recovering the U.S. Hispanic Literary Heritage,* eds. Ramón Gutiérrez and Genaro Padilla, 107–28. Houston: Arte Público Press.

——. 1994. *The Hispanic Almanac.* Detroit: Visible Ink.

Rodríguez, Clara E., ed. 1997. *Latin Looks: Images of Latinas and Latinos in the U.S. Media.* Boulder: Westview Press.

Tatum, Charles. 1982. *Chicano Literature.* Boston: Twayne Publishers.

Ybarra-Frausto, Tomás. 1977. The Chicano Movement and the Emergence of a Chicano Poetic Consciousness. *New Scholar* 6: 81–109.

5

Popular Literature

Chicano literature is a vast and interesting area of artistic expression that deserves its own book. I will limit myself in this chapter to the literature that, in my opinion, has appealed widely to readers over the past seventy years, with a concentration on popular writers since the mid-1960s. Not included in this chapter are the dozens of Mexican American writers who published in the hundreds of southwestern Spanish-language newspapers from the mid-nineteenth century through the mid-1970s. A few of these writers are discussed in chapter 4.

The first section includes only a handful of pre-1965 writers who could pass the litmus test of popularity. There are many writers not included simply because their works were not widely distributed among a Mexican American or Anglo readership. Often these writers languished in obscurity either because they published their own works and did not have available to them an effective distribution network or because their publishers did not aggressively market their works. Occasionally, literary texts would remain in manuscript form only to be discovered and published decades later through the efforts of organizations such as the Recovering the U.S. Hispanic Literary Heritage Project based at the University of Houston. The writers omitted in the first section should by no means be dismissed as less important than those who are included.

The second section includes many prose fiction (novel and short story) writers, poets, and dramatists whose works have become popular among general and Chicano readers. Unlike the period before 1965, in recent years many academic, small presses, and large commercial presses have published hundreds of Chicano literary works. The combination of distribution networks and aggressive marketing strategies has very effectively put Chicano literature on the U.S. literary map and has greatly contributed to its popularization.

Popular Writers Pre-1965

In this section, I present the following popular writers whose works were published in the 1950s and early 1960s: Sabine Ulibarrí, Fray Angélico Chávez, and José Antonio Villarreal.

Sabine Ulibarrí

Poet, essayist, and short story writer Sabine Ulibarrí holds an important place in pre-1965 Chicano popular literature. He was born in 1919 in Tierra Amarilla, a small village in northern New Mexico. Both his parents were descended from old New Mexico families. They graduated from college and instilled in their son and their other children a sense of pride and dignity in their culture, including speaking Spanish as their first language. As a high school student Ulibarrí read widely in literature and science, a practice that he would cultivate for the rest of his life.

He attended the University of New Mexico but dropped out for financial reasons and began teaching in the public schools. From 1942 to 1945 he served as a gunner in the U.S. Army Air Corps, then returned to the University of New Mexico thanks to the GI Bill, graduating in 1947 with degrees in English and American literature. He went on to graduate school at UCLA, where he received his Ph.D. in 1958. He spent his entire academic career at the University of New Mexico, where he distinguished himself as a teacher, scholar, creative writer, and popular lecturer.

Ulibarrí is best known for a popular collection of short stories, *Tierra Amarilla: cuentos de Nuevo México* (Tierra Amarilla: Tales of New Mexico), originally published in Spanish in 1964 and in English translation in 1971. In this and other works of short fiction, he chronicles and records the values, sentiments, relationships, and texture of the daily lives of his friends and family, the Hispanic inhabitants of his beloved childhood home of Tierra Amarilla.

The writer himself has commented that, in fact, he was trying to document the history of the Hispanics of northern New Mexico, a history not yet recorded by the scholars who have written otherwise excellent historical and anthropological studies about the region. Ulibarrí believes that these scholars do not understand at a deep level the Hispanic heritage that predates by hundreds of years the arrival of the Anglo soldier, settler, and businessman in the mid-nineteenth century.

Just as important, Ulibarrí's short stories were his attempt, as a purely personal objective, to regain his childhood experiences through creative memory. He felt as though he had been uprooted from his childhood and adolescence, and in documenting his memories of that phase of his life he was trying to resurrect for himself a repository of humanizing experiences. In answering questions about his people—how they were; what it meant to live in an environment where Spanish was the dominant language; the significance of living daily the values and traditions of the oldest non-Indian culture in the United States—he ultimately answers questions about himself: Who am I? Where do I come from? What have I lost? How much of it can I regain?

Fray Angélico Chávez

Fray Angélico Chávez was one of New Mexico's most distinguished writers. He was born Manuel Chávez in Wagon Mound, New Mexico, in 1910, on the day when Halley's comet made one of its rare and spectacular appearances. He grew up and attended public schools in Mora, where his teachers soon identified him as an outstanding student who read voraciously the histories of New Mexico and classics of English literature. He attended St. Francis Seminary in Cincinnati and colleges in the Midwest. On becoming a Franciscan friar in 1937, he changed his name to Fray Angélico Chávez. Chávez served as an Army chaplain in both World War II and the Korean War. In 1967, he left the Franciscan order to assume responsibilities as a parish priest in many small New Mexican towns (Colahan 1989, 85).

Chávez was a prolific writer of short fiction, most of which is published in two collections: *New Mexico Triptych: Being Three Panels and Three Accounts: 1. The Angel's New Wings; 2. The Penitente Thief; 3. The Hunchback Madonna* (1940) and *From an Altar Screen; El Retablo: Tales from New Mexico* (1957). Chávez highlights in both his historical writings and his prose fiction social aspects of life in New Mexico such as class differences that existed between Spanish officials and the common Spanish settlers. He also roundly condemns the abuses committed by the French Catholic hierarchy that the Vatican sent to New Mexico to quell the rebellious tendencies of Hispanic clergy such as Padre Martínez of Taos.

José Antonio Villarreal

José Antonio Villarreal has steadfastly maintained for more than forty years that he does not consider himself to be a Chicano writer. Yet there is a consensus among critics and literary historians that his popular 1959 novel *Pocho* is at least a bridge between the literature being written prior to the Chicano Movement of the mid-1960s and the literature written the decade after. Villarreal and his novel both deserve our attention.

Villarreal was born in Los Angeles after his parents fled the aftermath of the 1910–1920 Mexican Revolution. The family became seasonal farm-workers, traveling the length of the state for several years living in tents pitched on the edge of the agricultural fields. They settled in Santa Clara, California, in 1930, about the time that Villarreal was old enough to begin elementary school. In 1950, when he was in his mid-thirties, Villarreal received a B.A. in English from the University of California, Berkeley. He began a graduate degree at the same university but soon terminated his studies after deciding to dedicate himself to his writing.

Villarreal completed the writing of *Pocho* in 1956, and it was published in 1959 by Doubleday of New York City, the first Chicano novel in the twentieth century to be published by a major commercial mainstream publisher. He later published two other novels: *The Fifth Horseman* (1974) and *Clemente Chacón* (1984).

Pocho is structured around the lives of Juan Manuel Rubio, a Mexican immigrant, and his son Richard Rubio, the *pocho* (an assimilated Mexican) identified in the novel's title. The elder Rubio, an army colonel who fought alongside General Villa during the Mexican Revolution, arrives in Ciudad Juárez (across the U.S.–Mexican border from El Paso, Texas) from Mexico City, eventually crosses the border to El Paso, and migrates to California, where his wife Consuelo joins him. They try in vain to maintain their Mexican cultural traditions but soon the marriage itself fails.

The novel then shifts to Richard Rubio's personal development as he begins to agonize over questions such as the existence and immensity of God while at the same time suffering from the guilt of adolescent sexuality. His spiritual and emotional awakening is plagued by feelings of self-doubt and inadequacy, feelings made more complex by the changes occurring within his family. As his family disintegrates and he is thrust between Chicano and Anglo cultures, neither of which he completely accepts, Richard's suffering becomes more intense. Toward the end of the novel, he joins the Navy in an attempt to strike out on his own and try to find answers to his questions completely independent of his family and relationships in Los Angeles.

Pocho is an important novel for presenting the multiple dilemmas faced by many Mexican immigrants who abandon their own society and culture to adopt and fit into one that is very alien. It is not surprising that this work has continued to be very popular with both Chicano and non-Chicano readers since its publication more than forty years ago.

The Chicano Movement and the Forming of an Artistic Consciousness

I refer often in this book to the important influence that the Chicano Movement had on popular forms of artistic expression such as music and art, as well as on media such as newspapers, radio, television, and cinema. The influence on Chicano popular literature is no less profound. Especially influential was the 1969 First Annual Chicano Youth Conference organized in Denver by Rodolfo "Corky" Gonzales and the organization he had helped found, the Crusade for Justice. "El Plan Espiritual de Aztlán" (The Spiritual Plan of Aztlán), the document that emerged from this meeting, was particularly important to the formation of a Chicano artistic consciousness that was to guide many Chicano visual artists, musicians, filmmakers, writers, and others for years to come. The participants at the conference affirmed the importance of cultural nationalism and placed great emphasis on cultural regeneration. The artist was seen as playing an active and vital role in extending the political consciousness of his or her audience and in heightening its awareness of the world. Aztlán was at once a cultural, political, and mythological concept that undergirded much of the Chicano Movement's cultural nationalist agenda.

Popular Poetry of the 1960s

Two of the most influential poets of the Chicano Movement are Rodolfo "Corky" Gonzales and Alurista. Cofounder of the Crusade for Justice, Gonzales is best known for *I Am Joaquín,* a work that is as much political manifesto as poetry. Alurista is the epitome of the Chicano writer/activist and is noted for his melding of different languages in one poem.

RODOLFO "CORKY" GONZALES   Gonzales was largely responsible for founding the Denver-based Crusade for Justice and its most important event, the 1969 First Annual Chicano Youth Conference. He had already set the stage for the strong current of cultural nationalism that emerged from this conference with the publication in 1967 of his epic poem *I Am Joaquín.* This slim book of poetry was read widely by high school and college students at the time and would become one of the most important cultural documents associated with the Chicano Movement.

Gonzales was born in Denver in 1928 to Chicano parents who had worked the beet fields in Colorado for much of their lives. He took up boxing in 1943, eventually becoming a Golden Gloves winner. He gave up the sport ten years later and became active as an organizer in Democratic Party politics in Denver. He also began to write around the same time. He soon became the first Chicano district captain in Denver history and in 1960 was appointed coordinator of Colorado's Viva Kennedy presidential campaign and chairman of Denver's antipoverty program. Gonzales's politics took a radical turn in the mid-1960s, and by the time he had founded the Crusade for Justice in 1966, he had left the Democratic Party for good.

I Am Joaquín synthesizes many of the themes and motifs of Chicano poetry of the 1960s and early 1970s (Hancock 1973, 185–86):

- The identification of Chicanos with both contemporary Mexico and its indigenous Aztec and Mayan cultures
- An emphasis on urban working-class life in the barrio
- The family as a source of cultural continuity, strength, and love
- *Carnalismo* (brotherhood) among Chicanos
- Political action achieved through unity and solidarity in order to maintain Chicano identity and protect Chicano values

As Gonzales states in his introduction to the work, the poem is a search for identity and cultural roots (Gonzales 1972). He intends it to be the collective voice of the Chicano people who have resisted assimilation into Anglo society and subjugation to its oppressive forces and who have searched for strength in their cultural heritage in order to continue the struggle. Gonzales traces the history of Chicanos from their Spanish and Indian past throughout Mexican history to the present era in American history, offering a frank appraisal of "villains and heroes." Gonzales exalts the heroic dimensions of men such as Cuauhtémoc, Benito Juárez, Emiliano Zapata, and Joaquín Murieta; they are inspiring models for all Chicanos. Endurance is the poem's dominant theme. As Joaquín has survived many travails, conquests, wars, defeats, and so on, he will continue to endure in the future. Gonzales ends his poem with a crescendo, calling upon Chicanos to join in solidarity to seize their destiny in the contemporary world.

Looking back over the more than thirty years since the original publication of the poem, Chicano literary critics and historians have given much more value to *I Am Joaquín* as a cultural document than as a successful literary work. This, of course, was Gonzales's intention: to create a highly accessible and readable text that his contemporaries would read and readily understand, and that he hoped would inspire them to become involved in taking control of their own social and political futures. To what extent the poem has succeeded in this aim is difficult to determine, but it has endured as one of the most popular pieces of contemporary Chicano literature.

ALURISTA   More successful as a poet, although perhaps not as popular among the general Chicano population of the 1960s and 1970s, was Alurista, born Alberto Baltazar Urista Heredia in Mexico City in 1947. Tomás Ybarra-Frausto (1977, 86) singles him out as "a seminal figure in the contemporary florescence of Chicano poetry," in terms of his creative participation in the tumultuous phase of the Chicano Movement. He is notable as a poet for his bold experiments with bilingualism, the incorporation of indigenous themes in his work, and his key role as philosopher and ideologist in the formulation of the conceptual basis of the nationalist agenda of the movement.

Alurista's entire family emigrated to San Diego when he was thirteen. Alurista continued to speak his first language of Spanish in the home and continued to write in Spanish, a practice he had begun in second grade in Mexico. After his graduation from high school in 1965 he studied sociology, social welfare, and finally psychology in college, graduating with a B.A. from San Diego State University in 1970. He then earned an M.A. in 1978 from the same institution and in 1988 received a Ph.D. in literature from the University of California, La Jolla.

Alurista was already deeply immersed in barrio social causes as a high school student in San Diego. In college, his activities intensified as a member of the Brown Berets and as a counselor and psychiatric child-care worker from 1965 to 1968. In 1968 he cofounded the Chicano Studies Department at San Diego State University and a year later cofounded the Chicano Studies Center at the same university. He has taught at several colleges and universities.

Alurista has worked throughout his life to promote Chicano literature among students as well as a wider Chicano public. He has written poetry, given extensive public readings and lectures, cofounded *Maize,* a journal of literature and literary criticism, and been chief organizer of the annual Festival Floricanto, an event that over the years has attracted many writers and critics for several days of cultural and critical exchange. He also cofounded MECHA (Movimiento Estudiantil Chicano de Aztlán) in 1967.

Alurista was also instrumental in establishing the concept of Aztlán as a central cultural, political, and mythical symbol of the Chicano Movement. As already discussed, the concept is central to "El Plan Espiritual de Aztlán," the cultural and political manifesto that emerged from the 1969 Chicano Youth Conference in Denver. Alurista was largely responsible for writing this document.

Alurista has been more successful than any other contemporary Chicano poet in his linguistic experimentation with a combination of English, Spanish, Nahuatl (the language of the Aztecs, still spoken today by many Mexican Indian groups), and barrio slang. Such code-switching helps create the multicultural, multilingual mark of much of his early popular poetry. This experimentation has greatly enhanced the oral aspect of his poetry, which in turn has made him a highly popular reader and lecturer before Chicano and other audiences. The orality of his poetry is also in keeping with his view that a poet is a public figure who serves his community as one of its voices.

Post-1970s Poetry

Chicano poetry in general has not maintained the degree of popularity that it enjoyed from the late 1960s through the 1970s. This is due to the fact that the Chicano Movement—with which both Gonzales and Alurista were closely identified as poets who had a political and cultural agenda—began to wane rapidly. Even by the mid-1970s much of the political activism, excitement, and commitment to radical change had dissipated as leaders and their followers turned to trying to effect change by reforming the two-party system and established social institutions. This is not to say that poets and other writers did not remain committed to their ideals and to expressing these ideals through their literary works, but the public forum that had been available to them on college campuses, at festivals, and at demonstrations and rallies no longer existed. In addition, much of the poetry became less explicit in promoting a social agenda.

Poetry and poetry reading in general have become less a broad public activity and more one for smaller audiences. Ironically, the practice of Chicano poetry has increased dramatically as measured by the number of poetry collections published; however, only small numbers of these hundreds of books are actually printed and sold. Dozens of excellent Chicano poets have matured and distinguished themselves in the past thirty years: Jimmy Santiago Baca, Lorna Dee Cervantes, Ray Gonzalez, Juan Felipe

Herrera, Pat Mora, Alberto Ríos, Luis Omar Salinas, and Gary Soto to mention only a few. But none have achieved the level of popularity of either Gonzales or Alurista.

Luis Valdez and El Teatro Campesino

Contemporary Chicano popular theater began in 1965 when Luis Valdez, a young Chicano armed with a fresh undergraduate degree in drama from San Jose State College (now San Jose State University) and a season with the San Francisco Mime Troupe, an alternative theater group, founded El Teatro Campesino (The Farmworkers' Theater). Valdez was born to migrant farmworker parents in Delano, California, in 1940, the second in a family of ten brothers and sisters. Like thousands of other children of migrant families, his early schooling was interrupted repeatedly as his family was forced to move abruptly from one agricultural area to another in order to maintain their meager income.

As a young child Valdez began working alongside his parents and siblings, enduring many hours of physically draining stoop labor under an unrelenting sun. By the time he was twelve he had created a puppet show that he staged for his family and friends. After graduating from high school, he earned a scholarship to attend San Jose State College, where his interest in drama became fully developed.

Valdez epitomizes the socially committed artist envisioned in "El Plan Espiritual de Aztlán." A season with the Mime Troupe served as his apprenticeship in alternative theater. He then returned to Delano in 1965, twenty-five years after his birth there, to lend support to César Chávez, who was trying to organize the farmworkers under a union banner. Valdez's idea of organizing a theater whose writers, actors, and crew would be drawn from the agricultural fieldworkers themselves was revolutionary. This was an alternative theater of the proletariat, who would control the artistic as well as material aspects of an artistic enterprise that would benefit them in their own struggle. The theater would be organized in such a fashion that it could take the message of the strike directly to farmworkers in the fields.

The *acto* (a short improvisational one-act play with simple props, direct dialogue, and a hard-hitting theme) became the vehicle that El Teatro Campesino used during its first few years to take various messages to different groups of Chicanos. The form comes from the Italian commedia dell'arte (resurrected in the 1960s by the San Francisco Mime Troupe) and the Mexican *carpa* or tent presentations. But what made the acto characteristically Chicano was its bilingualism, the fact that it dealt solely with Chicano experiences, and that it addressed specific needs of Chicanos.

El Teatro Campesino created a stock of prototypical characters with signs around their necks—their only costumes—identifying them as El Huelguista (The Striker), the Cop, El Patrón (The Grower), El Coyote (The Labor Contractor), El Esquirol (The Scab), El Vendido (The Sellout), Juanito Raza, and Johnny Pachuco, Death, the Church, Union, Winter, Summer, and so on. The actors stood on improvised stages such as the flatbed of a truck, a slightly raised platform in a union hall, or a speaker's platform at a rally. No props were required except for an occasional chair or table or whatever might be handy. Everything—actors, props, language—was designed to make the presentation simple and direct in order to convey a clear message to the audience.

Two other characteristics of the early actos were their mobility and their portability; the actors needed to be able to set up their simple sets, do their short performance, and go on to another site in as little as thirty minutes. It was not uncommon for the theater group to pull up in a flatbed truck next to an agricultural field, coax the farmworkers out of the fields to the truck with a megaphone, perform on the flatbed, and move on before the local police or the growers' security men arrived to arrest or harass the actors.

In its earliest days, then, El Teatro Campesino dealt solely with the farmworkers' and the union's struggle against the growers. Valdez and his workers performed throughout the San Joaquin Valley and then began to travel to other agricultural areas in the state and eventually to other sites across the Southwest where the United Farm Workers Union needed the theater group to help in their struggle. They performed what had become after a couple of years some standard actos that the collective of workers/ actors had written themselves. *Las dos caras del patroncito* (The Two-Faced Boss) focuses on the hypocrisy of the grower and the innocence and vulnerability of the Mojado (Wetback). Many of the farmworkers were undocumented immigrants from Mexico brought to California as "scab" labor to help break the union strike. *La quinta temporada* (The Fifth Season) deals with the hated figure of the *coyote,* the labor contractor who delivered Chicanos, Filipinos, and Mexican nationals to the growers' fields in exchange for a set fee. The contractor, as portrayed in this acto, was often a ruthless and cruel individual.

The focus of El Teatro Campesino broadened in 1967 when it moved from Delano to Marina del Rey, California, where the troupe founded El Centro Campesino Cultural (The Workers' Cultural Center). The troupe's reputation had begun to spread well beyond the Southwest and even beyond U.S. borders. For example, they were invited to perform at the Seventh World Theatre Festival in France, where audiences received them enthusiastically. They continued producing actos about other aspects of the Chicano experience. They also began experimenting with the basic structure of the short one-act acto that had been their trademark since 1965.

In 1970, El Teatro Campesino turned its attention to the Vietnam War with the production of *Vietnam campesino* (Vietnam Farmworker), a longer five-scene acto that focused on the collusion between the growers and the Pentagon to exploit the Chicano farmworker both at home in the United States and in Vietnam. *Soldado razo* (The Chicano GI), first performed in 1971 at the Chicano Moratorium against the War in Vietnam, also makes a strong antiwar statement from a Chicano perspective. It revolves around a father and son's false concept of *machismo,* which they associate with serving their country by fighting in one of its foreign wars.

The year 1971 signaled a major change in the evolution of El Teatro Campesino. Luis Valdez and his troupe of actors moved to San Juan Bautista, California, and began experimenting with another dramatic form, the *mito,* which differs significantly from the acto. The mito is designed to explore the nature of Chicano culture whereas the acto concentrates on political issues expressed in the cultural terms of its target Chicano audience. El Teatro thus began de-emphasizing strictly sociopolitical content in favor of legends, myths, and religion. Valdez has called the acto and the mito twin forms (*cuates*) that complement each other.

Zoot Suit, one of the theater troupe's most popular plays, is a dramatic version of the events in 1942 that historians have labeled the Sleepy Lagoon murder. In the play, four young Chicanos represent seventeen *pachucos* indicted and found guilty of murdering a young man. They are sentenced to long prison terms. The play premiered at the prestigious Mark Taper Forum in Los Angeles in 1978. It was then revised and reopened at the same theater as part of its regular 1978–1979 season. After a few performances at the Aquarius Theater in Hollywood, it moved to the Winter Garden Theater on Broadway in New York City. The play received generally positive reviews on the West Coast but New York City critics treated it harshly. (As described in chapter 3, a movie version was also released in 1981; see figure 6.)

■ Fig. 6. El Pachuco (from the movie *Zoot Suit*) strikes a characteristically defiant stance. The hat, long coat, and pegged pants were characteristic of a pachuco's unorthodox dress. (1981 Universal City Studios movie poster used courtesy of David Maciel.)

Zoot Suit represented an important step forward for popular Chicano theater because, for the first time, a contemporary play by a Chicano had successfully made the transition from the barrio and the university campus to commercial theater. Valdez and his troupe were able to carry their hard-hitting message to a wider audience. At the same time, Valdez's decision to "mainstream" his troupe's plays ultimately led to the dissolution of the theater collective, which had held together since the mid-1960s. Rather than a collective, El Teatro Campesino is now more of a production company that produces plays for mainstream audiences (Broyles-González 1994, 217).

Other Regional Theaters

El Teatro Campesino was the major force in popular Chicano theater from the mid-1960s to the late 1970s. Its unique and dynamic nature as a collective that produced simple one-act plays with a strong social message spawned the formation of other Chicano popular theater groups in barrios and on college campuses across the Southwest.

It also led to the founding of TENAZ (El Teatro Nacional de Aztlán [The National Theater of Aztlán]), and to annual theater festivals. In 1970, El Teatro Campesino hosted the First Annual Festival de los Teatros Chicanos (Festival of Chicano Theaters), attended by sixteen theater troupes from all over the United States and one from Mexico. Among them were El Teatro del Piojo (The Flea Theater) from Seattle, El Teatro Mestizo from San Diego, Grupo Mascarones (Large Masks Troupe) from Mexico City, El Teatro Aztlán from San Francisco, and El Teatro Bilingüe (Bilingual Theater) from El Paso.

After El Teatro Campesino, El Teatro de la Esperanza (The Theater of Hope) was probably the most vital and influential Chicano popular theater ensemble during much of the 1970s. Formed in 1971 by Dr. Jorge Huerta (now a distinguished professor of drama at the University of California, San Diego) and other students at the University of California, Santa Barbara, El Teatro de la Esperanza performed first in the Santa Barbara area and then in gyms, halls, auditoriums, and community centers throughout southern California. Its short skits, like the *actos* of El Teatro Campesino, were based on prototypical and allegorical characters who represented different components of the Chicano community as well as Anglo society. Most of the skits were set in urban barrios rather than agricultural fields.

Other popular theater groups included El Teatro de la Gente (The People's Theater) formed in 1970 in San Jose by a group of students from San Jose State University; El Teatro de Aztlán founded in 1970 by students at California State University, Northridge; El Teatro Urbano (The Urban Theater), a community-based group formed in 1972 in East Los Angeles; and El Teatro Libertad (The Liberty Theater) founded in 1975 by a group of Tucson farmworkers, activists, students, and laborers. Teatros were also founded in the 1970s in Gary, Indiana; San Antonio and Austin, Texas; Denver and Greeley, Colorado; Seattle, Washington; and Pasadena, California.

The Legacy of El Teatro Campesino

The Chicano popular theater movement of the 1960s and 1970s left a legacy that has persisted through the 1990s and beyond. The two most important examples of this legacy are Latins Anonymous and Culture Clash, a second generation of Chicano/Latino theater actors and writers who inherited the political fervor and artistic commitment of the Chicano Movement.

LATINS ANONYMOUS Latins Anonymous was founded in 1987 by a group of young Latino actors: Luisa Leschin, Armando Molina, Rick Nájera, and Diane Rodríguez. Cristóbal Franco joined the group later. Reflecting the diverse native and immigrant makeup of Latino communities in California, these actors come from different backgrounds: Leschin, the daughter of a concert pianist and a Salvadoran politician, was raised in Guatemala and educated in Europe and New York City. Molina's family immigrated to the United States from Colombia and settled in New York City. The Franco family, originally from Mexico City, resettled in the San Fernando Valley. Nájera, a Chicano, was born and raised in San Diego; and Rodríguez, a Chicana, is from a performing family of ministers and singers from San Jose, California. Each of the actors has performed individually, taking on increasingly more public and prestigious roles in live theater, television, and film productions. They have also excelled in other areas of theater production. Still, as in the early years of El Teatro Campesino, Latins Anonymous has a collective identity, and its members work together to write and produce their plays. No one individual is singled out as the author or the lead actor.

The group's "signature" play, *Latins Anonymous,* is a series of comedic playlets, each satirizing Anglo culture while providing observations in a humorous vein about different aspects of the Latino condition in the United States. They have performed *Latins Anonymous* all over the United States and in Mexico at venues such as South Coast Repertory in Los Angeles, San Diego Repertory, Borderlands Theater in Tucson, Group Theater in Seattle, New World Theater in Amherst, Massachusetts, and a theater in Guadalajara, Mexico. They have performed their second play, *The La La Awards,* at the Japan American Center in Los Angeles, the San Diego Repertory, and the Guadalupe Arts Center in San Antonio. *The La La Awards* describes itself as "a satirical, up-to-the-minute look at the Latino presence in Hollywood" (Latins Anonymous 1996, 13). The play, which satirizes awards ceremonies (e.g., the Academy Awards or the Tony Awards), includes several characters based on Latino celebrities; for example, Cheech Marin County (Cheech Marin), Edward James Almost (Edward James Olmos), and Linda Roncha (Linda Ronstadt), as well as stereotypes such as Aztec Studs and Juan Valdez (the fictional Colombian coffee farmer). Among the group's other works, one playlet, *Machos of Omaha,* parodies machismo, and another, *Latin Denial,* pokes fun at Latinos who would prefer to be identified as European.

CULTURE CLASH   Culture Clash is another theater group that functions as a collective. It is made up of mainly northern Californian Latino actors and writers—Herbert Siguenza, Richard Montoya, Ricardo Salinas, and José Antonio Burciaga (deceased)—who came together around 1984 at the Galería de la Raza/Studio 24 in San Francisco to begin producing satirical theater. Siguenza, who was born in San Francisco of Salvadoran parents, has an art and design background. Salinas was born in El Salvador but grew up in San Francisco's Mission District, a heavily Latino barrio of the city. He was involved in Chicano Movement theater activities. Montoya was born in San Diego but raised in northern California. His parents were involved in Chicano Movement politics and artistic activities, and he was exposed early to El Teatro Campesino. Burciaga was an artist and poet who taught for many years at Stanford University. The name signifies for the group "the culture clash of Latinos against mainstream America, as well as the culture clash between the different Latino races" (Theatre Communications Group 1998, 3).

Initially, the group performed cabaret-style without a narrative script. Each actor would take a turn on stage performing individual material, although members did collaborate on sketches and played off of each other's jokes. More recently the group has cowritten and co-produced several plays including *The Mission* (1988), *A Bowl of Beings* (1991), and *Radio Mambo: Culture Clash Invades Miami* (1994). According to Ricardo Salinas, Culture Clash's first play, *The Mission,* is "a synthesis of many traditions ... a culmination of three separate lives coming together in a desperate plea to tell the world about our dilemma. It is a semi-autobiographical romp about three frustrated Latino actors from San Francisco's Mission District trying to break into show biz" (Theatre Communications Group 1998, 5). The play premiered in San Francisco in 1988 and has subsequently been performed at venues throughout the United States.

A Bowl of Beings, which premiered in 1991 in Los Angeles, is the group's tribute to the legacy of the Chicano Movement, and as such it is explicitly political in its content. It is a broad sweep through the history of Hispanics in the United States from the time of the European discovery of America forward. The play takes on a number of sacred cows, such as the historical figures of Columbus, Che Guevarra, Trotsky, and Frida Kahlo; Chicano popular icons such as Edward James Olmos; and folk myths such as La Llorona.

Radio Mambo: Culture Clash Invades Miami is unique in contemporary Chicano theater in that, although written and performed by a Chicano theater group, the play deals with Cuban, Haitian, African American, and Jewish themes within the distinctly non-Chicano city of Miami. It highlights a number of issues that both unite and separate different ethnic groups in the Miami area in an irreverent and humorous way. Culture Clash was commissioned to write the play after a successful performance in Miami of *A Bowl of Beings.* The play premiered in Miami in 1994 to very positive reviews and enthusiastic audiences.

Popular Fiction of the Chicano Movement

"El Plan Espiritual de Aztlán" was paralleled elsewhere by the establishment of writers' and artists' collectives, the founding of literary journals, and the opening of exhibit space for visual artists. In terms of popular literature, the most important association of writers was El Grupo Quinto Sol (The Fifth Sun Collective) established in Berkeley, California, in 1967. This group—which included writers, critics, artists, and some social scientists associated with the University of California, Berkeley—founded the journal *El Grito: A Journal of Contemporary Mexican American Thought* in the same year. In 1969, some of the founders/editors of El Grupo Quinto Sol and the journal established a small publishing company, Quinto Sol, and established an annual literary prize, El Premio Quinto Sol, to recognize outstanding works of literature by Chicanos. Tomás Rivera won the 1970 award for his novel . . . *Y no se lo tragó la tierra/. . . And the Earth Did Not Part;* Rudolfo A. Anaya won in 1971 for his novel *Bless Me, Ultima;*

Rolando Hinojosa won in 1972 for his work *Estampas del valle y otras obras;* and Estela Portillo Trambley won in 1975 for her collection of short stories *Rain of Scorpions and Other Writings.* The Premio Quinto Sol was very influential in inspiring many other novelists to submit works to Quinto Sol as well as to other Chicano and mainstream presses, leading to a very productive three decades of fiction writing that continues today. In this section, I will discuss these four award-winning works and several others that have achieved widespread popularity.

TOMÁS RIVERA   Tomás Rivera was born in Crystal City, Texas, in 1935. Both of his parents had emigrated from Mexico and spoke Spanish in their home. Before attending public school, Rivera learned to read and write Spanish in a barrio school in Crystal City. Much like other Chicano writers, musicians, artists, and filmmakers, his schooling was frequently interrupted by trips his family made every year in the migrant stream. As a child and adolescent, he spent many harvesting seasons working in fields under horrible conditions like thousands of other Chicano migrants. Despite repeated interruptions, he finished high school and attended first Southwest Texas Junior College and then Southwest Texas State University, where he received a B.A. degree in 1958. He later received an M.Ed. in administration from the same institution before pursuing his doctoral studies in Spanish literature at the University of Oklahoma, receiving his Ph.D. in 1969. Rivera taught at several universities before entering academic administration first as a dean and later as the executive vice president of academic affairs at the University of Texas at El Paso. In 1979 he was appointed chancellor of the University of California, Riverside, a position he occupied until his tragic and untimely death in 1984.

In addition to his career as a gifted teacher and inspiring academic administrator, Rivera was a fine writer. Winning the first Premio Quinto Sol (1970) for his novel . . . *Y no se lo tragó la tierra* launched his writing career in an auspicious way. He had already published some poetry and short fiction, but this novel gave him instant recognition throughout the Chicano literary world and beyond. The novel was translated into English, published in bilingual form, and has become one of the most popular and widely read Chicano novels of the past thirty years. It is found in small as well as mainstream bookstores throughout the country and is used in high school and college classes.

The novel focuses on Texas-based migrant farmworkers, a world that

Rivera knew well. The author's intent is not to preach social change by glorifying the Chicano farmworker and vilifying Anglos but to create, in his own words, "an artistic world . . . in which the literary characters must move, speak, and feel as true and complex creations" (Tatum 1982, 184). Rivera draws heavily on the lives of the people he knows best, while at the same time elevating their fears, struggles, and beliefs beyond the level of social protest. This is not to say that he ignores the cause of his people; rather, he gives their cause greater force and credibility by creating characters who are multidimensional. Rivera rejected the stock sociological or historical characters of inferior pulp fiction. He also avoided the trap of dividing the world into good and evil people, as he portrays both Chicanos and Anglos lying, cheating, robbing, and even killing their own people.

RUDOLFO ANAYA   Rudolfo Anaya's novel *Bless Me, Ultima* (1972) is probably the best-selling Chicano novel of the past thirty years. Like Rivera's novel, it is used extensively in high school and college classes and is found on bookstore shelves throughout the United States. It has been translated into Spanish, German, and Polish.

Anaya was born in 1937 in Pastura, a very small village in eastern New Mexico. He attended public schools in nearby Santa Rosa and in Albuquerque. He earned a B.A. (1963) and an M.A. (1968) in English from the University of New Mexico, where he was also a professor of creative writing until his retirement several years ago. He has published numerous novels, collections of short stories, and essays, and has received several important awards and recognitions. As discussed in a later section, he also has branched successfully into detective fiction.

Bless Me, Ultima revolves around a young boy growing up in rural New Mexico after World War II in a family whose roots go back to the original Spanish settlers. Antonio Márez, the young protagonist, is almost seven when he begins to have what can be described as a religious crisis. His first-person narrative ends almost a year later, after a period of intense spiritual growth. During this time the young boy is influenced by Ultima, a local *curandera* (folk healer) of indeterminate age whom Antonio's family has brought to live in their home. Anaya depicts Antonio's father, Gabriel Márez, as an intensely independent *llanero* (plainsman) who laments that he no longer lives on the *llano* and has not fulfilled his lifelong dream to move to California to seek a better way of life for his family. In contrast, Antonio's mother, María Luna Márez, comes from a long line of farmers who are firmly rooted in the land they have worked for generations. Critical of the wanderlust of her husband's side of the family, she hopes that Antonio will someday become a priest so she can vicariously live out a life of cultivation and learning that her marriage to Gabriel has not afforded her. Antonio's brothers, World War II veterans, are characterized as shiftless, unambitious young men who add to the keen disappointment their mother feels about her life. Antonio's sisters are barely mentioned.

Ultima's arrival in the family home saves Antonio from the probable torment and anguish of feeling torn between his mother's and father's attempts to influence his future. Ultima has a profound impact on Antonio as she invites him to see the possibilities of a magical world that is as much a part of him as his mother's faith in God and his father's sense of independence. She is his spiritual guide at a time when the death of people close to him leads Antonio to lose his faith in traditional Catholic beliefs. Ultima awakens in him the memory of the timeless, mythological figures that inhabit his past, teaching him a profound respect for the mystical legends and folk wisdom that have survived through the centuries. She explains to him the significance of the Golden Carp, a legendary, benevolent god who became a fish to be near his people.

ROLANDO HINOJOSA   Rolando Hinojosa intends all of his works, regardless of the genre, to form a part of a lifelong novel that he has called his Klail City Death Trip. He has created a fictional world—Klail City in Belken County, Texas—located somewhere in the Lower Rio Grande Valley. Klail City is filled with memorable characters whose ordinary lives take on tragicomic proportions as they go about their daily tasks, dealing with the conflicts arising out of generations of racial strife and cultural misunderstanding.

Born in Mercedes in the Lower Rio Grande Valley, Hinojosa comes from an old New Mexico family. His paternal ancestors arrived in the valley in 1749 as part of the Escandón expedition sent by the Spanish viceroy in Mexico City to settle New Spain's northern frontier. Hinojosa began writing when he was fifteen and still in high school. He pursued his writing after graduating from high school in 1946, spent a year at the University of Texas in Austin, then joined the Army and saw service in Korea. He returned to the University of Texas after being deactivated and graduated in 1954 with a degree in Spanish. He taught in a high school and held down other jobs for a few years before pursuing a graduate degree.

He received an M.A. in Spanish from Highlands University in Las Vegas, New Mexico, in 1963 and a Ph.D. in Spanish from the University of Illinois in 1969. He held several academic and administrative positions during his long career and recently retired from the University of Texas at Austin.

Several of the novels Hinojosa published over the past thirty years can be categorized as popular. I have singled out *Estampas del valle y otras obras* to discuss in this section and I will return to discuss his detective fiction in a later section.

Winner of the 1972 Premio Quinto Sol, Hinojosa's 1973 *Estampas del valle y otras obras* (published as *The Valley* in 1983) is a series of sketches (*estampas*) that form a tapestry of the Chicano community in and around Klail City. Each estampa forms an integral part of the complex mix of lives, joys, tragedies, and struggles of the community. The author tells us at the beginning of this work that his sketches are like individual strands of hair matted together with the sweat and dirt of generations of human toil. To separate them would be to interrupt the flow of vitality and spontaneity that surges through the work. The novel ranges in tone from a terse, direct presentation to a subtle folk humor. We follow dozens of characters through the pages almost as though we were listening to the running commentary of a group of old friends who are reminiscing about a lifetime of relatives and acquaintances, marriages, romances, scandals, elections, deaths, burials, births, divorces, and racial incidents.

■ The Ascendancy of Popular Writing by Chicanas

The first three Premio Quinto Sol awards were won by men. In 1975, Estela Portillo Trambley won the award for her stunning collection of short stories, *Rain of Scorpions and Other Writings*. Although several other Chicana writers had published fiction in the post-1960s era, the awarding of the prize signaled the ascendancy of Chicana literature. Many other female novelists and short-story writers have taken their place among the very best that contemporary Chicano literature has to offer. These writers include Kathleen Alcalá, Ana Castillo, Denise Chávez, Sandra Cisneros, Lucha Corpi, Roberta Fernández, Montserrat Fontes, Alicia Gaspar de Alba, Sylvia López-Medina, Demetria Martínez, Cecile Piñeda, Alma Villanueva, and Helena María Viramontes.

I have selected a few Chicana authors whose works I consider to have achieved a level of popularity in terms of readership of all ages: Estela Portillo Trambley, Denise Chávez, and Sandra Cisneros. Lucha Corpi is included in the section on the detective novel. Again, my sole criterion for choosing these authors is the popularity of their works; many other less-popular works are also of excellent quality.

Estela Portillo Trambley

I discuss Estela Portillo Trambley first because of the importance of *Rain of Scorpions and Other Writings* as an award-winning work of fiction. She was born in 1936 in El Paso, where she attended public school as well as college. She received a B.A. in English in 1956 and an M.A. in the same field in 1978 from the University of Texas at El Paso. She worked for many years for the Department of Special Services of the El Paso public schools and as a drama instructor, producer, and director in the El Paso Community College system. She passed away in December 1998. In addition to fiction, she published the play *Day of the Swallows* in 1971 and wrote the script for a musical comedy named *Sun Images. Day of the Swallows,* her first major publication, came about when Portillo Trambley's brother, a mail carrier, gave some of her manuscripts to an English professor who lived on his route.

Portillo Trambley stands out as a short-story writer for her sensitive treatment of a variety of themes as well as her finely crafted prose characterized by its lyricism and striking imagery. Her stories have been compared to morality plays in which conflicting forces clash, sometimes producing disharmony and other times resulting in a peaceful resolution. Although she was very involved with social causes and often an eloquent spokeswoman on behalf of various issues, in her writing she steadfastly avoided what she believed to be overtly political or social pamphleteering. Her insistence that the use of literature as a political tool would ultimately bind the creative work is reflected in her stories, which are generally free of strictly social messages.

Liberation of the human spirit is a common theme in *Rain of Scorpions and Other Writings.* Two stories, "The Paris Gown" and "If It Weren't for the Honeysuckle" are illustrative of her skill in developing this theme. "The Paris Gown" deals with the personal courage of Clo, a young woman who is out of step with the expectations and restrictions of the Mexican society in which she has been raised. Clo refuses to submit to the dictates of her parents, who insist that she marry an elderly widower. By way of defying her parents' expectations she appears nude at her formal engagement party. Her father accedes to her wish not to marry the widower and sends her to Paris to find herself. The second story is set in a rural Mexican hamlet where Beatriz, the central character, rebels against her husband's brutality by conspiring with another woman to poison him.

Sandra Cisneros

Sandra Cisneros's *The House on Mango Street* (1984) is one of the most popular works of Chicano fiction published in the past twenty years. It is used extensively in high school and college classes, is found in virtually all large national chain bookstores (such as Barnes and Noble and Borders), and selections of it have been included in many important anthologies. It has also been translated into Spanish. In 1985, the book was awarded the American Book Award by the Before Columbus Foundation.

Cisneros was born in Chicago in 1954 and was raised in a home with what she has described as "seven fathers," six brothers (two older, four younger) and a father. She felt that her brothers sometimes attempted to control her behavior in a traditional Mexican male way even though several of them were close to her own age. When she was a young girl, her family moved frequently from apartment to apartment in Chicago and also lived for a time in Mexico City, where her father's family was from. She received a B.A. from Loyola University in Chicago in 1976 and an M.A. from the prestigious University of Iowa Writers' Workshop in 1978. She has published two works of fiction, *The House on Mango Street* (1983) and *Woman Hollering Creek* (1991), a book of poetry, *My Wicked, Wicked Ways* (1987), and several essays on the creative writing process and other topics. She has worked as a high school teacher, college minority student recruiter and counselor, and guest university creative writing professor. She has given numerous public readings on college campuses and in other venues over the past ten years. Cisneros currently lives in San Antonio.

The House on Mango Street, a series of very short stories or vignettes, took five years to complete. Cisneros's central character, who speaks throughout the work, is Esperanza, a poor Chicana adolescent who longs for not only a room but a house of her own, like the house that Cisneros dreamed about as a child. The story "My Name" is very revealing. The narrator says, "In English my name means hope. In Spanish it means too many letters. It means sadness, it means waiting. . . . It is the Mexican records my father plays on Sunday mornings when he is shaving, songs like sobbing" (Cisneros 1983, 12). The young narrator traces her name back to her Mexican great-grandmother, who was "tamed" by her husband and spent most of her life looking out of a window. The young narrator inherited her great-grandmother's name but is quite clear that she does not want to inherit her position as a subservient, tamed woman. Esperanza would like to baptize herself under a new name like "Lisandra or Maritza or Zeze the X. Yes. Something like Zeze the X will do" (Cisneros 1983, 13). The new name will have an air of mystery and power about it, and its bearer will not be subject to the strictures of male-dominated Mexican society and, by extension, Chicano culture.

Denise Chávez

Denise Chávez is a playwright, prose fiction writer, and actress. She is best known for *The Last of the Menu Girls* (1986), a work that some critics consider a collection of short stories and others consider a novel. She was born in Las Cruces, New Mexico, where she received her undergraduate degree in 1971 from New Mexico State University. She also received an M.A. degree in drama from Trinity University in San Antonio in 1974 and an additional graduate degree in creative writing from the University of New Mexico almost ten years later. She has taught drama at the University of Houston and writing at New Mexico State University. She currently resides in Las Cruces.

Chávez's *The Last of the Menu Girls* is a semi-autobiographical, bittersweet work of seven interrelated sections. Like so many other popular Chicano works of prose fiction (e.g., José Antonio Villarreal's *Pocho,* Tomás Rivera's . . . *Y no se lo tragó la tierra,* and Sandra Cisnero's *The House on Mango Street*) this is a coming-of-age novel. Rocío Esquibel is the central character who functions as the artist/narrator. She is a first-year university student interested in creative writing. She recalls for the reader her childhood as well as the adolescent rites of passage that form the backdrop of her transition to adulthood. Much of the work, which is set in a Chicano barrio in a southwestern city along the U.S.–Mexican border, has to do with the everyday events and experiences of Rocío's life among her friends and family. The thread that unifies the interrelated stories is Rocío's search for models of what she will and should become as a woman growing up in a traditional culture. Many of the older women in her life, however, have grown disillusioned and even bitter because their own dreams have been shattered, due mainly to their relationships with men whom Chávez portrays as generally deceitful and egotistical.

As in Sandra Cisneros's *The House on Mango Street,* a house, Rocío's home, is a central metaphor throughout the novel. "It is a house full of memories of the past, of Great Aunt Eutilia who died, of her mother's first husband who was poisoned, and her own father who left to go north" (Eysturoy 1996, 115). As part of her growing maturity, Rocío discovers that her own mother, Nieves, is not just the soft, reliable woman who has always been available to comfort her but a woman with her own past, her own unfulfilled desires and frustrations.

■ Current Chicano Popular Literature

I include in this section a handful of writers who in my opinion have attained a significant level of popularity in the past ten to fifteen years. These include two writers of fictionalized biographies (Gary Soto and Víctor Villaseñor), one nonfiction writer (Gloria Anzaldúa), and five writers who have cultivated the mystery novel (Rudolfo Anaya, Lucha Corpi, Rolando Hinojosa, Michael Nava, and Luis Ramos). Again, I remind you that I have excluded many excellent Chicano writers who have published outstanding novels, collections of short stories or poetry, plays, and nonfiction or autobiographical works since the mid-1980s. A more extensive work on Chicano literature would surely discuss writers such as Oscar "Zeta" Acosta, Kathleen Alcalá, Ron Arias, Aristeo Brito, Norma Cantú, Ana Castillo, Monserrat Fontes, Dagoberto Gilb, Demetria Martínez, Max Martínez, Miguel Méndez, Pat Mora, Cherríe Moraga, Alejandro Morales, Cecile Piñeda, Alberto Ríos, Benjamin Saenz, Luis Urrea, Helena María Viramontes, and Bernice Zamora.

Nonfiction and Autobiographical Fiction

Many Chicano writers have drawn on their personal experiences to lend power to their prose. Two of Gary Soto's short story collections, *Living up the Street* and *Lesser Evils,* are strongly autobiographical. Victor Villaseñor even withdrew his book, *Rain of Gold,* from publication in part over the publisher's intent to present it as a work of fictional history. In *Borderlands/La Frontera,* Gloria Anzaldúa constructs her birthplace through prose and poetry.

GARY SOTO   Gary Soto is an award-winning poet with several books of poetry to his credit. He has also produced two short films and several anthologies. However, in terms of his popularity as a writer, it is his short stories that are of greatest interest, especially those in *Living up the Street: Narrative Recollections* (1985) and *Lesser Evils: Ten Quartets* (1988).

Soto was born in Fresno in 1952 and educated there through college. His father was killed in an industrial accident when he was only five years old. He grew up surrounded by Spanish in his family home and in the Fresno community but never formally studied the language. He graduated from high school in 1970 with an undistinguished academic record and entered Fresno City College in order to improve his academic record so that he could gain admission to Fresno State University. He succeeded, majoring first in geography and then in poetry, a life choice that he has never regretted. At Fresno State University, he studied with Philip Levine, one of the country's finest contemporary poets. In 1974 Soto graduated magna cum laude, and the next year he received an M.F.A. from the University of California, Irvine. He taught at the University of California, Berkeley, for many years and currently teaches at the University of California, Riverside. The awards he has won for his poetry include the 1977 *Poetry* magazine Bess Hokin Prize, a Guggenheim Fellowship in 1979, a National Education Association Fellowship in 1981, and the *Poetry* magazine Levinson Award in 1984. He also won the American Book Award in 1985 for his prose fiction work *Living up the Street.*

Living up the Street and *Lesser Evils* are autobiographical prose works that form a thematic continuity (Avalos Torres 1989a, 250). The first work includes stories of mischief from his childhood, his adventures as a young adult, and the increasing complexity of young adulthood. The seeming simplicity of his poetry is carried over into his prose, as Soto allows the reader to enter and be present in the scenes and anecdotes that are representative of his often difficult and troubled young life in Fresno. The details of the day-to-day travails and occasional victories are rooted very firmly in the soil of lived experience; they correspond to small but significant events that are artfully woven together from the writer's memories.

Lesser Evils deals with Soto's Catholicism, which is not treated in his first book. His observations and thoughts seem to have matured and become more introspective as he raises issues about life topics such as parenting, marriage, religion, women, responsibility, and teaching. Sometimes a humorous patina lightly covers a serious theme. The anger that sometimes surfaces in *Living up the Street* seems to have given way not to resignation, but to acceptance and a fair amount of tranquility.

VÍCTOR VILLASEÑOR   Victor Villaseñor's *Rain of Gold* took a difficult route to publication. The author had originally sold the completed manuscript to Putnam, a large New York–based commercial publisher. Villaseñor received $75,000 for U.S. publication rights, but the publisher wanted him to shorten the long manuscript and to change the title to something like "Rio Grande," which the editors thought would sell more books. They also wanted to publicize the book as fictional history. Villaseñor vigorously objected to having what was essentially a biography of his parents classified as fiction under a title with which he was profoundly uncomfortable. He bought back the book and all publication rights and tried without success to sell it to another New York publisher. Arte Público Press eventually agreed to publish the hardback edition in 1991 and at the same time it sold the paperback rights to Dell Publishing (Quality Paperbacks), which published a paperback edition in 1992.

Villaseñor was born in Carlsbad, California, in 1940 and was raised by his parents, both of Mexican descent, on a ranch in Oceanside. He attended schools in both the United States and Mexico, where he moved as an adolescent. He returned to the United States in 1960, where he began writing, combating his dyslexia, and supporting himself in construction work. He wrote almost obsessively, producing manuscripts for nine novels and more than sixty-five other pieces of fiction. Villaseñor has lectured widely throughout the United States on high school and college campuses, in prisons, and at the Smithsonian Institution in Washington, D.C.

Villaseñor's parents, Juan Salvador Villaseñor and Lupe Gómez, were married in 1929 in Santa Ana, California. Their respective families had fled the violence and deprivation of the Mexican Revolution to come north to the United States. In *Rain of Gold,* Villaseñor recounts the many travails each family encountered and overcame, including narrow escapes from death and serious injury. The author drew on the many stories he had heard from his parents and numerous other members of both families, as well as on research he conducted on the historical context and conflagration that forced them to leave Mexico in the first place. The author captures the deep dismay with which the Mexican rural poor and urban working class regarded the regime of Porfirio Díaz, Mexico's president during the last part of the nineteenth century and the first decade of the twentieth century. Díaz had encouraged foreign investment in sectors such as utilities, mining, and the railroads to such an extent that by the end of his many years in office much of the Mexican population had become disgruntled with their economic dependence on foreign interests. The exploitation of workers in the mines and factories and on large farms and ranches, combined with political opposition in Mexico City, eventually led to a full-scale revolution that drove Díaz from power and set in motion more than a decade of civil war as different political and military interests sought control of the country. Much of the country's population, especially the rural poor, found themselves buffeted between these interests and often were caught in the military cross fire that ensued.

The book's narrative alternates between the two families, focusing on Juan Salvador, depicted as volatile and impulsive, and Lupe, who is characterized as thoughtful and calming. The two families and thousands of other refugees flee to Ciudad Juárez, where they are forced to encamp. Villaseñor describes in vivid detail the harsh living conditions in the camps and the random acts of violence the refugees there were forced to witness. The families eventually cross into the United States. The Gómez family enters the migrant stream, and we follow Lupe's adjustment to an alien culture and her struggle to be accepted among her Anglo peers as she transfers from school to school. Salvador, on the other hand, manages to survive as a miner and then as a bootlegger. He is jailed but escapes. Lupe and Salvador are eventually brought together by a complicated set of circumstances and marry.

GLORIA ANZALDÚA   Anzaldúa has authored only one book, *Border-lands/ La Frontera: The New Mestiza* (1987), but it has had a major impact on scholars and students in Chicano studies, women's studies, and cultural studies. In addition, Anzaldúa has made numerous presentations not only at universities, conferences, and other academic venues but also in more public forums. She has been in the forefront of Chicana-feminist-lesbian politics.

Anzaldúa was born in 1942 on a ranch settlement in south Texas. She lived in a ranching environment until she was eleven, when her family moved to a small town where she attended the public schools. Her father died when she was fifteen. She worked in the agricultural fields even while earning a B.A. degree at Pan American University in Edinburgh, Texas (1969). She later received an M.A. in English and Education from the

University of Texas at Austin and a Ph.D. from the University of California, Santa Cruz. She has taught at several universities around the United States.

Borderlands is a difficult book to categorize. It is at once an autobiography, a spiritual journey, a theoretical work that opens up new spaces, and an expository essay in which Anzaldúa intentionally—even defiantly—mixes genres in a way that serves her purpose to instruct, challenge, scandalize, and provoke her reader and those who would try to reduce her and her writing to a neat label. Her tone is poetic, epic, and tragic (Avalos Torres 1989b, 13).

The book is divided into two major sections: a long essay, "Atravesando Fronteras/Crossing Borders," and a collection of poems, "Un agitado viento/Ehécatl, the Wind." Anzaldúa's historical construction of the place where she was born and raised draws on both research and many conversations she had with her family. She traces the history of her people over almost three thousand years from the first millennium before Christ through the experiences of her own family in Texas in the late twentieth century. Anzaldúa provides a critique of Western society while at the same time situating herself within it as a being divided between countries and cultures. The borderlands she and others inhabit are more spiritual than geographic states. It is fair to say that Anzaldúa's highly elliptical style might at times be difficult to follow but it is well worth the effort to do so.

The Chicano Mystery Novel

The Chicano mystery novel is a new genre that has emerged during the past decade. Established writers such as Rudolfo Anaya, Lucha Corpi, and Rolando Hinojosa, who were already well known as novelists or poets, have cultivated this genre with success. Michael Nava and Manuel Ramos are two writers who are best known for their detective fiction. In this section I will discuss works by all five authors.

RUDOLFO ANAYA Rudolfo Anaya has used his considerable talent as a novelist to produce three mystery novels since 1996: *Zia Summer* (1996), *Rio Grande Fall* (1997), and *Shaman Winter* (1999). In each, Sonny Baca, an Albuquerque-based Chicano private investigator, becomes involved in a mystery that leads the reader through a fascinating labyrinth of intrigue, myth, magic, and good old-fashioned crime investigation. Sonny is the supposed great-grandson of the legendary lawman Elfego Baca who helped tame the New Mexico territory at a time when gunslingers and rustlers were trying to take it over. Anaya sets these mysteries against a backdrop of urban Chicano culture and does not avoid raising social issues related to the deep divisions that still exist in the late twentieth century between Anglos and Americans of Mexican descent. He also draws on the spiritual dimensions of connectedness with the land that characterize his classic novel *Bless Me, Ultima*. His knowledge of and respect for the cultural traditions of both indigenous and Hispanic peoples is evident in all three mystery novels.

In *Zia Summer,* Sonny Baca, much of whose work involves mundane tasks such as tracking errant husbands or deadbeat dads, is suddenly thrust into a web of mysterious and baffling circumstances that affect him personally: the murder of his cousin Gloria Dominic. His investigation takes him into a world of dreams and myth. He discovers that Gloria had been in contact with a sun-worship cult from a nearby Indian pueblo that is planning to blow up a truck transporting nuclear waste to a dump site in southern New Mexico. Sonny foils the plot to blow up the truck and solves the mystery of his cousin's gruesome death, while at the same time revealing the power struggle for control of Albuquerque's financial and commercial future.

Rio Grande Fall focuses on a woman's fatal fall from a hot-air balloon. Sonny discovers that she has been murdered and that Raven, the leader of the violent sun-worship cult from the first novel and Sonny's nemesis, is implicated in the murder. Anaya has endowed Raven with superhuman qualities and has Sonny availing himself of the assistance of his guardian spirit, the Coyote, as he engages Raven for a second time in his epic struggle against evil. As in the first mystery novel, Anaya effectively foregrounds elements of New Mexico's old Hispanic culture and shamanistic magic even as the plot is played out in the context of a contemporary urban environment of political intrigue.

Shaman Winter is perhaps the most extreme of the three novels in terms of the incorporation of Native American and Hispanic spiritualism, myth, and magic as Sonny becomes aware of the power and presence of an ancestor Owl Woman, the daughter of a shaman who accompanied Juan de Oñate's expedition to New Mexico in 1598. An epic battle takes place between Sonny and Raven in a world of dreams as the private investigator's enemy repeatedly tries to enter his dreams in order to attack and carry off his soul. The antagonists also confront each other in the real world when Sonny discovers that Raven is the perpetrator of yet another heinous crime, part of a much larger plot to seize control of municipal, state, and national political and financial institutions. Sonny momentarily triumphs over Raven at the end of this mystery novel, but the reader is prepared for the battle between the two to continue in future novels.

ROLANDO HINOJOSA   In 1985 Hinojosa published *Partners in Crime: A Rafe Buenrostro Mystery,* a work that differs from his previous novels in that it lacks their collective focus, fragmented narrative structure, and heavy influence from the oral tradition. It is instead a novel that follows the pattern of many modern detective stories. Hinojosa's thorough research of police procedures and crime along the border and his use of a clipped, hard-boiled style give this novel much credibility as detective fiction. Rafa (Rafe) Buenrostro, the central character of this and Hinojosa's second mystery novel, is a detective lieutenant on the Belken County, Texas, homicide squad. Most of the novel takes place in the squad room of the Belken County Building as Buenrostro and his fellow detectives go about the often tedious work of solving homicides, answering phone calls, and filling out endless reports. They also cooperate with Mexican police officials across the border in Barrones to solve a horrible crime, the brutal slaying of an American and two Mexican nationals that they eventually link to a cocaine smuggling ring. Hinojosa has written a good piece of detective fiction in that he reveals the true order and meaning of events based largely on physical circumstances.

Hinojosa's second detective novel, *Ask a Policeman: A Rafe Buenrostro Mystery* (1998), like his first one, reflects the escalation of deadly violence associated with drug trafficking that takes places daily along the U.S.– Mexican border. Rafe Buenrostro, who has now been promoted to chief inspector of the Belken County Homicide Squad, is forced to deal with the tragic consequences of this violence when a former Mexican government official and convicted murderer is freed from jail by his henchmen. Once again, American and Mexican police officials cooperate closely to track down and incarcerate the perpetrators, who threaten civic order on both sides of the border.

LUCHA CORPI   Prior to publishing three mystery novels, Lucha Corpi was best known as a fine poet and novelist. Critics have a high regard for her bilingual collection of poetry, *Palabras de Mediodía/Noon Words* (1980), as well as her novel, *Delia's Song* (1989). She was born in 1945 in the

Mexican state of Veracruz and immigrated to the United States as a new-lywed when she was nineteen. She has lived and worked in the San Francisco Bay Area since then, where she has been active in organizing and participating in several arts groups and activities. She earned a B.A. from the University of California, Berkeley, and an M.A. from San Francisco State University.

Corpi brings a strong feminist perspective to her mystery novels. In 1992, she published *Eulogy for a Brown Angel: A Mystery Novel,* the first of three mystery novels whose central character is Gloria Damasco, a civil-rights activist who lives and works in the Bay Area. Gloria is not a private investigator either by training or inclination; she just happens to become involved in a crime: the murder of a young child on a Los Angeles street during a Chicano demonstration in 1970. She collects information about the victim and the circumstances of her death for several years until unexpected revelations lead her to the killer.

Corpi's second Gloria Damasco mystery novel, *Cactus Blood* (1995), involves the horrifying and bloody murders of three social activists as well as the rape of a young Chicana and her exposure to pesticide contamination many years previously. Damasco and a fellow Chicano detective follow several false leads until finally Damasco's extrasensory awareness links the three serial murders to the incident involving the young woman. This novel has a subplot as Damasco and Justin Escobar, the detective with whom she is working on the case, discover their romantic interest in each other.

In Corpi's most recent mystery novel, *Black Widow's Wardrobe* (1999), Gloria Damasco witnesses an assassination attempt on a woman who has just been released from prison. Against her better judgment, Damasco sets out to investigate the identity of the woman and the motive for the violent act against her. The more she probes, the more intricate and involved becomes the web of relationships and circumstances surrounding the initial act and its intended victim. In this novel, the reader is taken from California's Bay Area to the mountain town of Tepoztlán south of Mexico City. Damasco continues to uncover several levels of mystery as the novel progresses, until the solution ultimately leads her to Mexican national political intrigue.

MICHAEL NAVA   Michael Nava has published several mystery novels involving a San Francisco Bay Area criminal lawyer named Henry Ríos: *The*

Little Death (1986), *How Town* (1990), *The Hidden Law* (1992), *Goldenboy: A Mystery* (1996), *The Death of Friends* (1996), and *The Burning Plain* (1999). Nava was born in 1954 in Stockton, California. He received a B.A. from Colorado College in 1976 and a J.D. degree from Stanford University in 1981. He currently practices law in Los Angeles as a research attorney for the California Court of Appeals.

We first meet Henry Ríos in *The Little Death,* the first novel in the series. Ríos is ten years out of law school and has chosen criminal defense law over more comfortable and high-paying jobs in corporate law. Nava depicts Ríos as a principled individual dedicated to defending the downtrodden even when they seem to resent him. As an idealistic college student he went to law school in order to serve his community, and he has not forgotten or compromised his principles. Nava also handles Rios's homosexuality in a sensitive and natural way in all of his novels while raising issues such as homophobia and AIDS.

We follow Ríos's sputtering career over the next fifteen years through several excellent and compelling mystery novels. He begins in the public defender's office, but soon leaves to set up his own private criminal defense law practice. Still, the material conditions of his life as a lawyer never improve; he grows older but not more prosperous. Most of his clients are losers, down-and-outers, and desperate petty criminals who often cannot pay Ríos to represent them and rarely express their appreciation for keeping them out of jail. Nava does not spare us the gritty details of life on the streets, in the jails, or in the barrio, which Ríos confronts every day. The nature of his work takes him where his clients and the leads in their cases are to be found. He defends clients at trial, but he is also an unofficial private investigator who uses instinct, legal expertise, common sense, and persistence to get to the bottom of often baffling murders and other crimes that come up in the course of his practice.

MANUEL RAMOS Manuel Ramos, like Michael Nava, is a practicing lawyer who has written a series of mystery novels with a central character who is an idealistic lawyer. Ramos was born in 1948 in Florence, Colorado. His father, a labor organizer, was a native of Zacatecas, Mexico. His mother was born in the Colorado mining community of Chandler. Ramos attended public schools in Florence and Colorado Springs, received a B.A. with honors in 1971 from Colorado State University, and earned a J.D. degree from the University of Colorado in 1973. He currently lives in

Denver, where he is deputy director and litigation director for the Legal Aid Society of Metropolitan Denver. He has published four novels, all featuring the same protagonist, Luis Móntez: *The Ballad of Rocky Ruiz* (1993), *The Ballad of Gato Guerrero* (1994), *The Last Client of Luis Móntez* (1996), and *Blues for the Buffalo* (1997). In 1994 he won the Colorado Book Award presented by the Colorado Center for the Book. He was recipient in 1996 of the Law Alumni Distinguished Achievement Award from the University of Colorado School of Law and, in 1998, of the Jacob V. Shaetzel Award from the Colorado Bar Association.

The character of Luis Móntez whom Ramos presents to us in his first novel, *The Ballad of Rocky Ruiz,* is a middle-aged lawyer who was an idealistic student activist in the early 1970s but has become somewhat disillusioned that he and other friends have not remained faithful to their youthful ideals. Ramos immerses us in the ambience of the last stages of the Chicano Movement in Colorado when Móntez was a member of a militant group called Los Guerrilleros (The Warriors) battling for social justice. Móntez's life after law school has been mostly aimless on both a personal and professional level. He has had several divorces and has fathered a few children to whom he feels little connection. He spends much of his free time drinking in bars or at baseball games as his law practice limps along. In order to survive and stay one step ahead of the bill collector and his child support payments, he hustles cases, but many of his clients are too poor to pay him a legal fee.

In *The Ballad of Gato Guerrero,* Móntez regains some of the idealism, optimism, and self-confidence of the years he spent as a social activist. He has managed to put his law practice back on track. He once again establishes contact with his sons and becomes a more loving son to his own father. Always the loyal friend, he comes to the aid of Félix "Gato" Guerrero, a Vietnam veteran who has been falsely accused of murder. Móntez's investigation takes him to Colorado's San Luis Valley, which is portrayed as a place where Chicano values and traditions have managed to survive even in the face of tremendous poverty. The simple life of farmers, ranchers, and small businesspeople is contrasted to the corrupting influence that urban Denver has on Chicano families and their ability to raise their children to become productive citizens.

In *The Last Client of Luis Móntez,* the lawyer's life once again becomes chaotic when he is falsely accused of murdering a wealthy young client whom he has successfully defended against drug charges. He flees the police and goes from Denver to San Diego looking for a former police officer he is convinced holds the key to his client's death. Móntez solves the case but at the end of the novel he is described as psychologically drained and physically exhausted by both his professional and family responsibilities.

Blues for the Buffalo finds Móntez recovering from his weakened state on a beach in Mexico. He meets Raquel Espinoza, a beautiful young Chicana writer, before returning to Denver to try to revive his law practice, which he temporarily abandoned when he fled from the police in the previous novel. He soon discovers that Espinoza has disappeared in Mexico and he joins with Conrad Valdez, a private investigator hired by her father, to find her. He and Valdez, a fully assimilated Chicano, clash over values and politics but put aside their differences long enough to solve the mystery of Espinoza's disappearance.

■ Discussion Questions

1. Characterize the popular literature written by Chicanos prior to 1965.

2. Describe how the Chicano Movement was important in the formation of an artistic consciousness among Chicano writers.

3. What accounts for the decline in popularity of Chicano poetry after the mid-1970s?

4. Discuss what was unique about El Teatro Campesino's actos and the troupe's social role during the Chicano Movement.

5. What legacy did El Teatro Campesino leave in terms of Chicano theater of the 1970s and beyond?

6. Summarize the Premio Quinto Sol award-winning works of fiction.

7. Discuss the ascendance of Chicana writers beginning in the 1970s.

8. What do the autobiographical works of Soto, Villaseñor, and Anzaldúa have in common?

9. Do Chicano mystery novels seem to reflect mainstream or Chicano values?

10. What theory of popular culture best characterizes contemporary Chicano popular literature?

■ Suggested Readings

Broyles-González, Yolanda. 1994. *El Teatro Campesino: Theater in the Chicano Movement*. Austin: University of Texas Press.

Hancock, Joel. 1973. The Emergence of Chicano Poetry: A Survey of Sources, Themes, and Techniques. *Arizona Quarterly* 29 (1): 57–73.

Huerta, Jorge. 1982. *Chicano Theater: Themes and Forms*. Ypsilanti, Mich.: Bilingual Review/Press.

Kanellos, Nicolás. 1990. *A History of Hispanic Theatre in the States: Origins to 1940*. Austin: University of Texas Press.

Tatum, Charles. 1982. *Chicano Literature*. Boston: Twayne Publishers.

6

Art, Celebrations, and Other
Popular Traditions

In this chapter, I will discuss some important forms of Chicano popular culture that I have not covered in previous chapters: popular art, celebrations, and traditions. As you will read, all these forms of popular expression are as significant and vital as the forms discussed in previous chapters. As in the case of popular music, cinema, newspapers, radio, television, and literature, entire books and countless articles have been written about the many different aspects of popular expression covered in this chapter. My brief discussion of each will, I hope, serve to lead you to further investigation and a deeper understanding.

Popular Art

I have divided my discussion of Chicano popular art into two broad categories: religious art and secular (nonreligious) art. I recognize, however, that it is often difficult to separate the two: secular themes can be found in religious art contexts and vice versa.

Popular Religious Art

Any discussion of popular religious art in the Spanish-speaking Southwest must necessarily be put in the context of the Catholic Church and its role in the exploration, conquest, and settlement of New Spain's northern territories (the states of Texas, New Mexico, Arizona, Colorado, and California) from the sixteenth century onward. First under the Spanish crown and later (after Mexican independence) under the Mexican government, the Catholic Church, led by several of its religious orders, set up missions throughout the Southwest. In their attempts to convert indigenous peoples to Catholicism, these religious orders used popular religious traditions that they had brought from Spain as early as the sixteenth century.

Later in this chapter I will discuss some of these traditions, such as practices surrounding religious holy days and celebrations. In this section I will focus on a few popular religious art forms that grew out of these traditions and are still prevalent today: the *santero* tradition, which encompasses *retablos, reredos,* and *bultos;* home and roadside religious shrines; cemetery art; and *milagros.*

SANTOS AND SANTEROS   *Santos* are simply images of the Holy Family, the crucifix, saints, or other holy persons. Those painted on large pieces of cloth for altars are known as reredos, those painted on smaller wood or tin panels for churches are retablos, and three-dimensional carved figures in the round are bultos. As religious objects, santos originally were intended to be viewed within the confines of a church, but in the twentieth century many of these images have found their way into museums and galleries as well as into private homes throughout the Southwest (see figure 7).

Modern santeros (santo painters or carvers) come from a long tradition that began in the seventeenth century, particularly in northern New Mexico where it is still thriving (Quirarte 1973, 26–27). The hundreds of churches in New Mexico gave santeros gainful employment, and they produced various forms of religious images for strictly religious use within the churches. This situation changed in the late nineteenth century when the churches began to purchase commercially produced objects that were less expensive and more readily available (Quirarte 1973, 27–29). Nonetheless, the tradition continued because the general public remained interested in purchasing religious images for their homes. As early as the 1920s, santeros began painting panels and carving and painting three-dimensional figures for sale.

Today, the primary consumers of santos are collectors (both professional and personal), tourists, and museums, although churches sometimes still either purchase or accept santos as devotional gifts. Although santeros are found in other states, New Mexico continues today to be the center of the practice of this popular art form. Typically, the tradition has been passed down from generation to generation within specific families, but the popularity of santos has encouraged other craftspeople from outside these families to develop their painting or carving as a livelihood or to supplement their incomes. Santeros market the sacred painted and carved images either through small retail businesses (frequently out of their own homes), at annual events such as the Santa Fe Spanish Market frequented by thousands of buyers, or through third-party gallery and art store buyers.

The more established santeros try to maintain the authenticity of their nineteenth-century counterparts by adhering to established painting and

■ Fig. 7. "Retablo of José Cruz Soria" is a typical oil on metal retablo painting. José Cruz de Soria is a religious figure important to Mexican Americans and Mexican immigrants to the United States. (From *Miracles on the Border: Retablos of Mexican Migrants to the United States* by Jorge Durand and Douglas S. Massey. Tucson: University of Arizona Press, 1995. Reprinted by permission of Douglas S. Massey.)

carving practices such as the use of authentic materials, tools, and techniques. They have done extensive research and have carefully documented the finer aspects of the tradition. Others have modernized their craft. For example, some carvers use power tools instead of the original carving instruments or use commercially produced glues rather than making their own.

YARD AND ROADSIDE SHRINE ART   A common sight in Chicano neighborhoods in towns and cities from Brownsville to San Diego is the front-yard shrine (see figure 8) commonly referred to as a *gruta* (grotto) or *nicho* (recess). These shrines are generally half-domed structures simply constructed of bricks, stones, or plaster (commonly recycled materials) that range in size from a couple of feet to more than five feet across. Most shrines are built by the families themselves, but a few are commissioned

■ Fig. 8. A shrine typical of those commonly found in the front and side yards of Chicano family homes throughout the Southwest. This one is from a house located in southwestern Tucson, Arizona. (Photograph courtesy of James S. Griffith.)

and sometimes, depending on the family's financial status, the shrine might be surrounded by a well-tended garden or be adorned with columns and other architectural decorations. Found in the shrines are wooden, metal, or plaster statues of, most commonly, the Virgin Mary in her various popular apparitions (the Virgin of Guadalupe from the Mexican tradition, the Virgin of Fátima from Portugal, or the Virgin of Lourdes from France). It is also common to see different renditions of Christ and of saints such as Saint Jude and San Martín de Porres.

Families build and publicly display grutas for many different reasons but generally to fulfill a *manda* (vow) or *promesa* (promise) made by a family member who at some time in the past has appealed to the Virgin, Christ, or a saint to intercede on his or her behalf to, for example, grant a wish or cure a serious illness (West 1988, 224–25). Sometimes a family might dedicate a shrine to a suddenly departed member (e.g., a son killed in Vietnam) as a public sign of the family's grief.

As James Griffith (1992, 135–36) has observed in his study of beliefs and holy places in southern Arizona and northern Sonora, a shrine can evolve into a more public place of worship and devotion. For example, in a side yard of a Chicano home in South Tucson is a five-foot grotto dedicated to

St. Jude. A large three-foot statue of St. Jude is displayed within the half-domed grotto, which is in turn covered by a plastic and metal ramada. The cement slab kneelers and the ramada invite passersby to stop for a moment to visit the shrine and perhaps ask St. Jude to intercede on their behalf to grant a special favor.

Roadside shrines, similar in construction to yard shrines, or nichos cut out of the rock cliffs are also common in the Southwest, especially on the sides of secondary roads. Like yard shrines, they usually contain a statue of the Virgin, Christ, or a saint. Families build and maintain these shrines for many reasons that include building a visible and public memorial to a departed family member or dear friend or fulfilling a vow or promise. Given their placement in a public place, the shrines constitute an invitation to automobile occupants to stop at the side of the road for a moment to contemplate the personal and religious significance of the statues, images, and messages that are contained within. Unlike yard shrines, which are generally private and placed within a well-defined yard, roadside shrines are often filled with mementos, candles, holy cards, and *milagros* (miracles) that visitors have left behind in memory of their own dearly departed family and friends or in gratitude for an answer given to some prayer.

CEMETERY ART In addition to yards, semipublic locations, and roadsides, cemeteries are a location where shrines and other popular art forms are found. This is particularly true of cemeteries in small towns with a predominantly Chicano population or those in urban areas that have come to be identified as cemeteries where Chicanos bury their dead. Sometimes, a small shrine will be carved directly into the gravestone; other times it will be placed on top of the grave or twin shrines will be placed on either side of it (see figure 9). As in the case of yard shrines, the economic condition of the family is reflected in the simplicity or elaborateness of the shrine.

The Virgin Mary and Christ are the most common figures found in cemetery shrines, but both simple and decorated crosses are also common (see figure 10). Freestanding crosses made out of wood, stone, cement, iron (even painted industrial pipes) may serve as gravestones. These crosses range from very simple to very ornate, again reflecting a family's economic status (West 1988, 236).

MILAGROS Milagros (miracles) are tiny metal statues of religious figures or of objects such as parts of the human body (e.g., hands, feet, arms, eyes,

Fig. 9. A figure of El Santo Niño de Atocha painted on bright tile in Hurley Catholic Cemetery in New Mexico. (Photograph courtesy of Mildred Mead.)

and hearts), cars, houses, and even cows. They constitute another form of Chicano popular religious art that is omnipresent throughout the Southwest. They are found in Catholic churches on altars or by statues of the Virgin, Christ, or saints who are thought to have curative powers. They are also found in garden and roadside shrines. They are left in these places by

■ Fig. 10. Christ is often depicted in a red robe. This red-robed statue of Christ was photographed in the Lordsburg, New Mexico, cemetery. (Photograph courtesy of Mildred Mead.)

individuals who are either giving thanks or supplication for divine intercession to cure a disease or bring about some other favor (Oktavec 1995, xv).

Milagros fall into a category known as *ex-votos*, which in the Catholic Church are votive offerings left at a church or shrine to fulfill a vow to God, Christ, the Virgin, or a saint. In Mexico, one finds ex-votos in the form of retablos, not the kind painted on wood panels but ones painted on small pieces of tin, which is more durable than wood. It is common for those who believe in the power of miracles and divine intercession to leave life-size objects such as crutches, clothing, or even prosthetic devices at shrines such as the *santuario* (sanctuary) at Chimayo, New Mexico.

Silversmiths used to make the tiny milagros from silver and occasionally gold and sell them at their stores. Today, they are mass-produced by casting or stamping inexpensive gold or silver alloys, brass, copper, nickel, or occasionally aluminum. They can be purchased at a variety of stores, including religious supply stores located in or close to Chicano barrios (Oktavec 1995, 74).

Popular Secular Art

I begin my discussion of Chicano popular secular art in the twentieth century not because artists and artisans in the nineteenth century and earlier were not producing works of art, but because most of it was religious art. From among the many secular artists who have painted, sculpted, or used other forms of artistic expression, I have selected a few who seem the most representative of general trends in Chicano popular secular art and who have achieved widespread recognition. Much of the information on the following artists is taken from Jacinto Quirarte's pioneering book *Mexican American Artists* (1973).

MEL CASAS Mel Casas was born in El Paso in 1929, where he attended public schools and Texas Western College (now the University of Texas at El Paso), receiving a B.A. degree in 1956. He received his M.A. degree in 1958 from the University of the Americas in Mexico City. Casas has taught in El Paso and in other Texas cities. Television and movie screens are prominent in his art. For example, his well-known series of paintings called *Humanscapes,* along with more recent paintings, deal with cinema, television, and advertising and their power to teach rather than distort. His art during the 1970s was heavily focused on the sociopolitical and economic problems of the Chicano, the migrant, young people, and other groups of individuals he considered outsiders. He currently resides in San Antonio.

EDUARDO CARRILLO Eduardo Carrillo was born in Santa Monica in 1937. He attended Catholic grammar and high schools in Los Angeles and studied at UCLA, where he received a B.A. degree in 1962 and an M.A. degree in 1964. He began teaching at Sacramento State University in 1970 and was active in the Chicano Movement from the very beginning. He also taught at the University of California, Santa Cruz where, in 1981, he organized a conference for veteran Chicano artists. Carrillo has exhibited widely since 1962 throughout California, Texas, and Mexico. Many of his paintings comprise imaginary landscapes and figures. Critics have commented very favorably on his exquisite sense of space and spatial frameworks.

LUIS JIMÉNEZ   Luis Jiménez was born in El Paso in 1940. He studied architecture and art at the University of Texas at Austin, where he received a B.F.A. degree in 1964. He also traveled and studied in Mexico with the benefit of a scholarship from the National Autonomous University of Mexico. He has exhibited widely in one-man and group shows at museums and galleries on the East Coast, as well as in the Southwest. His commissioned sculptures are common sights outside both public and private buildings. His work has always been figurative, as reflected in some of his early murals and in the very large fiberglass and epoxy sculptures with high-gloss surfaces for which he is best known. He uses this medium to produce much larger-than-life human figures as well as modern machines such as cars and motorcycles, which he equates in his work with generative and destructive forces in nature. Jiménez lived for many years in New York but returned to New Mexico during the 1970s to devote himself to countering some of the negative stereotypes perpetuated by Western artists such as Frederic Remington. In this vein he created a series of memorable barrio types.

CÉSAR MARTÍNEZ   Born in Laredo in 1944, César Martínez is one of the most important and most active members of the contemporary Chicano art movement. He was educated through high school in the Laredo public schools. He received a B.S. degree from Texas A&I University in 1968. After several years in the Army, he moved to San Antonio, where he became active in the local arts scene as head of the cultural component of the Texas Institute for Educational Development. Along with San Antonio Chicano/a artists Amado Peña and Carmen Lomas Garza, he founded Los Quemados (The Burned-Out Ones) artists group. He began working with woodcuts in the 1970s, often focusing on Aztec themes and motifs. He is best known for his *Bato Series,* stunning depictions of street characters from the Chicano community. His paintings of *pachucos, batos* (young Chicano males), and *rucas* (young Chicana females) are composite recollections of individuals he has known rather than individual portraits. Martínez paints these figures as busts or half-figures against dark backgrounds that serve to emphasize their often proud and defiant demeanors. The figures' clothing and hairdos often are reminiscent of the 1940s and 1950s. The artist has based many of his characters on high school yearbooks, the media, and obituaries from these decades. Martínez is also well known for his *Mestizo Series,* a number of paintings in which he tries to capture the confluence of cultures that make up his own cultural heritage. In 1999, he accepted an invitation to become Visiting Artist at the University of Texas at San Antonio.

JUDITH BACA A pivotal figure in contemporary Chicano art, Judith Baca was born in 1946 in south-central Los Angeles but raised in Pacoima, where she spent her formative years in both public and Catholic schools. She received a B.A. degree from California State University, Northridge, in 1969 and an M.A. degree a few years later. She taught for a short time at the Catholic high school from which she had graduated, but she and several nuns and lay teachers were fired from their jobs for participating in anti–Vietnam War activities in the early 1970s. Baca worked for a time for the City of Los Angeles, teaching art to young people. She eventually organized a group of youth from different neighborhood gangs into an arts group that painted a mural in Hollenbeck Park. Her interest in mural art took her to Mexico City in the mid-1970s, where she studied mural materials and techniques. She also learned a great deal about the importance of Mexican muralism (which will be discussed later in the chapter) as a public and political act.

Upon her return to Los Angeles she organized the Citywide Mural Project, a project whose participants were youth from different ethnic and racial backgrounds. Baca supervised the painting of more than 250 murals throughout the city's poor neighborhoods. Her most ambitious and best-known project is the *Great Wall of Los Angeles,* a half-mile-long mural painted under her supervision on the concrete walls of a drainage canal. It is described in detail in the section on muralism.

At the same time that Baca was raising funds, hiring, and supervising the *Great Wall* project, she founded the Social and Public Art Resource Center (sparc) in Venice, California. The expressed purpose of this non-profit arts center is to involve artists, community groups, and young people in painting and preserving murals in multiethnic communities. In 1987,

Baca initiated her grand *World Wall: A Vision of the Future without Fear,* a portable mural made of seven very large panels painted by her and arranged in a one hundred–foot semicircle. She has toured with the mural in Finland and Russia, where she invited national artists to contribute to the mural by painting their own panels. Baca currently lives in Los Angeles, where she continues to promote and organize mural and other art projects among youth from different ethnic and racial backgrounds. She is also a professor of art at the University of California, Irvine.

CARMEN LOMAS GARZA   Born in Kingsville, Texas, in 1948, Carmen Lomas Garza was inspired artistically by her mother, a self-taught artist, and her father, a skilled artisan who worked in both sheet metal and wood. She received a B.A. degree from Texas A&I University in 1972, by which time she had already begun to establish her reputation as a fine artist with a unique style. She moved to California in the mid-1970s and continued her formal arts education at San Francisco State University, where she received an M.A. degree in 1980.

Using her trademark *monitos* (little figures), Garza's painting focuses almost exclusively on daily-life aspects of growing up surrounded by Chicano cultural traditions, both religious and secular. Her subjects have included cactus being gathered for Holy Week ceremonies, family activities such as board games, children playing, and home altars. Her paintings are like windows through which she invites the viewer to look and experience vicariously the ebb and flow of the life she remembers from growing up in south Texas. In her later work, she added much color to these scenes, but in the beginning they were starkly black and white.

Garza has exhibited her work widely but has also continued to identify herself strongly as a Tejana artist. She visits her home region frequently and exhibits her work in both local and urban museums in Houston and other cities. She has received several awards and fellowships from both public agencies and foundations, including the National Endowment for the Arts and the California Arts Council. Her first retrospective show, *Pedacito de mi corazón/A Little Piece of My Heart,* traveled to seven cities during 1992. She continues to be a productive artist and mentor to younger Chicanos who are interested in pursuing art as a career.

Muralism

Perhaps the most dynamic form of secular art is Chicano muralism: large paintings on the outside or inside walls of public buildings, schools, store-fronts, community and cultural centers, drainage channel walls, and just about any other space where art can be made available to the masses. By definition, this art is not hidden away in museums or in private collections. Mural art surged from the mid-1960s to the mid-1970s throughout the Southwest and particularly in California. It is still practiced today but in a less energetic way.

The name of this art form comes from the Spanish word for wall, *muro,* and its adjective form, *mural,* which is a cognate to the English adjective *mural.* Many cultures throughout history have practiced mural art, but Chicano muralism takes its inspiration from post-revolutionary Mexican muralism that, in turn, drew on the ancient artistic traditions of the Aztecs and other Mexican Indian civilizations.

MEXICAN MURALISM   The 1910–1920 Mexican Revolution was marked by a strong nationalist current that tended to reject European traditions in areas such as painting. Many of the young Mexican painters had histor-ically gone to France and other European countries to receive their artistic training, aspiring to incorporate into their own work the latest European trends. During and shortly after the revolution, they began returning to Mexico to join a nationalist wave that emphasized Mexico's indigenous cultures. Classically trained painters such as Diego Rivera, José Clemente Orozco, and David Alfaro Siqueiros—often referred to as *Los tres grandes* (The Three Great Ones)—joined the ranks of Mexican revolutionary cul-tural workers to resurrect the ancient muralist traditions. These and other painters rejected European gallery art in favor of public art. With the enthusiastic financial support and patronage of the new revolutionary gov-ernment and under the leadership of José Vasconcelos, its Minister of Education, they were encouraged to cover the exterior and interior walls of government buildings in and around Mexico City with paintings. Their murals emphasized revolutionary themes, including the exaltation of Mex-ico's indigenous cultures and the history of oppression that these cultures had suffered under the yoke of the Spanish (European) conquerors. The Mexican government has taken great care over the past eighty years to preserve these original murals as well as those painted later by Rivera, Orozco, Siqueiros, and many other muralists. The Mexican public today may view these paintings on the walls and staircases of several government ministries as well as on museums and schools in and around Mexico City.

All three Mexican muralists came to the United States at some point in their respective careers. Rivera was in the United states from 1930 to 1934. In 1931, he was contracted to paint several murals in the San Francisco Bay Area, including one on the wall of the San Francisco Stock Exchange Luncheon Club. He also painted a commissioned mural in the lobby of the Rockefeller Center in New York City in 1933. The mural was so controversial, in part because it contained the figure of Vladimir Lenin, that the Rockefeller family ordered it whitewashed just days after he unveiled it. (Rivera later re-created this mural at the Palace of Fine Arts in Mexico City.) Orozco spent the late 1920s and early 1930s in exile in the United States. In 1930 he accepted an art commission at Pomona College, where he painted Prometheus and other heroic figures. Siqueiros went into exile in 1930 and lived for a time in Los Angeles, where he taught mural painting at the Chouinard School of Art. He painted some controversial murals including one, *Meeting in the Street,* with a strong pro-union theme that caused an uproar in a city that was at the time strongly antiunion. His most famous Los Angeles mural, located in a barrio called Sonoratown, was called *Tropical America.* His depiction of a near-naked Indian boy on a cross surrounded by signs of the sixteenth-century Spanish conquest of Mexican Indians led to such a public outcry that local Los Angeles officials had the artist deported and the mural whitewashed.

THE INFLUENCE OF MEXICAN MURALISM ON CHICANO ARTISTS More than thirty years passed between these mural projects by Mexico's three master muralists and the Chicano art movement that began in the late 1960s. Some Chicano artists of the 1930s were, of course, familiar with Mexican muralism and at times studied under Rivera, Orozco, Siqueiros, and other muralists in Mexico and the United States. Most of the Chicano artists that were active during the 1960s and 1970s had not yet been born, however, and muralism had not continued as an unbroken artistic tradition in the United States in the intervening decades. Nonetheless, for reasons rooted deeply in the cultural nationalist ideology of the Chicano Movement, Chicano artists looked back on Mexican muralism in general and on its three masters for inspiration. The Marxist revolutionary themes of many of the works by Orozco, Rivera, and Siqueiros also resonated with the social activism of the Chicano Movement.

As discussed in chapter 5, the cultural nationalist ideology codified in "El Plan Espiritual de Aztlán," adopted at the March 1969 Chicano Youth

Conference in Denver, had a strong influence on different forms of Chicano popular culture. Art was also heavily influenced by the basic tenets of cultural nationalism, including its anti-Europeanism and the strong promotion of indigenous Indo-Mexican cultures. The plan also called for all Chicano artists to renounce their bourgeois values and to rededicate their artistic practices (music, media, visual arts, literature) to the people by producing art that appealed to the masses of Chicanos everywhere. At the same time, Chicano painters, graphic artists, sculptors, and photographers were influenced by the political agenda and artistic expression generated by Black Power and the American Indian Movement. Another influence was the strongly revolutionary messages conveyed through art—especially posters, billboards, and film—of the 1959 Cuban revolution that overthrew dictator Fulgencio Batista in 1959.

Young Chicano painters, energized by the political ferment of the 1960s, were encouraged to explore artistic traditions that supported their cultural nationalist philosophy, and Mexican muralism with its strong pro-Indian and social protest character provided a logical and compelling model. Artists began studying Mexican muralist painters and their brief but important presence in the United States in the 1930s. Siqueiros accepted several Chicano artists as interns at his Taller Siqueiros in Mexico City; one of the projects they assisted with was a poster devoted to the Chicano journalist Rubén Salazar, who had been killed in 1970 during the Chicano Moratorium anti–Vietnam War protest march in Los Angeles. Chicana painter Judith Baca was one of the Chicano painters who attended the Taller Siqueiros. Contemporary Mexican painter Rufino Tamayo also had a strong influence on Chicano artists, many of whom traveled to Mexico to view his large mural paintings at the Museum of Anthropology and elsewhere in Mexico City.

CHICANO MURALISTS' SOCIAL COMMITMENT Many artists, both ones with and without formal training, began mural projects throughout the Southwest in the late 1960s. According to Goldman and Ybarra-Frausto (1985, 83), Chicano muralism "began as a massive grassroots artistic explosion—the regional expression of a national phenomenon—that swept great numbers of trained and untrained people into artistic activity." The self-taught artist, the sign and billboard painter, the college art student, and the graffiti artist alike participated.

Unlike Mexican muralism of the 1920s and 1930s, which had been supported by government funding, Chicano muralism was a more spontaneous phenomenon. It began in urban neighborhoods where it enjoyed little financial and certainly no official government support. By 1985 there were more than two thousand murals in dozens of large and small cities in California alone, adorning buildings both inside and out. Other cities where murals are found are Crystal City, Dallas, San Antonio, Houston, Austin, and El Paso, Texas; Las Vegas, Santa Fe, and Albuquerque, New Mexico; Phoenix and Tucson, Arizona, Denver, Colorado; Chicago, Illinois; and several cities in Michigan. Some notable, professionally trained wall painters are Judith Baca and Willie Herrón of Los Angeles, Gilberto Guzmán of Santa Fe, Graciela Carrillo of San Francisco, Raúl Valdez of Austin, Rudy Treviño of San Antonio, Antonio Pazos and David Tineo of Tucson, Manuel Martínez of Colorado, and Leo Tanguma of Denver.

I should emphasize, however, that murals, at least most of those painted in the late 1960s and 1970s, were produced as collective works of art. A project typically would have an artistic director or consultant who would work with a small team of artists and/or community residents to produce a mural. Frequently, community input would be solicited to make sure that the mural's theme corresponded to community sentiments or accurately reflected their desires. Like El Teatro Campesino, the collective production of a work of popular art is very different from an individual painter working in the isolation of a studio to produce for a museum a work that reflects his or her worldview. At least in the beginning, muralists and their respective communities considered the production of mural art not as decorative but as art in the service of a social cause, a fundamentally revolutionary act that most frequently conveyed a strong and explicit message of social protest (see figure 11).

One of the earliest murals, painted by Antonio Bernal, covered the walls of the United Farm Workers union headquarters and paid tribute to César Chávez and his struggle to win better working conditions and a living wage for Chicano, Mexican, Filipino, and other migrant workers. In 1974, Mexican-born muralists painted a mural on the inside walls of the United Farm Workers union hall in San Juan, deep in the Lower Rio Grande Valley of Texas. It depicts the difficult life of farmworkers laboring under the watchful eye of the feared Texas Rangers, who are portrayed in the mural as overseers in complicity with the local growers. One side of the mural focuses on struggle while the other side celebrates victory as a Catholic priest witnesses the signing of a labor contract. Because the union

■ Fig. 11. Detail of a school mural, painted in the 1970s, depicting positive symbols of Chicano identity. Located in Tucson, Arizona. (Photograph courtesy of James S. Griffith.)

hall functions as a social center for the farmworkers, the mural attempts to make a strong connection with their plight by including them within the painting itself.

Murals figured early in the political struggles of urban barrios against established authority on any number of issues. One of the first known urban barrio murals was completed in 1970 in East Los Angeles by students at the UCLA Chicano Studies Center. This led to the formation in 1971 of the Mechicano Arts Center, made up of barrio artists who painted many murals throughout the area. One notable mural produced through the center is Willie Herrón's Ramona Gardens mural, which portrays through vivid colors the rage, anger, and frustration of youthful victims of drugs and police violence. The syringe is a dominant symbol in this and many other East Los Angeles murals. Another example of the treatment of urban issues in Chicano muralism is found in San Diego. Artists there painted murals in support of the Chicano Logan community, which was seeking more city-funded recreational space, including access to the ocean. One mural in a highly public place depicts unsightly junkyards; junkyards became the focus of the protest because they blocked access from Logan to San Diego Bay waters. In San Antonio, muralists painted a mural honoring a grassroots organization that had confronted the city council on numerous occasions on behalf of barrio dwellers (Romo 1992–1996, 141–43).

Malaquías Montoya, a Sacramento portrait and graphic artist, painted the first Chicano-produced mural in Mexico. The Colegio de la Frontera Norte and a local youth organization in Tijuana commissioned a mural at a schoolyard close to the Colegio and to the U.S.–Mexican border, a location that hundreds of Mexican and Central American undocumented workers pass by every day. The mural depicts a social history of Tijuana with emphasis on the powerful symbols of immigration, labor, and family. Montoya successfully depicts the thorny issue of immigration for both the Mexican and U.S. governments and how it affects not only the lives of dislocated undocumented workers but fundamentally life on the border itself.

Chicano muralists have often emphasized in their public art the exemplary heroism of both Mexican and Chicano leaders who have been in the forefront of resisting oppression. Mexican revolutionary heroes such as Pancho Villa and Emiliano Zapata figure prominently in murals, either in the foreground as central figures or in the background as part of a general tableau of Mexican history. For example, a large mural at an outdoor theater in Austin uses Zapata as a symbol of revolutionary struggle, a leader who can inspire the masses to political and military action. A mural in Houston shows *zapatistas* (Zapata's followers) resisting *federalistas* (Mexican federal troops) in one of the bloodiest confrontations of the Mexican Revolution. Los Angeles muralist Gil Hernández gives Zapata an exalted position next to Mexican muralist Siqueiros in an Estrada Court mural. Several murals in Los Angeles and San Antonio focus on Villa and his bravery during the many campaigns into which he led his famous cavalry, Los Dorados. Along with Zapata and Villa, Chicano folk heroes such as Juan N. Cortina and Gregorio Cortez have prominent roles in Chicano murals. One San Antonio mural depicts Cortina as a victim of the Texas Rangers who pursued him relentlessly after he organized an armed revolt against Texas authorities in 1859.

In addition to social and political scenes, many murals have religious themes and motifs, and some portray the Catholic Church very differently from the generally anti-ecclesiastical portrayals of the Mexican muralists. Rivera, Orozco, and Siqueiros tended to view the church and its agents (i.e., priests) as complicit with the Spanish crown and the military in subjugating Mexico's indigenous populations. Their views were very much in keeping with the official anti-ecclesiastical stances of Mexico's post-revolutionary governments and of the country's 1917 Constitution, which very drastically limited the power and influence of the Catholic Church in Mexico. Chicano muralists, on the other hand, tend to treat the church more benignly. When they do appear in murals, religious icons such as Christ, the Last Supper, the Apostles, and the Virgin of Guadalupe are generally portrayed positively. For example, Tucson muralist Antonio Pazos's mural, titled simply *Wall,* uses the Virgin of Guadalupe as a central organizing figure around which growing up young and Chicano in Tucson in the 1970s is the dominant theme.

Muralism continues to be a vibrant art form among Chicano artists and artistic communities today. Perhaps its best-known and most vigorous proponent is Judith Baca who, as previously mentioned, created the *Great Wall of Los Angeles* mural project. The giant mural, which narrates the multiethnic history of Los Angeles and the surrounding area from pre-historic times through about the 1950s, took around nine years to complete during the 1970s and 1980s. Painted on the concrete wall of the Tujunga Wash flood control channel in the San Fernando Valley, the mural is certainly about as distant as an artist could get from gallery or museum art. In addition to its subject matter, its venue, and its stunning colors, its collective nature—Baca supervised thirty artists who in turn worked with more than one hundred youths—was solidly in the tradition of both Mexican and Chicano muralism. In 1984, Baca and other muralists such as Willie Herrón and Frank Romero were commissioned to paint murals on freeway retaining walls, underpasses, and overpasses in honor of the 1984 Olympic Games in Los Angeles. The Social and Public Art Resource Center, which Baca founded in 1976, has continued to play an active role in training and sponsoring young mural artists and their projects throughout the city of Los Angeles and elsewhere in California. Two of these outstanding young artists are Yreina Cervántez and Juana Alicia, the latter a resident of San Francisco.

Graffiti Art

Like murals, graffiti is another form of popular art that is painted on exterior walls or other public surfaces. In 1990s, the general public, which knows little of the origins and development of graffiti, has come to associate it exclusively with the insignias that gangs use to designate their presence and territorial control in urban areas. This is, of course, one use of graffiti, but within Chicano culture graffiti insignias are a unique visual system developed by several generations of Chicano calligraphers.

GANG-RELATED GRAFFITI Marcos Sánchez-Tranquilino, an art historian who has studied this phenomenon, comments that graffiti is designed to keep a public check on the abuse of power in the streets. Based on his observations, he concludes that these insignias, known as *placas* or *plaqueasas,* are not random acts of vandalism. They are consciously written or spray-painted on external surfaces—usually buildings—on the periphery of youth gang territories, and their content follows an established system to convey information about the gangs that create them. The insignias are visible to everyone, but their content is encoded and can be read only by those individuals—typically gang members—who know and can interpret the code. To them, the graffiti conveys information about the name of the youth gang responsible for the inscriptions, its territorial size, and its fighting strength. The individual who has written or sprayed the placa on a surface identifies his or her nickname or battle name (e.g., El Gato [The Cat], La Loca [The Crazy One], El Oso [The Bear]) and status within the gang.

MURALISM AND GRAFFITI COMBINED For the past several decades, public officials and community groups have tried to discourage gangs from covering surfaces with their encoded graffiti. The whitewashing or erasure of the graffiti has been largely ineffective; soon after it is covered or removed from a public space, it reappears. In the 1970s with the popularization of mural art, officials in some cities launched projects supported by public funds to encourage barrio artists to replace graffiti with murals that convey a sense of cultural pride.

Sánchez-Tranquilino has carefully studied how this dynamic played out at Estrada Courts, one of the largest public housing projects in East Los Angeles. Between 1973 and 1978 the housing residents, with the assistance of trained Chicano artists, adorned many of the external walls of the project with marvelous murals ostensibly to cover up and replace graffiti that had existed on these walls since the project was built in 1941. In fact, as a result of the debate that ensued among artists, residents, and gang members, many of the Estrada Court murals incorporated placas in their visual portrayals of indigenous cultures, Mexican and Chicano history, revolutionary heroes, and social and political issues. Barrio calligraphers, who were quite adept at producing freestanding placas solely for gang use, were recruited as artists for the mural project. Rather than being co-opted by participating in a project to erase their own identity (the covering of placas), they became active contributors in creating a new art form that embedded insignias in murals (Sánchez-Tranquilino 1995).

What occurred at Estrada Courts and in other urban barrios of the Southwest puts another face on what the general public perceives to be the threatening nature of graffiti. I do not wish to imply that this perception does not have a strong basis in reality. Gang graffiti is not always art— perhaps rarely so—and most frequently it has no function other than to ward off opposing gangs from entering another gang's territory. But as illustrated in the Estrada Courts example, gang graffiti need not be perceived as always threatening but rather as an important component of post-1960s Chicano popular art.

Low Riders as Art

The adornment of cars, trucks, vans, motorcycles, and even bicycles with highly artistic figurative and symbolic paintings is another form of Chicano popular art that has proliferated in the past thirty years (see figure 12). The vehicle most commonly associated with this art is the lowrider car, which typically is decorated with a multicolor paint job, a crushed velvet interior, hydraulic suspension systems, a chain steering wheel, and other features that are dependent on the owner's ingenuity and ability to make a considerable investment in his or her car. Like graffiti and even mural art, the presence of low riders cruising "low and slow" through parks,

■ Fig. 12. Even bicycles are the objects of artistic expression. This highly chromed bicycle was exhibited at a 2000 Tucson lowrider car and truck show. (Photograph by Charles M. Tatum.)

boulevards, and shopping centers can produce either aversion or admiration in the onlooker. For the uninformed, low riders are often and mistakenly associated with youth gangs; for the admirer, these artworks on wheels signify prestige, mechanical expertise, and artistic competency. The car owners are not necessarily the mechanical wizards or artists responsible for converting a humdrum vehicle into a thing of beauty; there are talented mechanics and artists who specialize in creating such motorized marvels.

The interest in low riding surged in the late 1970s, primarily in Chicano urban communities of the Southwest, but low riders have existed since the late 1930s. Auto body repair shops in Sacramento and then in Los Angeles produced the first customized cars and trucks. Hydraulic lifts and a complex suspension system that give the driver the ability to raise, lower, and even bounce the car were not introduced until 1957. The media, including television, cinema, and newspapers, have given low riding much attention since the mid-1970s, and this attention has in part contributed to its popularity. Low riding spread quickly from California to small and large cities in Arizona, New Mexico, Colorado, and Texas. President Jimmy Carter declared National Low Riding Week in 1979. An unconfirmed rumor that circulated widely in the lowrider community was that he did so as a way to encourage drives across the country to decrease their speed and conserve gas by imitating low riders, who had established "low and slow" driving as a trademark (Museum of New Mexico 1999, 17).

The unlikely locale touted by some as the Low Rider Capital of the United States is Española, New Mexico, a very small city located within an hour's drive northwest of Santa Fe. Northern New Mexico in general has become "the hub for some of the most distinctive custom cars in the United States," states Carmella Padilla, who wrote the text for a stunning book of photographs of low riders and their vehicles published by the Museum of New Mexico (*Low 'n Slow,* 1999, 15). According to Padilla, the Smithsonian Institution recognized the importance of northern New Mexico low riders when its curators put a lowrider car from the area on permanent display in the National Museum of Natural History in Washington, D.C.

Low Rider Happening custom car shows in large southwestern cities have served to keep this phenomenon in the public eye and contribute to its thriving popularity among primarily Chicano car owners, custom car shops, and artists (see figure 13). It is common today to have lowrider vehicles of all types exhibited at Chicano celebrations on college campuses as well as at officially sanctioned community festivals such as at The Tucson Heritage Experience Festival, which recognizes the cultural contributions of the city's many and varied ethnic communities.

Low Rider Magazine has been in continuous publication since 1977. It provides news about the latest technical-mechanical innovations and a calendar of car shows and other activities of interest to low riders, as well as information on other popular cultural practices such as break dancing in the mid-1980s and hip-hop music in the 1990s. It has well more than 150,000 subscribers.

The rise of hip-hop music has also given renewed energy to the lowrider phenomenon because the vehicle is not only a portable mural but now also a motorized amplifier. It is common for low riders to outfit their cars, trucks, and even motorcycles with powerful and expensive amplification equipment that is turned on full blast as the low rider cruises a public street, park, or shopping center. The introduction of music in the lowrider repertoire provided a link to local radio stations, which often promote and even sponsor lowrider shows and other events while at the same time promoting the latest hip-hop release.

According to Brenda Jo Bright (1995, 109), who has studied various aspects of low riding, "For low riders, the car is a 'cultural vehicle.'" During the 1970s, many of the paintings on the bodies of lowrider vehicles

Fig. 13. The intricate patterns that adorn the sides, hood, and trunk of this lowrider car reflect the skill of the professional artists that are commissioned to display their works on cars and trucks. The car was exhibited at a 2000 Tucson lowrider car and truck show. (Photograph by Charles M. Tatum.)

incorporated themes of the Chicano Movement through images of the Virgin of Guadalupe, Aztec mythology, and Mexican Catholicism. Although these images persist more than twenty years later, they now compete with scenes of urban conflict and the depiction of contemporary Chicano and non-Chicano celebrities, such as the Joker from the 1989 *Batman* movie. In the movie, Jack Napier became the demented Joker when he was betrayed by his boss, the owner of a chemical plant. The particular lowrider mural cited by Bright is called the Joker's Revenge and its creator, an aerospace industry machinist—hardly a young, violent gang member—addresses the theme of the corporate-industrial world and its indifference to and often callous treatment of its employees. Bright views this and other paintings she has studied as "part of one current trend [1980s and 1990s] in low rider aesthetics toward the interpretation of experiences of alienation based upon metropolitan decline" (Bright 1995, 112).

In central Los Angeles, car murals "display unique and complex images that narrate metropolitan experience" (Bright 1997, 19). These murals tend to combine images from a variety of sources, including references to popular films as well as religious images, images that depict the wickedness of contemporary life (e.g., drugs, gambling, violence, police brutality), and images that exalt the family and *carnalismo* (brotherhood) (see figure 14). Bright also notes that the aesthetics of low riding—manifested in the degree of customization a vehicle undergoes, the sophistication of the paint-

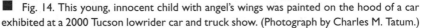 Fig. 14. This young, innocent child with angel's wings was painted on the hood of a car exhibited at a 2000 Tucson lowrider car and truck show. (Photograph by Charles M. Tatum.)

ings on its surface, the hydraulic system, and more recently the amplification system—change depending on the age and financial status of the owner. High school low riders tend to make less investment in their vehicles for two reasons: (1) they cannot afford the expensive equipment and adornments, and (2) they choose not to risk having their vehicles become targets of gang revenge. Older owners tend to have work and family demands that overshadow peer pressures, and they are generally more able to support their expensive pastime. The combination of murals, hydraulics, amplification systems, and other identifiable lowrider equipment and adornments becomes an extension of older owners' identity and status within their respective communities (Bright 1997, 19).

Performance Art

Not only is Chicano art painted on the exterior and interior walls of public and private buildings, the sides of concrete drainage channels, large portable panels, and motorized vehicles, but murals also became an essential part of another art form known as performance art, a combination of guerrilla or street theater, poetry, and art. One of the most important Chicano groups to practice mural/performance art was known as ASCO (nausea), founded by Willie Herrón, Gronk (Gluglio Nicandro), Patssi Valdez, and Henry Gamboa in 1972. Very much in keeping with the somewhat anarchistic and freewheeling "happenings" of the 1960s and early 1970s, ASCO's performances, such as *Walking Mural* or *Instant Mural,* were meant to shock and provoke the audience by juxtaposing actors' voices, art, and props in unconventional ways.

The group provided a very direct and explicit critique of social prejudice and racism directed at Chicanos as well as somewhat less severe indictments of Chicano artists who were perceived to practice mainstream art not in keeping with the social and artistic agenda of the Chicano Movement. Rather than being on stage or in venues normally defined as performance spaces, the group would perform on the streets and in full view of the public, even as part of a demonstration, picket line, or other form of protest. For example, when the police canceled an annual Christmas parade in East Los Angeles in 1971, ASCO staged a Christmas Eve procession down Whittier Boulevard, involving last-minute shoppers—most of them unwillingly—in their performance. They called their performance "Stations of the Cross" (a most holy Catholic ritual associated with Easter not Christmas) and featured one performer as Pontius Pilate, AKA Popcorn; Christ as *calavera,* or skeleton; and a zombie-like altar boy. This odd assemblage of performers walked a mile along one of the most upscale boulevards in Los Angeles, taunting and antagonizing consumers before placing their cardboard-box cross at the final station (of the cross), a U.S. Marine Corps recruiting station, and blessing the site with popcorn. The pun on *stations* conflated Christianity and the Vietnam War.

The following year, ASCO once again marched down Whittier Boulevard in their performance of "Walking Mural." The actors/performers/muralists were dressed as absurd mural characters: the Virgin of Guadalupe-in-

Black, a multifaced mural, and a Christmas tree wearing three inverted chiffon dresses. Among other things, this performance was intended to critique muralism as an inadequate strategy for reclaiming public spaces (Gamboa 1998, 9–10).

ASCO would typically use leaflets, picket signs, and graffiti as props in the service of their essentially subversive project to undermine established authority and question conventional social practices. ASCO also aimed its criticism at so-called progressive politicians and ideologues, including Chicano cultural nationalists, whom it criticized for ignoring gender and sexuality issues. After the group broke up in the late 1980s, all of its members continued producing murals or other art, and Gamboa and Herrón even founded Los Illegals, a punk rock band.

HARRY GAMBOA JR.   Harry Gamboa, one of the four members of ASCO, was born in the 1950s in Los Angeles. As one of the leaders of the Garfield High School walkouts (one of the six East Los Angeles high schools to participate in what is commonly referred to as the Blowout) in 1968, he committed himself early to political, artistic, and social causes. He became a practicing artist in the early 1970s as a student at California State University, Los Angeles, when he bought a camera with the aid of his Education Opportunity Grant and began taking pictures on the streets of East Los Angeles. In 1971, he became editor of *Regeneración* (Regeneration), a progressive Chicano campus/community newspaper and invited fellow students Patssi Valdez, Willie Herrón, and Gronk to collaborate on the artwork. Soon thereafter, the four students formed ASCO. In the 1970s, Gamboa was active in the emerging Los Angeles art scene. In 1978, he cofounded Los Angeles Contemporary Exhibitions (LACE), an artist-run gallery funded by the Comprehensive Employment and Training Act (CETA).

Gamboa functioned as an artist and social critic at the edge of what remained of the Chicano Movement and the artistic explosion to which it had given birth. Max Benavídez, a fellow Chicano artist, has identified him as being "at the edge, a card-carrying member of 'the elite of the obscure,' a transient celebrity from a phantom culture," whose schizophrenic satire serves as a metaphor for "the fractured age of unreason" (Gamboa 1998, 5).

ASCO's brand of performance art put Gamboa at odds with the established galleries and museums. The Los Angeles County Museum of Art rejected not only ASCO but also the request that Gronk, Gamboa, and Herrón made in 1972 to have the museum include Chicano art in its collection and exhibitions. Completely in keeping with their character as radical artists, ASCO responded by spray-painting the museum with their signatures. As Noriega has noted, Gamboa "has been a pioneer of multimedia and hybrid formats for nearly three decades, from photo-based to mixed-media performance to conceptual video" (Gamboa 1998, 7). Gamboa has also written more than seventy essays, dramatic pieces, fiction works, and poetry, which Noriega has collected in an informative and insightful book (Gamboa 1998).

GUILLERMO GÓMEZ-PEÑA   Guillermo Gómez-Peña is another important Chicano performance artist whose performance works, like those of Gamboa, are designed to shock, provoke, and lead his audiences to question established values, conventions, politics, and practices. He was born in Mexico City and came to the United States in 1978. He works with the San Diego Border Art Workshop in mounting installations and producing theater that deals with U.S.–Mexican border issues. Gómez-Peña's performance art also deals with border issues but in a more conceptual and abstract way. The border becomes a multifaceted cultural encounter that produces multiple identities on both sides of the border. He is one of the editors of *High Performance* magazine and of the *Drama Review*. He has received many awards and recognitions, including a MacArthur Fellowship (1991), the Prix de la Parole award at the International Theater Festival of the Americas, and an American Book Award for his book *The New World Order* (1997).

Chon Noriega (2000, 13) observes that Gómez-Peña's self-identification as a "cross-cultural diplomat" is important because it does not tie him to either Chicano nationalism or to the border as a specific site as is the case for other Chicano writers and intellectuals whose view of the dynamics of the border is more narrowly proscribed.

Chicano Art in Museums and Cultural Centers

Up to this point, I have emphasized Chicano art that is, by its very nature, public, as well as Chicano artists who have produced art for a primarily non-elite Chicano audience. Although there were exceptions—I have noted a few in my discussion of individual artists—by and large Chicano art, especially art with strong social content, was excluded from private galleries and from the permanent collections of public and private museums until the late 1980s. The same is generally true of exhibitions from about 1965 to 1980 that were organized, staffed, and curated by Chicano artists affiliated with community art galleries, cultural centers, or artists' groups. In most cases, little public or private funding was available to mount exhibitions of Chicano work.

The earliest exhibitions were organized, as would be expected, in large urban areas such as San Francisco, Los Angeles, and San Antonio under names that referred to the organizers' and artists' strong commitment to social justice: "Pintores de la Nueva Raza" (Painters for a New People), "Mexican American Liberation Art Front," "Con Safos and Los Quemados," "Mujeres Muralistas" (Women Muralists), and "Arte de la Jente (sic)" (Art of the People). Later, Chicano curators and art historians succeeded in arranging for cultural centers and university museums and galleries to exhibit Chicano art, and eventually a small number of large public museums agreed to host modest exhibitions.

The CARA Exhibit

Unprecedented in its time was the *Chicano Art: Resistance and Affirmation, 1965–1985* exhibit (most commonly known by its acronym CARA). This very large touring exhibition was unique in at least four ways:

1. From the earliest planning phase, a large number of Chicano artists, university professors, art historians, and community leaders gave input in developing the conceptual framework for the exhibition and the selection of artists who would eventually be included.

2. The staff of a major university gallery, the UCLA Wight Art Gallery, agreed to partner with CARA's various committees and groups: the National Executive Committee, the National Selection Committee, the Editorial Board, the regional chairs, several national task forces, the mayors' group, and the Mexican consuls general.

3. The exhibition's 1990–1993 tour was national in scope and included public museums in ten cities: Los Angeles (it opened at the UCLA Wight Gallery), Denver, Albuquerque, San Francisco, Fresno, Tucson, Washington, D.C., El Paso, the Bronx, and San Antonio.

4. Its scope was large, featuring 128 pieces of art and 54 mural images by 140 Chicano and 40 Chicana artists.

In her book-length study of the entire process of organizing, selecting, and curating the CARA exhibition, Alicia Gaspar de Alba (1998, 8) comments that its "unique significance and contribution to the history of Chicano/a art exhibitions, then, is not just its presence in public museums across the country, but rather . . . its resistance to traditional museum and market practices, its complex organizational structure, its politics of self-representation, and its reception by the different communities that it addressed and/or confronted."

■ Celebrations

Celebrations continue to be important events in the religious and civic life of Chicano communities. They provide a visible and effective way of maintaining and even strengthening traditions that have their roots in Spanish and later Mexican popular cultural practices. At the same time, they serve an important social function of allowing communities to maintain a collective identity as a people separate from the mainstream culture.

Religious Celebrations

Perhaps the most important and vital celebrations are those festive activities associated with the Christmas season (December 12 to January 16). Popular religious dramas are performed annually along the U.S.–Mexican border during this time. Another very important religious celebration is El Día de los Muertos (Day of the Dead). It is celebrated on November 1 (All Saints' Day) and November 2 (All Souls' Day).

CHRISTMAS SEASON CELEBRATIONS *Las Posadas* (the inns) is a religious drama performed in many rural towns and villages as well as in urban Spanish-speaking parishes either two weeks before Christmas or on Christmas Eve, often as a prelude to another Christmas drama *Los Pastores* (the shepherds). The Virgin Mary and Joseph's search for an inn prior to the birth of the Christ Child is reenacted: Groups of parishioners follow actors from house to house only to be denied lodging at each, until one designated house or the parish church itself welcomes them in. At each house, the refrain "No habrá posadas" (There is no room at the inn) is repeated until finally a welcoming response is given. Sometimes the denials and the welcome are sung. In some communities, a manger is set up either inside or outside (depending on the weather) the designated house or parish church as part of the welcoming ceremony.

Traditionally, bonfires called *iluminarias* were lit at each house to guide the actors and the parishioners (symbolically, to guide Mary and Joseph). These bonfires evolved into *luminarias* when paper sacks became available early in the eighteenth century. The paper sacks were filled with enough sand to provide balance and to keep a lit candle in place. Today, luminarias have been adopted as Christmas ornaments by the general population, and in some households the driveway and pathway leading to the main entrance of the house are lined with them. It is also quite common to see stores and whole shopping malls adopt the practice, except that electric lights in plastic facsimiles of paper bags substitute for candles and paper bags.

Los Pastores is probably the most popular religious folk drama and the most widespread throughout the Southwest. It is also performed in parts of the Rocky Mountain area and the Midwest where there are concentrations of Chicanos. Sometimes the play is performed by professional theater troupes, but most frequently the actors are local parishioners.

This popular folk drama follows in a general way the version of the Christmas story contained in the second chapter of the Gospel of Luke in the New Testament. Sometimes it incorporates *Las Posadas*. For example, once Mary and Joseph have been rejected at the various "inns," they seek shelter in a cave or in a stable near Bethlehem. After the angel announces the birth of the Christ Child, the shepherds appear on stage. (The stage for this and other folk dramas is not always the traditional proscenium stage we might imagine but rather an improvised setup.) The shepherds make their way to the birthplace guided by a star, bring gifts to the Christ Child, and sing his praises. In some versions, Lucifer and his allies make an appearance and try to impede the progress of the shepherds to Bethlehem. Some versions are serious and reverent whereas others are humorous, sometimes even raucous.

Borderlands Theater, an alternative theater located in Tucson, Arizona, has for the past few years performed its own version entitled *A Tucson Pastorela.* As a socially committed theater, Borderlands each year changes the script to incorporate references to local and regional events and political figures. Needless to say, Lucifer—who is sometimes a man, sometimes a woman—embodies not simply evil in an abstract biblical sense, but evil in terms of some particularly heinous act of criminality or injustice that may have occurred in Tucson during the past year. *A Tucson Pastorela,* which invites active audience participation, is energetic, uplifting, and filled with song and good humor. It is an excellent enactment of an age-old folk drama, a vital example not only of the survival of traditional Spanish folk drama but of its ability to adapt to contemporary circumstances. Although each year the play contains much social satire, it never loses sight of its essentially religious character, and at the end it returns to the central event: the celebration of the birth of Christ.

THE DAY OF THE DEAD CELEBRATION El Día de los Muertos is when many devout Catholic families congregate at *camposantos* (graveyards) across the Southwest to honor and commune with their dead. They bring tools to clean the gravesites, shrines, crosses, and gravestones, and flowers to adorn the final resting places of the dearly departed.

The custom of paying tribute to the dead is worldwide and is celebrated by different cultures on various dates of the year, including October 1 and the Lunar New Year (West 1988, 153–54). The cleaning of the graves and gravesites has a practical function in the Southwest that is related to the generally low economic status of working-class Chicanos. Most either cannot afford or prefer not to bury their dead in cemeteries that hire grounds-keepers to perform these duties.

Following a practice firmly rooted in Mexican culture and still practiced on a limited basis in Mexico, many Chicano families also occasionally celebrate a meal at the gravesites once they have been cleaned and restored to their original state. This practice is strongly associated with the belief that on All Souls' Day, the souls of the loved ones come "home" for a visit and therefore should be welcomed with a meal. And even if families no longer partake of a meal at the cemetery, they still buy and consume *pan de muertos* (bread of the dead) in memory of the deceased. These large, round, flat loaves of cakelike bread are readily available at traditional Mexican bakeries in southwestern cities such as Houston, San Antonio, El Paso, Tucson, and Los Angeles. Another delicacy that is readily available in Mexico and in some southwestern towns and cities are *calaveras,* spun-sugar skulls, often with children's names written across the foreheads. Calaveras are given as gifts to children just like any other candy or delicacy given on a special day. They may be purchased at bakeries, candy stores, or from vendors outside of cemeteries. Calaveras are also sent to friends and public figures to poke fun at their foibles or politics, much as a comic birthday card or valentine might be sent in mainstream culture. The calaveras serve as a stark reminder that all of us, regardless of our temporary positions of power or state of wealth, will eventually become skeletons—death is the great leveler (West 1988, 155–56).

Some of the Day of the Dead practices may seem morbid to non-Chicanos, and some Chicanos may themselves not be entirely comfortable with the practices. The same is true in Mexico whence the Day of the Dead celebration springs. It would be simplistic to say that Mexicans in general have a different concept of death and a more comfortable relationship with the dead than Anglos. Still, the Day of the Dead is in general a happy celebration of family and fond memories of loved ones.

Secular Celebrations

Among the most important popular secular celebrations are *fiestas patrias* (patriotic fiestas) and *charreadas* or *fiestas charras* (equestrian events). *Piñatas, cascarones,* and paper flowers are not properly speaking celebrations in their own right, but they are so closely associated with several religious and secular celebrations that they deserve a brief mention.

FIESTAS PATRIAS   The fiestas patrias that Chicanos celebrate are firmly tied to the two most important Mexican national holidays: Cinco de Mayo (May 5) commemorates the victory of Mexican troops over French invading forces at the Battle of Puebla on May 5, 1862; and Dieciséis de Septiembre (September 16) celebrates Mexico's independence from Spain on September 16, 1821. Both celebrations have experienced a substantial growth in popularity since the mid-1960s, when many Chicanos experienced a process of politicization and a renewed pride in their Mexican cultural traditions. They have become rituals of ethnic solidarity. It is common for the Mexican flag to be flown proudly along with the U.S. and state flags. Cities such as San Antonio, Tucson, Los Angeles, and San Francisco celebrate these important dates in Mexican history in a variety of ways. Common to all of them, however, are speeches by politicians, Mexican music of different types, including *mariachi* and *norteña* (more recently, rock music and Latin American music such as *salsa, merengue,* and *cumbia* are played), and foods associated with the northern Mexican states. Examples are tamales, enchiladas, *carne adobada* (meat marinated in red chile), *barbacoa* (barbecue), and the omnipresent corn or flour tortillas.

It is also common to see other symbols of Mexico such as the *charro* (Mexican cowboy) dressed in an elegantly tailored jacket and pants and large hat, and his partner, the *china poblana,* dressed in a white peasant blouse and wide red skirt featuring the Mexican eagle. The Sixteenth of September holiday may also feature the *grito,* or patriotic speech, which simulates the 1810 rallying cry issued by Miguel Hidalgo y Costilla, a Catholic priest whom Mexicans and Chicanos consider as having initiated the Mexican struggle for independence from Spain. It is also common for the Chicano community to sponsor a parade that features strolling mariachis, charros and chinas poblanas mounted on horseback, floats representing different clubs and groups, and politicians and community leaders waving to the admiring crowds from the backs of convertibles (Nájera-Ramírez 1994, 335–36).

CHARREADAS Charreadas or fiestas charras are equestrian events somewhat analogous to rodeos but with greater pomp and ritual. *Charrería* originated in Spain and has persisted in Mexico and in the American Southwest, where it is enormously popular today. In the border states of Texas, New Mexico, Arizona, and California, associations were formed in the 1950s and 1960s for the practice and promotion of charreada. Such associations, which thrive across the Southwest today, provided a way of maintaining strong cultural ties with Mexico while continuing the tradition of skilled horsemanship. Today there are almost a hundred associations in the United States that sponsor hundreds of charreadas every year.

Despite this impressive activity, these celebrations are largely unknown outside of the Chicano community. According to Kathleen Mullen Sands (1993, 4) who has written a fine book on the subject:

> Charreada is a public demonstration of a complex folk tradition that dates back to seventeenth century Mexico and finds its sources in medieval Spain. It incorporates and upholds basic Mexican norms of bravery and patriotism, discipline and mastery of complex equestrian skills, folk arts in the elaborately decorated horse trappings and costumes, family and community cooperation, and the value of work in rural ranching society; and it fosters an enduring ethnic identity.

Charreadas typically take place on Saturday and Sunday afternoons, when competitors, their friends and family, and spectators gather at a *lienzo* (arena) for several hours of competition in different events followed by a dinner. The charro dresses in a tailored shirt with a butterfly tie, tight chaps over pants with embroidered designs, a waist-length suede jacket, and a wide-brimmed hat. The female counterpart of the charro, the *esca-ramuza,* wears a colorful, highly decorated dress, high boots, and a high-crowned sombrero. With highly tooled saddles and stirrups, colorful saddle blankets, and finely worked reins and bits, the horses' trappings are as elegant as those of their riders. Before the competition starts, the riders parade around the lienzo and before the judges who signal the start of the charreada.

The events of the charreada are all rooted in the dominance of man (women participate in other events of the charreada) over animal, in this case, horses and bulls. Teams rather than individuals compete against each other in several events.

POPULAR DECORATIVE ARTS   Piñatas, cascarones, and paper flowers are associated with a variety of fiestas. Piñatas are hollow, hanging papier-mâché figures (animal, vegetable, mythological, architectural, human, almost anything goes) covered with strips of brightly colored paper. Filled with candy, small toys, and other objects including coins, they are designed to keep young children entertained at birthday parties and other celebrations (e.g., Las Posadas during the Christmas season).

Typically, the piñata is suspended from a rope looped over a ceiling beam or tree branch. An adult has the role of raising or lowering the piñata as blindfolded children (the very youngest are not blindfolded) take turns swinging at the suspended figure with a bat or wooden stick until one of them succeeds in tearing a hole in the soft papier-mâché body and the candy and other goodies come spilling out. At that point, all the young children leap into the fray to collect as much as they can from the remnants of the piñata. Mishaps may occur when one of the participants strays too close to the blindfolded child and gets whacked, or when an overly aggressive child becomes too physical in collecting more than his or her share of the goodies.

Cascarones are colored and sometimes brightly decorated eggshells filled with confetti. Families prepare for months before a celebration by carefully blowing out the contents of each egg through a small hole in the bottom. The eggshells are then dried, decorated, filled with confetti, and saved for the celebration (usually but not exclusively Easter), when children take their store of cascarones and smash them over the heads of other children and adults. Occasionally, some mischievous individual slips an uncooked egg in with the confetti-filled ones, and somebody is forced to leave the celebration early to clean up.

Artificial flowers made from paper and other materials are also found at many religious and secular celebrations. They are used to decorate food booths at fiestas, floats in parades, and to cover arches and bowers at wedding receptions and anniversaries, but their most important use is on altars and graves. In southern Arizona, Chicanos as well as members of the Yaqui and Tohono O'odham nations make the flowers from colored tissue paper, ribbon, yarn, or bits of discarded plastic, or they may purchase commercially produced plastic or silk blossoms imported from Southeast Asia (Griffith 1988, 34–35).

Other Popular Traditions

Chicanos have a rich oral tradition. Many popular folktales are still part of a thriving storytelling tradition in rural areas such as the Texas Rio Grande Valley, northern New Mexico, and southern Colorado as well as in urban areas such as San Antonio, Tucson, and Los Angeles. Another fascinating aspect of the popular folk culture of the Southwest is its deep reservoir of proverbs or popular sayings (*dichos* or *refranes*) and jokes.

FOLKTALES Chicanos have maintained a long tradition of popular folktales rooted in the traditional Spanish and (later) Mexican tales that have been passed on from generation to generation since the arrival of the Spanish in the Southwest in the sixteenth century. Between the 1930s and the 1950s several folklorists set about collecting and analyzing these tales. In general, folklorists discovered that all types and classes of folktales found in Spain were also found in the Southwest: riddle tales, moral tales, religious tales, tales of adventure, demon and ogre tales, tales of persecuted women, picaresque (trickster) tales, animal tales, and others. Although most of the surviving tales have evolved over the centuries, their similarity to original Spanish versions of the sixteenth century and earlier attest to the continuous Hispanic presence in the Southwest since the 1700s.

La Llorona (the wailing woman) is one category of tales that is found throughout the Southwest. Hundreds of local versions exist, most of which revolve around the mysterious appearance of a grieving woman who supposedly has returned from the dead in search of the children whom she herself has killed. Many versions associate the grieving woman with a body of water (e.g., a lake or river) where she is supposed to have drowned her children. Some versions have the woman returning to search for and destroy the man who is responsible for driving her to kill her children. Other times, she is depicted as a sinful woman who killed her children to pursue her own selfish interests. Much like the bogeyman in other cultures, La Llorona is used by parents to scare their children into desired behaviors (e.g., "If you don't come home by dark, La Llorona is going to get you." "If you continue playing by the irrigation ditch, La Llorona is going to drown you.").

PROVERBS AND JOKES   It is often said that a people's values, attitudes, philosophy of life, and worldview are embedded in its language. From small mountain villages in southern Colorado or northern New Mexico to the barrios of Los Angeles, dichos and refranes are a thriving component of Chicano oral culture.

The majority of dichos are proverbs that express truisms. They have relatively fixed forms and have some of the characteristics of traditional poetry, such as rhythm, rhyme, and alliteration. Folklorists have documented that many Chicano dichos are derived from the rich peninsular Spanish folk tradition that came to the New World. It is therefore common to hear these dichos spoken in Spain as well as throughout Spanish America today. Some dichos spoken in Mexico or the Southwest are adaptations of the original Spanish proverbs, and others are original to particular areas such as the Texas-Mexican border or California.

The most common dichos heard among Chicano speakers of Spanish are words of wisdom or advice (West 1988, 39). These popular proverbs acquire greater meaning when they are used in conversation or in writing within a specific set of circumstances. Proverbs are often used to embellish upon a point or to make a point in a conversation more dramatically or more concisely. Sometimes parents use them in conversation with their children in order to give them a moral lesson or perhaps an easily remembered formula that could guide them in their lives.

Linguists and aware educators are always concerned that the rich mix of popular tales, sayings, jokes, and other forms of popular speech will disappear if Chicanos do not maintain their proficiency in Spanish. This is especially true of younger second- or third-generation Chicanos who as children were exposed to Spanish in the home because their older relatives spoke it to them on a regular basis, but who have become less proficient as English supplanted Spanish during their formative years in school. On the other hand, the influx of Mexican and other Latin American immigrants together with family visits to Mexico are likely to continue to reinforce proficiency in Spanish even among young Chicanos. Spanish is quickly becoming the second language of the United States, and in some regions along the border it is arguably the first language. I am therefore optimistic that Spanish in all its richness will not only be maintained but strengthened in the twenty-first century.

◼ Discussion Questions

1. Describe the different purposes that popular religious art has served historically as well as in contemporary society.

2. What contributions has Judith Baca made to contemporary Chicano popular art?

3. Discuss the origin of Chicano muralist art.

4. What theory of popular culture best explains Chicano muralism and graffiti art?

5. In what way is the creation of Chicano muralism similar to El Teatro Campesino's production of actos?

6. Describe the content of Chicano muralism.

7. What are the similarities and differences between muralism, graffiti, and the art that adorns lowrider cars, trucks, and other vehicles?

8. What is performance art and what different art forms does it draw on?

9. Discuss what was unique about the CARA exhibit and how it was organized.

10. Describe some popular Chicano religious and secular celebrations that have survived into the twenty-first century.

◼ Suggested Readings

Bright, Brenda Jo. 1995. Remappings: Los Angeles Low Riders. In *Looking High and Low: Art and Cultural Identity,* eds. Brenda Jo Bright and Liza Bakewell, 89–123. Tucson: University of Arizona Press.

Goldman, Shifra, and Tomás Ybarra-Frausto, comp. 1985. *Arte Chicano: A Comprehensive Annotated Bibliography of Chicano Art, 1965–1981.* Berkeley: University of California, Berkeley, Chicano Studies Library Publications Unit.

Griffith, James S. 1988. *Southern Arizona Folk Arts.* Tucson: University of Arizona Press.

——. 1992. *Beliefs and Holy Places: A Spiritual Geography of the Pimería Alta.* Tucson: University of Arizona Press.

Griswold del Castillo, Richard, Teresa McKenna, and Yvonne Yarbro-Bejarano, eds. 1991. CARA. *Chicano Art: Resistance, and Affirmation.* Los Angeles: UCLA Wight Gallery.

Quirarte, Jacinto. 1973. *Mexican American Artists.* Austin: University of Texas Press.

West, John O. 1988. *Mexican-American Folklore: Legends, Songs, Festivals, Proverbs, Crafts, Tales of Saints, of Revolutionaries, and More.* Little Rock: August House.

Conclusion

I hope that you have enjoyed this rapid journey through Chicano popular culture and that you have come away from it with a greater awareness of popular culture as a fascinating and intellectually challenging field of study. In particular I hope you have gained a deeper appreciation for and understanding of the multiple ways that a people struggles mightily to survive, resist, and give expression to its values, traditions, beliefs—its very being—in the face of the continuous threat of domination by another culture. I have tried to show that Chicanos successfully established themselves culturally very early on in their history by drawing on deeply rooted traditions and that they have persisted as an identifiable ethnic minority group in the United States over the past 150 years. They continually developed new and creative forms of popular expression in response to difficult socioeconomic circumstances or to new media and technologies in a rapidly changing world.

I recognize that my survey of Chicano popular culture has been neither comprehensive nor thorough. Although I have attempted to include many of the forms of popular expression that are the most important culturally and historically, I have had to omit others due to limitations of space. There is plenty of material to fill an expanded volume or even a second book on Chicano popular culture. I might, for example, have included an extensive discussion of the origins, preparation, and evolution of the seemingly infinite varieties of food consumed throughout the Southwest as well as in population centers in the Northwest, Midwest, and East Coast where there are significant concentrations of Americans of Mexican descent. I might also have devoted a chapter to a more systematic treatment of humor (although I did touch on this aspect of Chicano culture in several chapters). Along with humor, I would naturally discuss Chicano comedians and comedic traditions. I might also have included a chapter on sports and sports figures.

My intent has been to give you a taste of popular culture, not a full meal. As I have reminded you frequently throughout this volume, scholars have thoroughly studied many aspects of each popular culture form I have chosen to discuss. I have drawn very heavily on the work of these scholars and invite readers to consult the "Suggested Readings" and "Works Cited" sections if they wish to explore a particular topic in more depth. In fact, perhaps the measure of my success in writing this book will be the extent to which I have stimulated your intellectual curiosity sufficiently to motivate you to do your own research.

■ Works Cited

Adorno, Theodor W. 1975. Culture Industry Reconsidered. *New German Critique* 6: 495–514.

Althusser, Louis. 1971. *Lenin and Philosophy and Other Essays.* New York: Monthly Review Press.

Alurista. 1971. *Floricanto en Aztlán.* Los Angeles: Chicano Studies Center of UCLA.

——. 1972. *Nationchild Plumaroja.* San Diego: Toltecas en Aztlán Publications.

——. 1976. *Timespace Huracán: Poems, 1972–1975.* Albuquerque: Pajarito.

Anaya, Rudolfo. 1972. *Bless Me, Ultima.* Berkeley: Quinto Sol Publications.

——. 1976. *Heart of Aztlán.* Berkeley: Editorial Justa.

——. 1979. *Tortuga.* Berkeley: Editorial Justa.

——. 1992. *Albuquerque.* New York: Warner Books.

——. 1995. *Zia Summer.* New York: Warner Books.

——. 1996. *Rio Grande Fall.* New York: Warner Books.

——. 1999. *Shaman Winter.* New York: Warner Books.

Anzaldúa, Gloria. 1999. *Borderlands/La frontera.* 2d ed. San Francisco: Aunt Lute Books.

Avalos Torres, Héctor. 1989a. Gary Soto. In *Dictionary of Literary Biography.* Vol. 82. *Chicano Writers,* eds. Francisco A. Lomelí and Carl R. Shirley, 246–52. First Series. Detroit: Gale Research.

——. 1989b. Gloria Anzaldúa. In *Dictionary of Literary Biography.* Vol. 122. *Chicano Writers,* eds. Francisco A. Lomelí and Carl R. Shirley, 8–16. Second Series. Detroit: Gale Research.

Barrios, Greg. 1985. Alambrista! A Modern Odyssey. In *Chicano Cinema: Research, Reviews, and Resources,* ed. Gary D. Keller, 165–67. Tempe, Ariz.: Bilingual Review/Press.

Bright, Brenda Jo. 1995. Remappings: Los Angeles Low Riders. In *Looking High and Low: Art and Cultural Identity,* eds. Brenda Jo Bright and Liza Bakewell, 89–123. Tucson: University of Arizona Press.

——. 1997. Nightmares in the New Metropolis: The Cinematic Poetics of Low Riders. *Studies in Latin American Popular Culture* 16: 13–29.

Broyles-González, Yolanda. 1994. *El Teatro Campesino: Theater in the Chicano Movement.* Austin: University of Texas Press.

Burr, Ramiro. 1995. Growth of Labels: Radio and Mass Merchandizing Cap a Fifth Year of Phenomenal Growth. *Billboard Magazine* September 2: 39, 42, 44, 46.

Campa, Arthur L. 1946. *Spanish Folk Poetry in New Mexico.* Albuquerque: University of New Mexico Press.

Castro, Rafaela. 1982. Mexican Women's Sexual Jokes. *Aztlán* 13 (1–2): 275–93.

Chávez, Denise. 1986. *The Last of the Menu Girls.* Houston: Arte Público Press.

Chávez, Fray Angélico. 1940. *New Mexico Triptych. Being Three Panels and Three Accounts: 1. The Angel's New Wings; 2. The Penitente Thief; 3. The Hunchback Madonna.* Patterson, N.J.: St. Anthony Guild Press.

———. 1957. *From an Altar Screen; El Retablo: Tales from New Mexico.* New York: Farrar Straus and Cudahy.

———. 1974. *My Penitente Land: Reflections on Spanish New Mexico.* Albuquerque: University of New Mexico Press.

Christian, Jane McNab, and Chester C. Christian Jr. 1966. Spanish Language and Culture in the United States. In *Language Loyalty in the United States,* ed. Joshua Fishman. The Hague: Mouton and Co.

Christon, Lawrence. 1991. Breaking the Chains. *Los Angeles Times,* Calendar section, 1 September: 4ff.

Cisneros, Sandra. 1983. *The House on Mango Street.* Houston: Arte Público Press.

Cockcroft, Eva Sperling, and Holly Barnet-Sánchez, eds. 1996. *Signs from the Heart: California Chicano Murals.* Albuquerque: University of New Mexico Press; Venice, Calif.: Social and Public Art Resource Center.

Colahan, Clark. 1989. Sandra Cisneros. In *Dictionary of Literary Biography.* Vol. 82. *Chicano Writers.* eds. Francisco A. Lomelí and Carl R. Shirley, 86–90. First Series. Detroit: Gale Research.

Corpi, Lucha. 1982. *Eulogy for a Brown Angel.* Houston: Arte Público Press.

———. 1995. *Cactus Blood.* Houston: Arte Público Press.

———. 1999. *Black Widow's Wardrobe.* Houston: Arte Público Press.

Corwin, Miles. 1989. A Voice for Farmworkers. *Los Angeles Times* 20 August: 3, 33.

De León, Arnoldo. 1983. *They Called Them Greasers: Anglo Attitudes Towards Mexicans in Texas, 1821–1900.* Austin: University of Texas Press.

Doss, Yvette C. 1998. Choosing Chicano in the 1990s: The Underground Music Scene of Los(t) Angeles. *Aztlán* 23 (2): 191–202.

Espinosa, Aurelio. 1927. Los tejanos. *Hispania* 27: 219–314.

———. 1985. *The Folklore of Spain in the American Southwest. Traditional Spanish Folk Literature in Northern New Mexico and Southern Colorado.* ed. J. Manuel Espinosa, Norman and London: University of Oklahoma Press.

———, ed. 1907. Los comanches. *University of New Mexico Bulletin* 1 (1): 5–46.

Espinosa, J. Manuel. 1937. *Spanish Folk Tales from New Mexico.* Memoirs of the American Folklore Society 30. New York: G. E. Strechert and Co.

Eysturoy, Annie O. 1996. *Daughters of Self-Creation: The Contemporary Chicana Novel.* Albuquerque: University of New Mexico Press.

Fiske, John. 1989. *Reading the Popular.* Boston: Unwin and Hyman.

Fregoso, Rosa Linda. 1990. Born in East L.A. and the Politics of Representation. *Cultural Studies* 4 (3): 264–80.

———. 1993. *The Bronze Screen: Chicana and Chicano Film Culture.* Minneapolis: University of Minnesota Press.

Gamboa, Harry Jr. 1998. *Urban Exile: Collected Writings of Harry Gamboa, Jr.* Chon A. Noriega, ed. Minneapolis: University of Minnesota Press.

García Canclini, Néstor. 1982. *Las culturas populares en el capitalismo.* México, D.F.: Editorial Nueva Imagen.

Gaspar de Alba, Alicia. 1998. *Chicano Art Inside/Outside the Master's House: Cultural Politics and the* CARA *Exhibition.* Austin: University of Texas Press.

Goldman, Shifra, and Tomás Ybarra-Frausto. 1991. The Political and Social Contexts of Chicano Art. In CARA. *Chicano Art: Resistance and Affirmation,* eds. Richard Griswold del Castillo, Teresa McKenna, and Yvonne Yarbro-Bejarano, 83–96. Los Angeles: UCLA Wight Gallery.

——, comp. 1985. *Arte Chicano: A Comprehensive Annotated Bibliography of Chicano Art, 1965–1981.* Berkeley: University of California, Berkeley, Chicano Studies Library Publications Unit.

Gonzales, Rodolfo "Corky." 1972. *Yo soy Joaquín/I Am Joaquín.* New York: Bantam Books.

Gonzales-Berry, Erlinda, ed. 1989. *Pasó Por Aquí: Critical Essays on the New Mexican Literary Tradition, 1542–1988.* Albuquerque: University of New Mexico Press.

Grajeda, Ralph. 1979. José Antonio Villarreal and Richard Vásquez: The Novelist Against Himself. In *The Identification and Analysis of Chicano Literature,* ed. Francisco Jiménez, 329–57. New York: Bilingual Press.

Grebler, Leo, Joan Moore, and Ralph Guzmán. 1970. *The Mexican American People.* New York: The Free Press.

Greenberg, Bradley S., and Pilar Baptista-Fernández. 1980. Hispanic Americans: The New Minority on Television. In *Life on Television: Content Analysis of U.S. TV Drama,* ed. Stanley S. Greenberg, 117–26. Norwood, N.J.: Ablex Corp.

Griffith, James S. 1988. *Southern Arizona Folk Arts.* Tucson: University of Arizona Press.

——. 1992. *Beliefs and Holy Places. A Spiritual Geography of the Pimería Alta.* Tucson: University of Arizona Press.

——. 1995. *Folklife in the Arizona-Sonora Borderlands.* Logan, Utah: Utah State University Press.

Griswold del Castillo, Richard, Teresa McKenna, and Yvonne Yarbro-Bejarano, eds. 1991. CARA. *Chicano Art: Resistance and Affirmation.* Los Angeles: UCLA Wight Gallery.

Gutiérrez, David G. 1995. *Walls and Mirrors: Mexican Americans, Mexican Immigrants and the Politics of Ethnicity.* Berkeley: University of California Press.

Gutiérrez, Félix F., and Jorge Reina Schement. 1979. *Spanish-Language Radio in the Southwestern United States.* Austin: Center for Mexican American Studies.

Hall, Stuart. 1980. *Culture, Media, Language.* London: Hutchison.

Hall, Stuart, and Paddy Whannel. 1964. *The Popular Arts.* London: Hutchison.

Hancock, Joel. 1973. The Emergence of Chicano Poetry: A Survey of Sources, Themes, and Techniques. *Arizona Quarterly* 29 (1): 57–73.

Herrera-Sobek, María. 1993. *Northward Bound. The Mexican Immigrant Experience in Ballad and Song.* Bloomington and Indianapolis: Indiana University Press.

Higuera, Jonathan J. 2000. A Marriage of Equals. *Hispanic Business* March: 26.

Hinojosa, Rolando. 1973. *Estampas del valle y otras obras/Sketches of the Valley and Other Works.* Berkeley: Quinto Sol Publications.

——. 1985. *Partners in Crime: A Rafe Buenrostro Mystery.* Houston: Arte Público Press.

——. 1998. *Ask a Policeman: A Rafe Buenrostro Mystery.* Houston: Arte Público Press.

Huerta, Jorge. 1982. *Chicano Theater: Themes and Forms.* Ypsilanti, Mich.: Bilingual Review/Press.

Kanellos, Nicolás. 1990. *A History of Hispanic Theatre in the States: Origins to 1940.* Austin: University of Texas Press.

——. 1993. A Socio-Historic Study of Hispanic Newspapers in the United States. In *Recovering the U.S. Hispanic Literary Heritage,* eds. Ramón Gutiérrez and Genaro Padilla, 107–28. Houston: Arte Público Press.

——. 1994. *The Hispanic Almanac.* Detroit: Visible Ink.

Keller, Gary D. 1985. *Chicano Cinema: Research, Reviews, and Resources.* Tempe, Ariz.: Bilingual Review/Press.

——. 1994. *Hispanics and United States Film: An Overview and Handbook.* Tempe, Ariz.: Bilingual Review/Press.

Lamadrid, Enrique. 1986. Los Corridos de Río Arriba: Two Ballads of the Land Grant Movement, 1965–70. *Aztlán* 17 (2): 31–62.

Latins Anonymous. 1996. *Plays.* Houston: Arte Público Press.

Leal, Luis. 1989. The Spanish Language Press: Function and Use. *The Americas Review* 17 (3–4): 157–62.

Levine, Paul G. 1982. Remember the Alamo? John Wayne Told One Story. PBS's "Seguín" Tells Another. *American Film* (Jan.–Feb.): 47–48.

Lichter, S. Robert, and Daniel R. Amundson. 1996. *Don't Blink: Hispanics in Television Entertainment.* Report prepared for the National Council of La Raza. Washington, D.C.: Center for Media and Public Affairs.

Lichter, S. Robert, Linda S. Lichter, and Stanley Rothman. 1991. *Watching America.* New York: Prentice Hall.

Limón, José. 1992. *Mexican Ballads, Chicano Poems: History and Influence in Mexican-American Social Poetry.* Berkeley and Los Angeles: University of California Press.

List, Christine. 1992. Self-Directed Stereotyping in the Films of Cheech Marin. In *Chicanos and Film: Essays on Chicano Representation and Resistance,* ed. Chon Noriega, 183–94. Minneapolis: University of Minnesota Press.

——. 1996. *Chicano Ethnicity: Refiguring Ethnicity in Mainstream Film.* New York: Garland Publishing.

Lomas, Clara. 1978. Resistencia cultural o apropriación ideológica. *Revista Chicano-Riqueña* 6 (4): 44–49.

Lomelí, Francisco, and Carl R. Shirley, eds. 1989. *Dictionary of Literary Biography*. Vol. 82. *Chicano Writers*. First Series. Detroit: Gale Research.

———. 1992. *Dictionary of Literary Biography*. Vol. 122. *Chicano Writers*. Second Series. Detroit: Gale Research.

———. 1999. *Dictionary of Literary Biography*. Vol. 209. *Chicano Writers*. Third Series. Detroit: The Gale Group.

Loza, Steven. 1993. *Barrio Rhythm: Mexican American Music in Los Angeles*. Urbana and Chicago: University of Illinois Press.

Lubenow, Gerald. 1987. Putting the Border Onstage. *Newsweek* 4 May: 79.

Meyer, Doris. 1978. Early Mexican-American Responses to Negative Stereotyping. *New Mexico Historical Review* 53 (1): 75–91.

Miller, Elaine K. 1973. *Mexican Folk Narrative from the Los Angeles Area*. Austin: University of Texas Press.

Morales, Alejandro. 1985. Expanding the Meaning of Chicano Cinema: *Yo soy chicano, Raíces de sangre, Seguín*. In *Chicano Cinema: Research, Reviews, and Resources*, ed. Gary D. Keller, 121–37. Tempe, Ariz.: Bilingual Review/Press.

Mukerji, Chandra, and Michael Schudson, eds. 1991. *Rethinking Popular Culture: Contemporary Perspectives in Cultural Studies*. Berkeley and Los Angeles: University of California Press.

Museum of New Mexico. 1999. *Low 'n Slow: Low Riding in New Mexico*. Santa Fe: Museum of New Mexico Press.

Musser, Charles. 1991. Ethnicity, Role-Playing, and American Film Comedy: From *Chinese Laundry Scene* to *Whoopee* (1894–1930). In *Unspeakable Images: Ethnicity and the American Cinema*, ed. Lester D. Friedman, 39–81. Urbana and Chicago: University of Illinois Press.

Nájera-Ramírez, Olga. 1994. Fiestas Hispánicas: Dimensions of Hispanic Festivals and Celebrations. In *Handbook of Hispanic Cultures in the United States: Anthropology*, ed. Thomas Weaver, 194–211. Houston: Arte Público Press.

Nava, Michael. 1986. *The Little Death*. Boston: Alyson Publications.

———. 1990. *How Town*. New York: Ballantine Books.

———. 1992. *The Hidden Law*. New York: Ballantine Books.

———. 1996a. *The Death of Friends*. New York: G. P. Putnam's Sons.

———. 1996b. *Goldenboy: A Mystery*. Ballantine Books.

———. 1999. *The Burning Plain*. New York: Bantam Books, 1999.

Nordholm, Monique. 1988. The Future of Spanish-Language Radio. *Hispanic Business* December: 62–63.

Noriega, Chon A., ed. 1992. *Chicanos and Film: Essays on Chicano Representation and Resistance*. Minneapolis: University of Minnesota Press.

———. 2000. *Shot in America: Television, the State, and the Rise of Chicano Cinema.* Minneapolis: University of Minnesota Press.

Noriega, Chon A., and Ana M. López, eds. 1996. *The Ethnic Eye: Latino Media Arts.* Minneapolis: University of Minnesota Press.

Oktavec, Eileen. 1995. *Answered Prayers: Miracles and Milagros along the Border.* Tucson: University of Arizona Press.

Olivares, Julián. 1996. Sandra Cisneros' *The House on Mango Street* and the Poetics of Space. In *Chicana Creativity and Criticism: New Frontiers in American Literature,* eds. María Herrera-Sobek and Helena María Viramontes, 231–44. Albuquerque: University of New Mexico Press.

Padilla, Genaro. 1989. The Social Allegories of Fray Angélico Chávez. In *Pasó Por Aquí: Critical Essays on the New Mexican Literary Tradition, 1542–1988,* ed. Erlinda Gonzales-Berry, 215–30. Albuquerque: University of New Mexico Press.

Paredes, Américo. 1958. *With His Pistol in His Hand: A Border Ballad and Its Hero.* Austin: University of Texas Press.

———. 1966. The Anglo-American in Mexican Folklore. In *New Voices in American Studies,* 113–17. West Lafayette: Purdue University Press.

———. 1993. *Folklore and Culture on the Texas-Mexican Border.* Ed. Richard Bauman. Austin: Center for Mexican American Studies.

Patoski, Joe Nick. 1996. *Selena: Como la flor.* New York: Berkeley Boulevard Books.

Peña, Manuel. 1985. *The Texas-Mexican Conjunto: History of a Working-Class Music.* Austin: University of Texas Press.

———. 1992–1996. Música fronteriza/Border Music. *Aztlán* 21 (1–2): 191–225.

———. 1999a. *The Mexican American Orquesta. Music, Culture, and the Dialectic of Conflict.* Austin: University of Texas Press.

———. 1999b. *Música Tejana.* College Station: Texas A&M University Press.

Portillo Trambley, Estela. 1975. *Rain of Scorpions and Other Writings.* Berkeley: Tonatiuh International.

Quirarte, Jacinto. 1973. *Mexican American Artists.* Austin: University of Texas Press.

———. 1991. Exhibitions of Chicano Art: 1965 to Present. In CARA. *Chicano Art: Resistance and Affirmation,* eds. Richard Griswold del Castillo, Teresa McKenna, and Yvonne Yarbro-Bejarano, 163–80. Los Angeles: UCLA Wight Gallery.

Quirarte, Jacinto, and Carey Clements Rote, eds. 1999. *César A. Martínez: A Retrospective.* Austin: Marion Koogler McNay Art Museum.

Rael, Juan B. 1977. *Cuentos Populares de Colorado y Nuevo México.* 2d ed. 2 vols. Santa Fe: Museum of New Mexico Press.

Ramírez Berg, Charles. 1996. Ethnic Ingenuity and Mainstream Cinema: Robert Rodríguez's *Bedhead* (1990) and *El Mariachi* (1993). In *Latino Media Arts,* eds. Chon A. Noriega and Ana M. López, 107–28. Minneapolis: University of Minnesota Press.

Ramos, Manuel. 1993. *The Ballad of Rocky Ruiz.* New York: St. Martin's Press.

———. 1994. *The Ballad of Gato Guerrero.* New York: St. Martin's Press.

———. 1996. *The Last Client of Luis Móntez.* St. Martin's Press.

———. 1997. *Blues for the Buffalo.* New York: St. Martin's Press.

Rebolledo, Tey Diana. 1989. Las Escritoras: Romances and Realities. In *Pasó Por Aquí: Critical Essays on the New Mexican Literary Tradition, 1542–1988,* ed. Erlinda Gonzales-Berry, 199–214. Albuquerque: University of New Mexico Press.

Reyes, David, and Tom Waldman. 1998. *Land of a Thousand Dances: Chicano Rock 'n' Roll from Southern California.* Albuquerque: University of New Mexico Press.

Richard, Alfred Charles Jr. 1992. *The Hispanic Image on the Silver Screen: An Interpretive Filmography from Silents into Sound, 1898–1935.* New York: Greenwood Press.

Ríos, Herminio. 1973. Toward a True Chicano Bibliography—Part II. *El Grito* 5 (4): 38–47.

Ríos, Herminio, and Guadalupe Castillo. 1970. Toward a True Chicano Bibliography: Mexican-American Newspapers, 1848–1942. *El Grito* 3 (4): 17–24.

Rivera, Tomás. 1971. *. . . Y no se lo tragó la tierra/. . . And the Earth Did Not Part.* Berkeley: Quinto Sol Publications.

Robb, John Donald. 1980. *Hispanic Folk Music of New Mexico and the Southwest.* Norman: University of Oklahoma Press.

Rodríguez, Clara E., ed. 1997. *Latin Looks: Images of Latinas and Latinos in the U.S. Media.* Boulder: Westview Press.

Rodríguez, Juan. Jorge Ulica y Carlo de Medina: escritores de la Bahía de San Francisco. *La Palabra* 2 (1): 25–46.

Rodríguez, Richard. 1982. *Hunger of Memory: The Education of Richard Rodríguez.* Boston: Godine.

Romo, Ricardo. 1992–1996. Borderland Murals: Chicano Artifacts in Transition. *Aztlán* 21 (1–2): 125–54.

Rosales, F. Arturo. 1996. *Chicano! The History of the Mexican American Civil Rights Movement.* Houston: Arte Público Press.

Saldívar, Ramón. 1990. *Chicano Narrative: The Dialectics of Difference.* Madison: University of Wisconsin Press.

Sánchez-Tranquilino, Marcos. 1995. Space, Power, and Youth Culture: Mexican American Graffiti and Chicano Murals in East Los Angeles, 1972–1978. In *Looking High and Low: Art and Cultural Identity,* eds. Brenda Jo Bright and Liza Bakewell, 55–88. Tucson: University of Arizona Press.

Sands, Kathleen Mullen. 1993. *Charrería Mexicana: An Equestrian Folk Tradition.* Tucson: University of Arizona Press.

Sheehy, Daniel. 1999. Popular Mexican Musical Traditions: The Mariachi of West Mexico and the Conjunto of Veracruz. In *Music in Latin American Culture: Regional Traditions,* ed. John M. Schechter, 34–79. New York: Schirmer Books.

Soto, Gary. 1985. *Living up the Street: Narrative Recollections.* San Francisco: Strawberry Hill Press.

——. 1988. *Lesser Evils: Ten Quartets.* Houston: Arte Público Press.

Strachwitz, Chris. 1974. *Una Historia de la Música de la Frontera: Texas-Mexican Border Music.* Vol. 1. El Cerrito, Calif.: Arhoolie Productions.

Strinati, Dominic. 1995. *An Introduction to the Theories of Popular Culture.* London and New York: Routledge.

Suberví-Vélez, Federico. 1999. The Mass Media and Latinos: Policy and Research Agendas for the Next Century. *Aztlán* 24 (2): 131–47.

Suberví-Vélez, Federico, and Susan Colsant. 1993. The Televised Worlds of Latino Children. In *Children and Television: Images in a Changing Sociocultural World,* eds. Gordon L. Berry and Joy Keiko Asamen, 211–23. Newberry Park, Calif.: Sage Publications.

Suberví-Vélez, Federico, et al. 1997. Hispanic-Oriented Media. In *Latin Looks: Images of Latinas and Latinos in the U.S. Media,* ed. Clara E. Rodríguez, 225–37. Boulder: Westview Press.

Tatum, Charles. 1982. *Chicano Literature.* Boston: Twayne Publishers.

Theatre Communications Group. 1998. *Culture Clash: Life, Death and Revolutionary Comedy.* New York: Theatre Communications Group.

Treviño, Jesús. 1982. Chicano Cinema. *New Scholar* 8: 167–80.

TRPI. 1999. *Missing in Action: Latinos in and out of Hollywood.* Report Commissioned by the Screen Actors Guild. Claremont, Calif.: Tomás Rivera Policy Institute.

Ulibarrí, Sabine. 1971. *Tierra Amarilla: Cuentos de Nuevo México.* Albuquerque: University of New Mexico Press.

——. 1997. *Mi abuela fumaba puros y otros cuentos de Tierra Amarilla.* Berkeley: Quinto Sol Publications.

Valdez, Luis. 1990. *Early Works.* Houston: Arte Público Press.

——. 1992. *Zoot Suit and Other Plays.* Introduction by Jorge Huerta. Houston: Arte Público Press.

Vallejos, Tomás. 1989. José Antonio Villarreal. In *Dictionary of Literary Biography.* Vol. 82. *Chicano Writers,* eds. Francisco A. Lomelí and Carl R. Shirley, 282–88. First Series. Detroit: Gale Research.

Veciana-Suárez, Ana. 1987. *Hispanic Media, U.S.A.: A Narrative Guide to the Print and Electronic Hispanic News Media in the United States.* Washington, D.C.: Media Institute.

Villarreal, José Antonio. 1959. *Pocho.* New York: Doubleday and Co.

Villaseñor, Víctor. 1991. *Rain of Gold.* New York: Dell.

Weigle, Marta. 1995. *Cuando Hablan los Santos: Contemporary Santero Traditions from Northern New Mexico.* Albuquerque: Maxwell Museum of Anthropology, University of New Mexico.

West, John O. 1988. *Mexican-American Folklore: Legends, Songs, Festivals, Proverbs, Crafts, Tales of Saints, of Revolutionaries, and More.* Little Rock: August House.

Yarbro-Bejarano, Yvonne. 1979. From *Acto* to *Mito:* A Critical Appraisal of the Teatro Campesino. In *Modern Chicano Writers: A Collection of Critical Essays,* eds. Joseph Sommers and Tomás Ybarra-Frausto, 176–85. Englewood Cliffs, N.J.: Prentice Hall.

Ybarra-Frausto, Tomás. 1977. The Chicano Movement and the Emergence of a Chicano Poetic Consciousness. *New Scholar* 6: 81–109.

Zate, María. 1998. Hispanic Ad Budgets Explode. *Hispanic Business* December: 58–60.

Index

canción (song), 15–16; canción ranchera, 15–16

Canclini, Néstor García, 10–11

Cannibal and the Headhunters (music group), 36

Carbajal, Jesús (filmmaker), 85

Carr, Vikki (singer), 46–47

Carrillo, Eduardo (artist), 160–61

Carrillo, Leo (actor), 53

Carrillo, Randy (mariachi musician), 46

Carrillo, Steve (mariachi musician), 46

Casa, David Zamora (filmmaker), 85

Casas, Mel (artist), 160

cascarones (eggshell craft), 186

Castilian caballero films, 52

Catholic Church, 153

celebrations, 181–87; charreadas, 185–86; Christmas, 181–83; Day of the Dead, 183–84; fiestas patrias, 184–85; popular decorative arts, 186–87

Cervantes, Lorna Dee (poet), 125

Cervántez, Yreina (artist), 171

Chacón, Felipe Maximiliano, 97

charreadas, 185–86

Chávez, Fray Angélico, 118, 120

Chávez, César (union leader), xxi, xxii–xxiii, 83, 98, 126

Chávez, Denise (author), 140–41

Chávez, Dennis (senator), xxi

Chicago Art: Resistance and Affirmation (CARA, art exhibit), 180–81

Chicano Moratorium (activist group), xx

Chicano: term defined, xii

Chicano, El (rock and roll band), 38

Chicano Movement, xxi–xxvi; formation of, xxii; and forming of artistic consciousness, 122–30; history of, xxi–xxii, xxv–xxvi; manifestations of, xxii–xxiv; negative side of, xxvi;

newspaper publishing and, 97–100; popular culture and, xxii; popular fiction and, 133–41; popular music and, 37; and re-emergence of the family, 28

Chicano mystery novels, 145–51

Chicano popular art: discussion questions, 189; graffiti art, 171–72; lowriders, 172–76; muralism, 163–71; museums and cultural centers, 179–81; performance art, 176–79; religious art, 153–60; secular art, 160–81; suggested readings, 189–90

Chicano popular cinema: actors and roles, 54–57, 81–82; current state of, 81–82; discussion questions, 87–88; distinguished from Hollywood films, 62; documentaries and short films, 82, 86–87; feature-length films, 59–81; features of, 60–62; history of race and ethnicity in, 50–52; Hollywood portrayal of Mexican American actors, 52–59; Latino audience for, 81–82; stereotypes presented by, 81; suggested reading, 88

Chicano popular literature: current, 141–51; discussion questions, 151; female writers, 137; mystery novels, 145–51; popular writers, pre-1965, 118–21; suggested readings, 152

Chicano popular music: discussion questions, 48–49; mariachi music, 44–46; on West Coast in 1960s, 36–37; in 1970s, 37–39; in 1980s, 39–43; in 1990s, 43–44; suggested reading, 49

Chicano popular theater: Culture Clash, 132–33; *Latins Anonymous,* 131–32; parodies of Chicano life, 132; regional theater groups, 130–33; El Teatro Campesino, 126–30

Frankfurt School, 4
Fregoso, Linda (film critic), 78

Gadsden Purchase treaty, xiv
Galán, Hector (filmmaker), 84
Gallardo, Carlos (actor), 73
Gamboa, Henry, Jr. (filmmaker), 86, 177, 178–79
gangs, 77–78, 171–72
Garza, Carmen Lomas (artist), 161, 163
Garza, Eligio de la (Congressman), xxi
Garza, Juan (filmmaker), 85
Gaspar de Alba, Alicia (art curator), 181
Gómez-Peña, Guillermo (performance artist), 71, 85, 179
Gonzales, Rodolfo ("Corky"; poet), xxi, 82, 122–24; *I Am Joaquín,* 122–23
González, Henry B. (Congressman), xxi
González, Pedro J. (radio programmer), 71–73, *72,* 101
Gonzalez, Ray (poet), 125
Gorras Blancas, Las, xvi
graffiti art, 171–72
Gramsci, Antonio (scholar), 4, 10
greaser as character in films, 53
Griffith, D. W. (filmmaker), 51
Griffith, James (folklorist), 156–57
Grijalva, Frank (mariachi musician), 46
Gronk (Gluglio Nicandro), 177, 178
Grupo Quinto Sol, El (writers' collective), 133–34, 137
Guerrero, Eduardo "Lalo" (musician), 31, 32–34, 40
Guevara, Ruben (musician), 39
Guevarra, Che (revolutionary leader), 99, 133

Gutiérrez, Efrain (filmmaker), 84
Gutiérrez, José Angel, xxi, xxiv
Guzmán, Leopoldo Blest (filmmaker), 86

Hall, Stuart (cultural populist), 10
Hayworth, Rita (Latina actress), 53
Hernández, Gil (muralist), 169
Hernández, Little Joe (orquesta musician), 28–29
Herrera, Juan Felipe (poet), 125–26
Herrón, Willie (muralist), 169, 170, 177, 178
Hidalgo, David (musician), 40
Hidalgo y Costilla, Miguel (Catholic priest), 185
Hinojosa, Rolando (author), 134, 136–37, 147
Hispanic: term defined, xii
historical background of Mexican culture, xiii–xvi
Holly, Buddy (musician), 34
Hollywood films with Chicano themes, 77–81
Homestead Act of 1862, xv
Horkheimer, Max (scholar), 4, 10
House on Mango Street, The (Cisneros), 139–40, 141
Huerta, Dolores (union leader), xxi, xxiii

I Am Joaquín (epic poem), 82, 122–23
immigration. *See* Mexican immigration

Jacobo, Daniel (filmmaker), 85, 86
Jarrico, Paul (film producer), 55
Jessop, Colin (filmmaker), 84
Jesus Christ in popular religious art, 156, 157, 158, *159*
Jiménez, Luis (artist), 161

media: Hispanics represented in, 111–16; common stereotypes in, 112–13; discussion questions, 116–17; suggested readings, 117
Medrano, Adán (filmmaker), 86
Mejía, Rosa (film character), 63
Mendoza, Lydia (Tejana singer), 15–16
Mendoza, Vicente (scholar), 14
Mexican: term defined, xii
Mexican Americanism, xix–xxi
Mexican American Legal Defense and Education Fund (MALDEF), 58
Mexican American Movement (MAM), xx
Mexican Americans: Chicano Movement and, xxi–xxvi; denial of rights of, xiv–xv; failure to assimilate, xviii–xix; historical background of, xiii–xxv; immigration by, xvi–xviii; nativist attacks on, xviii; political success of, xx–xxi; resistance to injustice, xvi
Mexican American Youth Association (MAYO), xxiv
Mexican immigration, xvi–xviii; illegal, as portrayed in films, 65–66; and maintenance of separate identity, xviii–xix; mutual aid societies and, xix; numbers for 1900 and 1930, xvii; reasons for, xvii–xviii
Mexican Voice, The (newspaper), xx
migrant workers, 74–75, 85–86
milagros (miracles), in religious art, 157–60
"Mi Raza" (Ayllón), 95–96
Molina, Armando (actor), 131
Mondragón, M. Padilla (poet), 96
Montalbán, Ricardo (actor), 58
Mora, Pat, 126
Montoya, Joseph (senator), xxi
Montoya, Malaquías (muralist), 169

Montoya, Richard (actor), 132
Morales, Alejandro (film critic), 67
Morales, Hugo (radio network owner), 105
Morales, Sylvia (filmmaker), 59, 86
Mosqueda, Fernando (music promoter), 40
movies. See Chicano popular cinema
Muñoz, Susana (filmmaker), 87
muralism, 163–71; and Chicano folk heroes, 169–70; controversial, 165; current state of, 170–71; influence of, 165–66; Mexican, 164–65; and political struggles, 167–70; school mural, 168; and social activism, 166–70
Murieta, Joaquín (social bandit), xvi; and I Am Joaquín, 122–23; life of, 91–92
museums and cultural centers, 179–81
música Tejana, 22–30, 85
Mutrux, Floyd (screenwriter), 77

Nájera, Rick (actor), 131
names, anglicizing of, 34, 37, 57
National Chicano Moratorium (antiwar group), xxv
National Council of La Raza (NCLR), 33, 58, 111
National Farm Workers Association, xxii–xxiii
National Latino Media Council, 115
nativism: rise of, xviii, xxvi
Nava, Gregory (film director), 70, 75
Nava, Michael (author), 148–49
Navaira, Emilio (Tejana musician), 30
Navarro, Fernando (radio personality), 102
NCLR (National Council of La Raza), 33, 58, 111

newspapers. *See* Spanish-language newspapers

Noriega, Chon (film critic), 60–61, 65, 71, 77, 178, 179

Norte, El (film), 70–71

Nosotros (Latino organization), 33, 58

Olmos, Edward James (actor), 31, 40, 59, 66, 132, 133; and *American Me,* 77–78; and *Ballad of Gregorio Cortez, 19,* 68, 69; and *Selena,* 75; and *Zoot Suit,* 76

Once in a Lifetime (film), 60

Onda Chicano, La (orquesta music group), 27, 28–29

Orozco, José Clemente (artist), 164, 165, 170

orquesta Tejana, 27–28. *See also* música Tejana

Ozuna, Sunny (orquesta musician), 28, 29

Pacheco, Manuel (university president), xxv–xxvi

Pachon, Harry P., 115

pachucos: film portrayal of, 76–78, 128–30

Padilla, Benjamín, 91, 92, 93

Padilla, Carmella (author), 174

paper flowers, 186–87

Pardo, María Esperanza (newspaper writer), 94

Paredes, Américo (cinema scholar), 10–11, 12, 14, 18

Pastores, Los, 182

Pazo, Antonio (muralist), 170

Pellicer, Pina (actor), 54

Peña, Amado (artist), 161

Peña, Federico (cabinet officer), xxvi

Peña, Manuel (Tejano scholar), 23, 24, 26–27, 28–29

Penichet, Carlos (filmmaker), 84

Penichet, Jeff (filmmaker), 84

Pereda, Laura de (newspaper writer), 93–94

Pérez, Louie (musician), 40

Pérez, Severo (film director), 74, 84, 86

performance art, 177–79

Phillips, Lou Diamond (actor), *35,* 78

piñatas, 186

Plan Espiritual de Aztlán, El, 122, 125, 133, 165–66

Pocho (Villarreal), xvii, 120, 121

poetry: popular, in 1960s, 122–25; popular, since 1980, 125–30; in Spanish-language newspapers, 94–97, 98, 99

politicians, Mexican-American: list of xxi

politics: Chicano Movement and, xxi–xxvi

Polk, James K., xiv

popular culture: conclusions about, 191–92; cultural populists and, 5, 9–12; defined, 3–4; discussion questions, 5–6, 13; dominant ideology and, 4–5; feminist definition of, 5; folk culture and, 4; Frankfurt school and, 4; high culture, 3–4; low culture, 3–4; mass-culture theorists and, 6–9; reasons for studying, xi; suggested readings, 13; theoretical approaches to, 5–13

Portillo, Lourdes (filmmaker), 87

Portillo, Rose (actress), 74

Posadas, Las, 181, 182

prison life, 77–78

prose in Spanish-language newspapers, 91–94

proverbs (dichos), 188

punk rock music: examples of Chicano groups, 40

About the Author

DR. CHARLES M. TATUM is professor of Spanish and dean of the College of Humanities at the University of Arizona. He was born in El Paso, Texas, and raised in Parral, Chihuahua, Mexico. His mother, Eloisa Aínsa, a Mexican American, was born and raised in El Paso. Tatum received his B.A. from the University of Notre Dame, his M.A. from Stanford University, and his Ph.D. from the University of New Mexico. He is the author of a monographic study, *Chicano Literature* (1982)—published in translation in Mexico in 1986—and coauthor of *Not Just for Children: The Mexican Comic Book in the Late 1960s and 1970s* (1992). Cofounder and coeditor of the journal *Studies in Latin American Popular Culture,* Tatum has also edited three volumes of *New Chicana/Chicano Writing* (1991–1993) for the University of Arizona Press and has coedited a volume of essays, *Recovering the U.S. Hispanic Literary Heritage,* vol. 2. A member of the advisory board of the Recovering the U.S. Hispanic Literary Heritage Project, Tatum's published book chapters and articles include studies on Latin American prose fiction, Chicano literature, and Mexican popular culture. He is currently working on a book on Chicano literature, which will appear in the Mexican American Experience series, published by the University of Arizona Press.

Chicano Popular Culture is a volume in the series The Mexican American Experience, a cluster of modular texts designed to provide greater flexibility in undergraduate education. Each book deals with a single topic concerning the Mexican American population. Instructors can create a semester-length course from any combination of volumes, or may choose to use one or two volumes to complement other texts.

Additional volumes deal with the following subjects:

Mexican Americans and Health
Adela de la Torre and Antonio Estrada

Mexican Americans and the U.S. Economy
Arturo González

Mexican Americans and the Law
Reynaldo Anaya Valencia, Sonia R. García, Henry Flores, and José Roberto Juárez Jr.

Chicana/o Identity in a Changing U.S. Society
Aída Hurtado and Patricia Gurin

Mexican Americans and the Environment
Devon G. Peña

For more information, please visit
www.uapress.arizona.edu/textbooks/latino.htm